John Donne's Sermons

on the Psalms and Gospels

JOHN DONNE'S
SERMONS ON THE
PSALMS AND GOSPELS

With a Selection of
Prayers and Meditations

Edited, with an Introduction, by
EVELYN M. SIMPSON

UNIVERSITY OF CALIFORNIA PRESS
BERKELEY, LOS ANGELES, LONDON

UNIVERSITY OF CALIFORNIA PRESS

BERKELEY AND LOS ANGELES, CALIFORNIA

UNIVERSITY OF CALIFORNIA PRESS, LTD.

LONDON, ENGLAND

ISBN: 0-520-00340-3

LIBRARY OF CONGRESS CATALOG CARD NUMBER: 63-16249

MANUFACTURED IN THE UNITED STATES OF AMERICA

4   5   6   7   8   9

Prefatory Note

THE TEXT of Donne's sermons in this volume has been reprinted from the standard University of California Press edition of 1953–1962 by G. R. Potter and E. M. Simpson. I am indebted to the Oxford University Press for permission to quote a passage from *The Business of Criticism* (1959) by Helen Gardner, and also for permission to reprint some sentences from my own *A Study of the Prose Works of John Donne* (2d edition, 1948). I must thank Mrs. G. R. Potter and Mrs. R. T. Holtby for their help.

Contents

Introduction

DONNE's sermons are admittedly unique. Charles Eliot Norton wrote of them, "They are as unlike any other sermons as his poems are unlike any other poetry." Coleridge was deeply interested in them and wrote profuse annotations in the margin of a copy of the 1640 Folio of Donne's *LXXX Sermons*. T. S. Eliot has told us that he prefers the sermons of Bishop Andrewes, Donne's greatest contemporary rival as a preacher, which are indeed full of intellectual power, but they have not the wide appeal which Donne's personality made on his hearers. F. P. Wilson has lately written, "For every reader of Andrewes there are, I suppose, a hundred of Donne.... One reason why the one is so much more read than the other may be that John Donne was once Jack Donne, whereas Andrewes was always Lancelot."[1]

For modern readers Donne has the advantage over Andrewes in that he was a poet who did not lose his poetical imagination when he entered the pulpit. Whenever he was deeply moved, his style caught fire, and he employed the images, the repetitions, and even sometimes the rhythms of poetry.[2] Moreover, during the forty-two years of his life before he entered the ministry, he had a wide and varied experience of life as a law student at Lincoln's Inn, a traveler in France and Italy, a gentleman adventurer in two naval expeditions led by the Earl of Essex against Spain, a secretary in the London house of Sir Thomas Egerton, the Lord Keeper, and finally, after his romantic marriage and subsequent disgrace, as an impoverished husband trying to maintain his growing family by hackwork for various patrons. While his more academic contemporaries, who subsequently became bishops, were presumably studying Aristotle and Plato, Donne was reading Dante, Rabelais, Pico della Mirandola, and Reuchlin.

There were long years of hesitation before Donne finally decided to enter the ministry after his hopes of a diplomatic or political career

---

[1] *Seventeenth Century Prose* (Berkeley and Los Angeles, University of California Press, 1960), p. 97.

[2] See pp. 12, 20, 25–26 of the present volume.

had been blighted. After his marriage his life had become regular, he was devoted to his wife and family, and he read voraciously books on the canon law, on casuistry, and commentaries on the Scriptures and the Fathers. He was also passionately excited by the discoveries of Kepler and Galileo, which established the truth of the Copernican theory that the earth and the other planets revolved around the sun. Donne was neither a scientist nor a philosopher, but unlike most of his contemporaries he appreciated the significance of these scientific discoveries which revealed that the earth was not the center of the universe, and he voiced his bewilderment and concern in his two fine poems, the *Anniversaries*.

These middle years were also years of religious emotion, of penitence for the sins of his youth and of anguish for his present unworthiness. Helen Gardner has demonstrated that sixteen out of the nineteen *Holy Sonnets* must have been written about 1609, before Donne started the writing of his prose treatise *Pseudo-Martyr*.[3] Most readers are startled by the intensity of religious feeling in such sonnets as "Oh my blacke Soule! now thou art summoned," "What if this present were the worlds last night?," "Batter my heart, three person'd God"; or "Thou hast made me, And shall thy worke decay?" The man who wrote these poems was clearly one who might some day become a great preacher.

Yet there was a delay of almost six years before Donne relinquished all hopes of a career in diplomacy or politics, and took Holy Orders in the Church of England. When he had taken the final step he devoted himself to his new calling with intense earnestness. As the years went by he realized that he had found his true vocation in the ministry.

Few preachers have impressed their personality on their sermons so vividly as Donne. He was no recluse, unable to feel for human weakness, and no hypocrite, claiming a saintliness which he did not possess; but a man of like passions with his hearers, a man whose history they all knew, whose penitence was as real as his sins had been, whose experience had taught him humility, compassion, and trust in the mercy of God.

---

[3] *John Donne, Divine Poems* (Oxford, Clarendon Press, 1952), pp. xxxvii–lv. *La Corona* and *A Litanie* are probably a little earlier, but they belong to the same period in Donne's life.

It is this note of intense personal religious experience which gives to the sermons their unique power. Behind their eloquence and elaborate rhetoric we hear the voice of a human soul, tortured at times by remorse for past sins, agonizing with his hearers to rescue them from temptations of which he knows the awful power, but inspired also by a great hope and a great devotion. The sermons of Andrewes or Tillotson or South seem cold beside this ardor of penitence, this glowing love to the person of Christ, this yearning desire for the souls of men. Donne never glosses over the sinfulness of his past life, but in the fact that God has had mercy on his own soul, he sees encouragement and hope for the most despairing of his hearers.

Thus speaking in joyful expectation of the resurrection of the dead, he rests all his confidence on Christ's merits.

> Christ shall bear witnesse for me, in ascribing his righteousnesse unto me, and in delivering me into his Fathers hands, with the same tendernesse, as he delivered up his owne soule, and in making me, who am a greater sinner, then they who crucified him on earth for me, as innocent, and as righteous as his glorious selfe, in the Kingdome of heaven.[4]

His sense of the mercy of God shown in the person of Christ leads to some of the most passionate outbursts in the *Sermons:*

> Earth cannot receive, Heaven cannot give such another universall soul to all: all persons, all actions, as Mercy. And were I *the childe of this Text,*[5] that were to live *a hundred yeares,* I would ask no other marrow to my bones, no other wine to my heart, no other light to mine eyes, no other art to my understanding, no other eloquence to my tongue, then the power of apprehending for my self, and the power of deriving and conveying upon others by my Ministery, the Mercy, the early Mercy, the everlasting Mercy of yours, and my God.[6]

More colloquial, but perhaps even more moving, is a short passage in a late Easter Day sermon:

> I doubt not of mine own salvation; and in whom can I have so much occasion of doubt, as in my self? When I come to heaven, shall I be able to say to any there, Lord! how got you hither? Was any man lesse likely to come thither then I?[7]

---

[4] *Sermons,* IV, 162.
[5] *Isaiah* 65.20: "The child shall die a hundred years old."
[6] *Sermons,* VII, 357.
[7] *Sermons,* VIII, 371.

This volume contains ten of Donne's most representative sermons on texts taken from two important sections of the Bible, the *Psalms* and the *Gospels*. The range of his sermons is very wide. He preached on texts from *Genesis* and *Exodus*, from *Job* and *Proverbs* and *Ecclesiastes*, from *Isaiah, Jeremiah, Ezekiel*, and several of the minor prophets, from *Acts*, from the *Epistles* of St. *Paul*, from St. *James*, and from *Revelation*. He knew the Scriptures from end to end, as the references, approximately eight thousand in number, in the complete edition of the *Sermons* can testify.[8] Yet he preached most eloquently on those books which were nearest to his own heart. He loved the *Psalms* more than any other book of the Old Testament, and we learn from his own testimony that he thought that the best sermons were those which were preached on Christ's own words.[9] It would be possible to quote a single fine passage from every one of Donne's 160 sermons which have been preserved, but too often such a passage is embedded in pages of tedious arguments or embittered controversy. Donne rises to his greatest heights when he has a great theme, and he found two such themes in the thought of death and the thought of love, the love shown by Christ on the Cross.[10]

Donne's intense affection for the *Psalms* is shown by the fact that of his extant 160 sermons thirty-four were preached on this book. He tells us himself that it was his favorite book of the Old Testament, and that one reason for this preference was that the Psalms are poetry, and that the metrical form appealed to him as a poet.[11]

---

[8] See University of California Press edition, *Sermons*, X, 295–296, for a rough analysis of the figures.

[9] See *Sermons*, V, 263: "... the best texts we can take, to make Sermons upon, are as this text is, some of the words of Christs owne Sermons."

[10] He joined these themes in his last great sermon, *Deaths Duell*, on *Psalms* 68.20 (*Sermons*, X, No. 11).

[11] *Sermons*, II, 49–50: "Almost every man hath his *Appetite*, and his *tast* disposed to some kind of meates rather then others; He knows what dish he would choose, for his first, and for his second course. We have often the same disposition in our *spirituall Diet*; a man may have a particular love towards such or such a book of Scripture, and in such an affection, I acknowledge, that my spirituall appetite carries me still, upon the *Psalms of David*, for a first course, for the Scriptures of the Old Testament... God gives us, not onely that which is meerly necessary, but that

Another reason which Donne gives for his preference for the
Psalms is that St. Augustine, his favorite among the Fathers, also
professed a passionate love for the book. Donne has many references
to Augustine's sermons and homilies on the *Psalms*,[12] and indeed he
studied Augustine's works with a remarkable intensity. He calls the
saint "that blessed and sober Father," "that tender blessed Father,"
and he found in Augustine's *Confessions* a striking parallel with his
own stormy and licentious youth. He looked on the *Psalms* as being
a treasury of devotion for the penitent, and he devoted twenty-four
sermons to three series of expositions on three of the Penitential
Psalms—the Sixth, Thirty-second, and Thirty-eighth in the Authorized Version, as well as a single sermon on the Fifty-first Psalm.

Donne delighted in the *Psalms*. He read them in the original
Hebrew, in the Latin of the Vulgate, and in the English of Coverdale
(Prayer Book version), the Geneva Bible, and the King James Bible.[13]
In his third Prebend Sermon he brings together the various English
translations and compares them (*Sermons*, VII, 248, 253). He even
goes back to Wycliffe's translation, and approves that. As for the
Vulgate, it had been the Bible of his childhood, and he must have
known many of the Psalms in Latin by heart, for he constantly quotes
the words of the Vulgate when the English alone would have been
quite sufficient.

Like so many other famous Christians Donne found in the *Psalms*
an unequaled treasury of devotion. In penitence there were no words
so fitting as those of the Fifty-first Psalm, and in joy he exclaimed
with the psalmist "Bless the Lord, O my soul, and forget not all his
benefits." He made the comment "How plentifully, how abundantly
is the word *Beatus, Blessed,* multiplied in the Booke of Psalmes?

---

which is convenient too . . . he gives us our instruction in cheerfull forms,
not in a sowre, and sullen, and angry, and unacceptable way, but cheerfully, in *Psalms . . .*

[12] See *Sermons,* X, 346–358, and 376–386.

[13] Donne's knowledge of Hebrew is best shown in the twenty-two sermons which he preached on the Sixth, the Thirty-second, and the Thirty-
eighth Psalms. He was not a great Hebrew scholar like Bishop Andrewes,
but he seems to have had a fairly competent knowledge of Hebrew, considering that his early training had been legal, not theological. On the
other hand his knowledge of New Testament Greek was very scanty.

Blessed, and Blessed in every Psalme, in every Verse; The Booke seems to be made out of that word, *Blessed,* And the foundation raysed upon that word, *Blessed,* for it is the first word of the Booke."[14] At other times when melancholy oppressed him he could use the *De Profundis,* "Out of the deep have I called unto thee, O Lord: Lord, hear my voice...I look for the Lord, my soul doth wait for him; and in his word is my trust...O Israel, trust in the Lord, for with the Lord there is mercy: and with him is plenteous redemption" (Prayer Book version). The last two words are quoted again and again by Donne, *"copiosa redemptio,* plenteous redemption," as though they were a charm against all melancholic fears.[15]

Since Donne is not always an easy writer,[16] a few suggestions about his method of composition of his sermons may perhaps be helpful. Sermons at St. Paul's were generally expected to be at least an hour long, and at St. Paul's Cross they might be prolonged to two or even three hours. The preacher began by dividing his discourse into two or three parts, and by enumerating the several branches into which each part was to be enlarged. Donne accepted this rigid framework, which was a great aid to the memory of both preacher and congregation. He never read his sermons, but neither did he preach extempore.

---

[14] *Sermons,* VII, 243.

[15] He quoted them in *A Sermon of Valediction at my going into Germany* (Vol. II, 379) when he was feeling qualms of anxiety about what might have proved a dangerous journey, and ten years later, in his Easter sermon of 1629, he reiterates them: "And, since with the Lord there is *Copiosa Redemptio, Plenteous Redemption,* that overflowing mercy of our God...that plenteous Redemption, may hold even in this particular blessednesse...there is plenteous redemption...this plenteous Redemption" (Vol. VIII, 370).

[16] Misinterpretations of his meaning may be found in the work of some professed Donne scholars. Thus when Donne, preaching by the King's order at St. Paul's Cross, took as his text, "They fought from heaven; the stars in their courses fought against Sisera," Gosse surprisingly identifies Sisera with King James. "The text seems unluckily chosen to illustrate the supposed defiance of the King by the Puritans—'The stars in their courses fought against Sisera'—but Sisera was highly pleased with his Dean's defence." (Gosse, *Life and Letters of John Donne* (1899), II, 161). In the sermon Donne tells us that the stars represent the ministers of the Gospel, and that *"Sisera* is *Error."*

He prepared his sermons very carefully, made voluminous notes, and then committed the whole discourse to memory.

When he preached on the *Psalms* or on any other book of the Old Testament, Donne generally used the threefold method—literal, moral, and "spiritual" or anagogical—which had been used by preachers and commentators from the time of Origen and Clement of Alexandria to the Renaissance. In the sixteenth and seventeenth centuries this method was beginning to look a little old-fashioned, and many of Donne's contemporaries were abandoning it in favor of a more historical approach. However, Donne himself announced in two sermons preached at Lincoln's Inn on the Thirty-eighth Psalm that this method was to be the basis of his series of six sermons. Having announced his text [*Psa.* 38.3] he says:

Which words we shall first consider, as they are our present object, as they are historically, and literally to be understood of *David;* And secondly, in their *retrospect,* as they look back upon the first *Adam,* and so concern *Mankind collectively,* and so *you,* and *I,* and all have our portion in these calamities; And thirdly, we shall consider them in their *prospect,* in their future relation to the *second Adam,* in *Christ Jesus . . ."*[17]

And in the next sermon he puts it more briefly:

First then, all these things are *literally* spoken of *David:* By *application,* of us; and by *figure,* of Christ. *Historically, David; morally,* we; *Typically,* Christ is the subject of this text.[18]

Though Donne frequently makes use of the moral and anagogical senses of Scripture, he is quite definite in asserting the supremacy of the literal sense, and thus he avoided the absurdities into which some of the earlier commentators fell. In his Christmas sermon of 1621 at St. Paul's he says:

Therefore though it be ever lawfull, and often times very usefull, for the raising and exaltation of our devotion . . . to induce the *diverse senses* that the Scriptures doe admit, yet this may not be admitted, if there may be danger thereby, to neglect or weaken the *literall sense* it selfe. For there is no necessity of that *spirituall wantonnesse* of finding more then necessary senses; for, the more *lights* there are, the more *shadows* are also cast by those many lights. And, as it is true in religious duties, so is it in interpre-

---

[17] *Sermons,* II, 75.
[18] *Ibid.,* p. 97.

tation of matters of Religion, *Necessarium & Satis convertuntur;* when you have done that you ought to doe in your calling, you have done enough ... so when you have the *necessary sense,* that is the meaning of the holy Ghost in that place, you have senses enow, and not till then, though you have never so many, and never so delightfull.[19]

In the nineteenth century this method was denounced as absurd by Biblical critics of various schools of thought, such as Matthew Arnold, Jowett, Dean Farrar, and Bishop Charles Gore. Farrar summed up the work of the Alexandrian Fathers by saying: "They do but systematize the art of misinterpretation. They have furnished volumes of baseless application without shedding upon the significance of Scripture one ray of genuine light."[20] The twentieth century has seen a revulsion from this wholesale condemnation. While some commentators may still desire "a single plain sense of Scripture" there has been a widespread return to the symbolical interpretation of Old Testament literature. A modern lay writer, Professor C. S. Lewis, in his *Reflections on the Psalms* (London, 1958, pp. 99–138), devotes three chapters to an eloquent re-statement of the position that Christians may rightly interpret the Old Testament, and especially the *Psalms,* as symbolizing and anticipating the life and death of Christ.

In handling texts from the Gospels Donne used a variety of methods. Occasionally he preached two or three sermons on a single text, as he did on *John* 1.8, while at other times (as in Sermon 7 of this volume) he based a single sermon on three texts, though only one (*John* 11.35) is placed at the head of the sermon, and the other texts (*Luke* 19.41 and *Heb.* 5.7) are enumerated in his third paragraph, and form the subject of the second and third parts of his sermon. Two sermons in the present volume show an interesting variation from Donne's usual direct approach to his text. Seventeenth-century sermons were almost invariably divided into two, three, or more parts, and each part might have several branches. This division

---

[19] See Sermon 6, p. 134 of this book.

[20] Helen Gardner, *The Business of Criticism* (Oxford, 1959), p. 89. The two chapters on "The Drunkenness of Noah," pp. 79–100, and "The Historical Sense," pp. 127–157, are valuable for those readers who would like to pursue this subject further, and pp. 136–142 deal specifically with Donne.

was clearly summarized early in the sermon, and Donne had no wish to upset his hearers by disregarding the usual practice. However, there are many texts in the Gospels for which this detailed dissection is inadvisable. Many sermon hearers have been distressed by the way in which a magnificent verse from the Gospels has been cheapened and its power lessened for them by unwise elaboration and repetition on the part of the preacher. In Sermons 6 and 10 Donne avoided this difficulty by studying carefully the whole passage in which his chosen theme is stated and then selecting as his actual text a verse which would lead up to and suggest the verse which he actually wished to impress on the minds of his hearers. Thus in Sermon 6 his theme is Christ the Light, and this is most fully expressed in *John* 1.9, "That was the true light, which lighteth every man that cometh into the world," but he must have surprised the congregation by announcing the preceding verse, which refers to John the Baptist, "He was not that light, but was sent to bear witness of that light." We must remember that both verses formed part of the Gospel appointed for Christmas Day,[21] and since Holy Communion was always celebrated at St. Paul's on the morning of that day, Donne's audience had already heard this Gospel read aloud a few minutes earlier, so that when he repeated his text, its final words, "... witness of that light," their minds would inevitably move on to the succeeding verse, "That was the true light..." Thus they would grasp that Donne's real theme was the whole passage describing Christ as the Light.

If the Psalms were Donne's treasury of song, the Gospels represented the sheet-anchor of his faith. He was a great evangelical preacher. When he spoke of the love of Christ, his words became full of a fire and a passion which were lacking in his treatment of some parts of the Christian faith. The Cross of Christ was at the heart of his religion. Coleridge noted this in his judgment on Jeremy Taylor: "The Cross of Christ is dimly seen in Taylor's work. Compare him in this respect with Donne and you will feel the difference

---

[21] *John* 1.1–14. This is the great prologue to the Fourth Gospel. The Roman Church reads it in the Latin of the Vulgate, the English Church in the English of the Authorized Version. Donne throughout the sermon quotes both the Latin and the English words of his text.

in a moment."[22] This is evident in Donne's *Divine Poems* as well as in the *Sermons*. See in particular such poems as *"Goodfriday, 1613. Riding Westward," "La Corona, 5.* Crucifying," *"Holy Sonnets, 9."*

Donne's love of the Gospels seems to have developed steadily during the sixteen years of his ministry.[23] His gospel teaching is based equally on *Matthew,* representing the first three Gospels, and *John.* He preached sixteen sermons on *Matthew,* only two on *Mark,* three on *Luke,* and sixteen on *John.* He liked the majesty of *Matthew* with its picture of Christ as the new Lawgiver delivering the Sermon on the Mount to his disciples as Moses had given the Law from Sinai. He liked also the compact discourses into which *Matthew* has packed so many parables and maxims which are scattered in the other two Synoptists. When Donne quoted a text which occurs in two or three of the Gospels he generally gave the reference to *Matthew* alone. He preached three good sermons on texts taken from the Sermon on the Mount.[24]

John was perhaps the Gospel on which Donne meditated most fruitfully. He loved the great prologue, in which Christ is set forth as the Word (the Logos) and the Light. He was profoundly affected by the symbolism of this Gospel, in which we find the seven great affirmations, "I am the bread of life," "I am the light of the world," "I am the resurrection and the life," and so on. Seven, as Donne often tells us, is the number of infinity, and so these affirmations suggest the infinite riches of Christ. The first words of *John,* "In the beginning"

---

[22] *Table Talk* (1835), 1. 168.

[23] This fact was not evident till the sermons were arranged chronologically in the University of California Press edition. Thus in the nine sermons of Volume I, preached from 1615 to 1618, there is only one sermon preached on a text from the Gospels. In Volume II, from 1618 to March, 1620, there are five sermons out of eighteen; in Volume IV there are four out of fifteen; in Volume VII there are eight out of eighteen. Volumes IX and X cannot be reckoned, since they consist largely of undated sermons.

[24] These are on *Mat.* 5.8: "Blessed are the pure in heart" (*Sermons,* VII, No. 13); *Mat.* 6.21: "For where your treasure is, there will your heart be also" (IX, No. 7); and *Mat.* 5.16: "Let your light so shine before men, that they may see your good works, and glorify your Father which is in heaven" (X, No. 3).

are set beside the same first words of *Genesis* again and again in Donne's sermons.[25]

There is symbolism in all four Gospels, but *John* has certain symbols peculiar to itself, such as Christ the True Light (1.9), the Ladder set up from earth to heaven (1.51), the Crucified Serpent (3.14),[26] the True Vine (15.1), and others. The symbolism of numbers meant much to Donne, as he explained in his *Essays in Divinity* (ed. Simpson, pp. 52–61).

In Sermon 1 of this volume, which was preached on Easter Day, 1619, Donne's favorite themes of love and death are both exemplified, but there is here no mention of the worms or skeletons which are currently associated with Donne's idea of death. Instead we have a wonderfully beautiful passage on the mystical death of rapture:

...The contemplation of God, and heaven, is a kinde of buriall, and Sepulchre, and rest of the soule; and in this death of rapture, and extasie, in this death of the Contemplation of my interest in my Saviour, I shall finde my self, and all my sins enterred, and entombed in his wounds, and like a Lily in Paradise, out of red earth, I shall see my soule rise out of his blade, in a candor, and in an innocence, contracted there, acceptable in the sight of his Father.[27]

Sermon 2 in this volume is undated, but since it is described in the Folio as "Preached at S. Pauls," it is almost certainly later than Donne's election as Dean in November, 1621, while there are several passages in it which seem to refer to the Elector's series of defeats in the years 1620–1621. The most probable year for it is 1622.

Throughout the sermon Donne dwells on the virtue of praise. Of the Book of *Psalms* he says, "The Book is Praise, the parts are Prayer. The name changes not the nature; Prayer and Praise is the same

---

[25] See p. 129 of this volume and compare it with *Sermons*, II, 246: "*Moses* his *in principio*, that beginning, the creation we can remember; but St. *Johns in principio*, that beginning, eternity, we cannot..."

[26] Donne devotes a whole sermon to Jacob's vision of the Ladder, and its application to Christ (*Sermons*, II, No. 10), and he also has a very beautiful meditation on that vision (quoted on p. 242 of this present volume). He gives another sermon, and also a set of verses, to the contrast between Satan, the Serpent of Guile, and the Crucified Serpent, Christ (*Sermons*, X, No. 8 and *Poems*, ed. Grierson, I, 398–400).

[27] Sermon I, pp. 42–43.

thing." Prayer and praise "accompany one another ... they meet like two waters, and make the streame of devotion the fuller." Prayer consists as much of praise for the past as of supplication for the future.

It is the counsell of the Wise man, *Prevent the Sunne to give thanks to God, and at the day-spring pray unto him.* You see still, how these two duties are marshalled, and disposed; First Praise, and then Prayer, but both early: ... Rise as early as you can, you cannot be up before God; no, nor before God raise you: Howsoever you prevent this Sunne, the Sunne of the Firmament, yet the Sonne of Heaven hath prevented you, for without his preventing Grace you could not stirre.[28]

This joy we shall see, when we see him, who is so in it, as that he is this joy it selfe. But here in this world, so far as I can enter into my Masters sight, I can enter into my Masters joy. I can see God in his Creatures, in his Church, in his Word and Sacraments, and Ordinances; Since I am not without this sight, I am not without this joy.[29]

Here Donne's imagination is fired, and he mounts on wings. He had chosen a happy text, "O satisfy us early with thy mercy, that we may rejoice and be glad all our days." This combined two of the thoughts that were dearest to him—the everlasting loving kindness of God and the beauty of the dawning of the day. He himself was an early riser,[30] and he loved to remember that God's mercies were new every morning, fresh and sparkling as the dewdrops in the sunlight. In the passages quoted above, the texture of the writing is as rich and laden with meaning as the lines of his poems. There is his favorite word-play on "the Sunne of the Firmament" and "the Sonne of Heaven," which runs through half a page, and lightens with humor his rebuke to those sluggards who have come to church without having said their morning prayers in private at home. There is his well-chosen quotation from the Book of *Wisdom,* and his glancing allusion to Christ's parable of the talents in the antithesis—"so far as I can enter into my Masters sight, I can enter into my Masters joy."

---

[28] Sermon 2, p. 58 of the present volume. *Prevent* is here used in the archaic sense "go before, anticipate."

[29] Sermon 2, p. 64.

[30] "Nor was his age onely so industrious, but in the most unsetled dayes of his youth, his bed was not able to detain him beyond the hour of four in the morning." Walton, *Lives* (1670), Life of Donne, pp. 61-62.

Prayer and praise make an alliterative chime throughout the sentences, and this world and the next keep each other in view. "Gods house in this world is called the house of Prayer; but in heaven it is the house of Praise: No surprisall with any new necessities there, but one even, incessant, and everlasting tenor of thanksgiving."[31]

Sermon 3 was the first sermon which Donne preached before Charles the First. Donne was given very short notice by the Lord Chamberlain, and he wrote to his friend Sir Robert Ker asking him to be allowed to spend a little time in Ker's rooms at court before the service, so that he might prepare himself for the ordeal. Ker answered kindly and invited Donne to dine with him first, for the sermon was to be preached in the afternoon, but Donne refused, writing "But, in good faith, I do not eat before, nor can after ... so much hath my this years debility disabled me, even for receiving favours. After the Sermon, I will steal into my Coach home, and pray that my good purpose may be well accepted, and my defects graciously pardoned."[32]

The young King, who was very pale and grave, listened attentively and devoutly to the sermon, so the courtiers observed. He showed his approval by quickly ordering that it should be published. This was done speedily, and it appeared in a beautifully printed little quarto volume. Like the other sermons which were published in Donne's lifetime, it was excluded from the Folios, probably for reasons of copyright, and it was omitted by Alford. Consequently the anthologists have left it alone, and I have included it here partly because of its intrinsic merit, but also because it is so little known.[33]

---

[31] Pp. 48–59. These are only a few passages taken from a number of pages in which we find the following images: the Morning Star, the dawn, sunrise, the sun in its strength, showers of rain on the thirsty earth, associated with the thought of God's mercy and man's response in songs of praise. Compare also the great passage on God's mercy, pp. 182–184.

[32] *Letters* (1651), pp. 311, 313–314; Gosse, *Life and Letters of John Donne*, II, 219–220.

[33] Readers may be surprised that I have not included in this section on the *Psalms* the famous *Deaths Duell* on *Psalms* 68.20, but it has been reprinted so often that I have deliberately omitted it. Some critics who have apparently read no other complete sermon of Donne's, write of it as if its references to worms and skeletons were characteristic of all the other 159 sermons.

No. 4, the Second Prebend Sermon, is one of Donne's finest discourses, and it has furnished the anthologists with many extracts. Gosse admired it immensely. He described it as "a long poem of victory over death," and as "one of the most magnificent pieces of religious writing in English literature." Of its peroration he wrote that "it closes with a majestic sentence of incomparable pomp and melody, which might be selected as typical of Jacobean, or rather early Stuart, prose in its most gorgeous and imperial order."[34]

During the second half of 1625 London had suffered from a terrible epidemic of plague. The King and Queen with the Court had moved to Hampton Court, which became infected, to Windsor, and finally to Woodstock where they remained while Parliament sat at the neighboring city of Oxford during August. Rich and poor fled from stricken London, so that at last almost all the shops were shut and the streets were as deserted at midday as they were ordinarily at three in the morning. Meanwhile the scum of the great city set about looting the empty city, and Donne has left a vivid picture of the misery and desolation in the first sermon which he preached at St. Dunstan's "after our Dispersion, by the Sickness" on January 15, 1625/6.[35]

The Second Prebend Sermon was preached a fortnight later, and in it and the sermons which succeeded it Donne set to work to cheer and uplift his depressed and dispirited congregations. Other preachers had insisted that the plague was God's judgment on sin, and had chosen such texts as "There is wrath gone out from the Lord; the plague is begun" to emphasize their strictures on the iniquities of London. Donne did not dispute this general belief, but he thought it more important to insist that London, in spite of its sins, might still be called, like Jerusalem of old, "the holy City," and that God's mercy was available for its afflicted people. There is a pleasant passage in a sermon preached a few weeks after the Prebend Sermon in which he says, "Who but my selfe can conceive the sweetnesse of that salutation, when the Spirit of God sayes to me in a morning, Go forth to day and preach, and preach consolation, preach peace, preach mercy,

---

[34] Gosse, *Life and Letters of John Donne*, II, 239.
[35] *Sermons*, VI, No. 18. See especially pp. 359–360.

And spare my people, spare that people whom I have redeemed with my precious Blood, and be not angry with them for ever ... "[36]

In this Prebend Sermon Donne notes "an extraordinary sadnesse, a predominant melancholy, a faintnesse of heart, a chearlesnesse, a joylesnesse of spirit" as one of the characteristics of the time, and therefore he says, "I would always raise your hearts, and dilate your hearts, to a holy Joy, to a joy in the Holy Ghost."

"Joy" is the keyword of this sermon. With its derivatives "joyful," "rejoice," and the like, it recurs thirty-nine times. And it is closely associated with "glory," as in the following passage, where Donne uses his favorite metaphor of the map:

If you looke upon this world in a Map, you find two Hemisphears, two half worlds. If you crush heaven into a Map, you may find two Hemisphears too, two half heavens; Halfe will be Joy, and halfe will be Glory; for in these two, the joy of heaven, and the glory of heaven, is all heaven often represented unto us. And as of those two Hemisphears of the world, the first hath been knowne long before, but the other, (that of America, which is the richer in treasure) God reserved for later Discoveries; So though he reserve that Hemisphear of heaven, which is the Glory thereof, to the Resurrection, yet the other Hemisphear, the Joy of heaven, God opens to our Discovery, and delivers for our habitation even whilst we dwell in this world.[37]

This joy takes full account of the manifold afflictions of the world. It does not depend on circumstances, but is derived from the unchanging nature of God himself. "Fixe upon God any where, and you shall finde him a Circle; He is with you now, when you fix upon him; He was with you before, for he brought you to this fixation; and he will be with you hereafter, for *He is yesterday, and to day, and the same for ever."*[38] We hear Donne's characteristic note in the words: "All our life is a continuall burden, yet we must not groane; A continuall squeasing, yet we must not pant; And as in the tendernesse of our childhood, we suffer, and yet are whipt if we cry, so we are complained of, if we complaine, and made delinquents if we call the times ill."[39] For Donne there is no safe abiding place for the soul anywhere but in God.

---

[36] *Sermons*, VII, 133.
[37] Sermon 4, p. 112.
[38] Sermon 4, p. 95.
[39] Sermon 4, p. 97.

Under the shadow of his wings, you may, you should, rejoyce... And
then thinke also, that if God afford thee the shadow of his wings, that is,
Consolation, respiration, refreshing, though not a present, and plenary
deliverance, in thy afflictions, not to thanke God, is a murmuring, and
not to rejoyce in Gods wayes, is an unthankfulnesse. Howling is the noyse
of hell, singing the voyce of heaven; Sadnesse the damp of Hell, Rejoycing the serenity of Heaven. And he that hath not this joy here, lacks
one of the best pieces of his evidence for the joyes of heaven...[40]

From this point Donne enters upon his peroration, which recalls
a passage in *The Second Anniversary,* where he had written of the
soul set free by death, and ascending to heaven:

> Thinke thy shell broke, thinke thy Soule hatch'd but now.
> And think this slow-pac'd soule, which late did cleave
> To a body, and went but by the bodies leave,
> Twenty, perchance, or thirty mile a day,
> Dispatches in a minute all the way
> Twixt heaven, and earth; she stayes not in the ayre...
> For th'Element of fire, she doth not know,
> Whether she past by such a place or no;
> She baits not at the Moone, nor cares to trie
> Whether in that new world, men live, and die...
> Who, if she meet the body of the Sunne,
> Goes through, not staying till his course be runne...
> But ere she can consider how she went,
> At once is at, and through the Firmament....
> So by the Soule doth death string Heaven and Earth.[41]

So here Donne continues to speak of the faithful soul:

This joy shall not be put out in death, and a new joy kindled in me in
Heaven; But as my soule, as soone as it is out of my body, is in Heaven,
and does not stay for the possession of Heaven, nor for the fruition of the
sight of God, till it be ascended through ayre, and fire, and Moone, and
Sun, and Planets, and Firmament, to that place which we conceive to be
Heaven, but without the thousandth part of a minutes stop, as soone as it
issues, is in a glorious light, which is Heaven... As my soule shall not goe
towards Heaven, but goe by Heaven to Heaven, to the Heaven of
Heavens, So the true joy of a good soule in this world is the very joy of
Heaven; and we goe thither, not that being without joy, we might have
joy infused into us, but that as Christ sayes, *Our joy might be full,*

---

[40] Sermon 4, pp. 112–113.
[41] *Poems,* ed. Grierson, I, 256–257.

perfected, sealed with an everlastingnesse; for, as he promises, *That no man shall take our joy from us,* so neither shall Death it selfe take it away, nor so much as interrupt it, or discontinue it, But as in the face of Death, when he layes hold upon me, and in the face of the Devill, when he attempts me, I shall see the face of God, (for, every thing shall be a glasse, to reflect God upon me) so in the agonies of Death, in the anguish of that dissolution, in the sorrowes of that valediction, in the irreversible-nesse of that transmigration, I shall have a joy, which shall no more evaporate, then my soule shall evaporate, A joy, that shall passe up, and put on a more glorious garment above, and be joy super-invested in glory.[42]

Sermon 5, which is placed at the beginning of the Gospel section, is undated, but there are several reasons for placing it comparatively early among Donne's sermons.[43] It has certain peculiarities of style and arrangement which set it apart from most of the sermons, and which have suggested to me that it may have been intended for one of Donne's country parishes, such as Sevenoaks in Kent or Blunham in Bedfordshire. The sentences are shorter and simpler than usual, and all the marginal headings are in English instead of Latin. Most of the sermon is free from the usual quotations from the Fathers. It is only in the last few pages that St. Augustine, St. Jerome, and the rest make their appearance. The sermon is shorter than average, as would befit a country church. Yet Donne certainly took pains over the sermon. In the paragraph quoted below, each short sentence has a wealth of thought and experience behind it, and the whole para-graph is lighted up by the final simile in which Donne, the affec-tionate father of many "gamesome children," as he called them in one of his letters, compares God's reception of prayer to a father's play with his children.

Almost every meanes between God and man, suffers some adulteratings and disguises: But prayer least: And it hath most wayes and addresses. It

---

[42] Sermon 4, pp. 113–114.

[43] These are set forth in detail in *Sermons,* V, 18–20. Of these reasons the most important is that it is found in the two MSS *E* and *M* in company with a number of dated sermons, all of which belong to the earlier part of Donne's career as a preacher, ranging from December, 1617 to April, 1622. Another reason is that the style of the sermon has some affinity with that of *Essays in Divinity,* a work written before Donne's ordination.

may be mentall, for we may thinke prayers. It may be vocall, for we may speake prayers. It may be actuall, for we do prayers. For deeds have voyce; the vices of *Sodome* did cry, and the Almes of *Toby*. And if it were proper for St. *John,* in the first of the *Revelations* to turne back to see a voyce, it is more likely God will looke down, to heare a worke. So then to do the office of your vocation sincerely, is to pray.... Since then every rectified man, is the temple of the Holy Ghost, when he prays; it is the Holy Ghost it selfe that prays; and what can be denyed, where the Asker gives? He plays with us, as children, shewes us pleasing things, that we may cry for them, and have them. Before we call, he answers, and when we speak, he heares ..."[44]

Sermon 6 was preached on Christmas Day, 1621, at St. Paul's, and it was the first of Donne's sermons as Dean. It was a splendid sermon, which Donne intended to be a manifesto that during his tenure of office his essential theme would be Christ as Light of the World, the Divine Word from all eternity who became incarnate at Bethlehem. It is longer than the majority of Donne's sermons, and it has a few weak passages which could well have been pruned away, but the Londoners who heard it must have been moved by his passionate eloquence and his evident sincerity.

On Christmas Day and certain other festivals the service at St. Paul's was attended by the Lord Mayor of London, the aldermen and sheriffs, and the chosen representatives of the twelve great livery companies, who rode together in procession to their cathedral. It was to them in particular that he addressed his peroration:

But to you the *Day starre,* the *Sunne of Righteousnesse,* the Sonne of God is risen this day. The day is but a little longer now, then at *shortest;* but a *little* it is. Be a little better now, then when you came, and mend a little at every coming, and in lesse then seaven *yeares apprentissage,* which your occupations cost you, you shall learn, not the Mysteries of your *twelve Companies,* but the Mysteries of the *twelve Tribes,* of the *twelve Apostles,* of their *twelve Articles,* whatsoever belongeth to the *promise,* to the performance, to the *Imitation* of Christ Jesus. He, who is *Lux una,* light and *light alone,* and *Lux tota,* light and *all light,* shall also, by that light, which he sheddeth from himselfe upon all his, the light *of Grace,* give you all these Attestations, all these witnesses of that his light; he shall give you *Lucem essentiæ,* (really, and essentially to be incorporated into him, to be made partakers of the Divine Nature, and the same Spirit with the Lord, by a Conversation in Heaven, here) ... *Lighten our darknesse,*

[44] Sermon 5, pp. 116–117.

we beseech thee, O Lord, with all these lights; that in thy light we may see light; that in this Essential *light, which is Christ, and in this* Supernaturall *light, which is* grace, *we may see all these, and all other beames of light, which may bring us to* thee, *and* him, *and that blessed Spirit which proceeds from both. Amen.*[45]

The symbolism of light which Donne used here was particularly suitable for a Christmas sermon. Soon after the winter solstice, when the sun seems to have sunk to its lowest point, the Church keeps the feast of the birth of the Sun of Righteousness, who rises with healing in his wings. At Christmas the London of Donne's day was plunged for nearly sixteen hours out of the twenty-four into a darkness which cannot be realized by modern city dwellers for whom night is turned into day by the brilliance of electric standards and flashing neon lights. Oil lamps, candles, and torches were the sole means of lighting the houses and streets. In the narrow lanes the height of the overhanging houses almost blocked out the sky, so that even the light of moon or stars on a clear night could hardly penetrate the murky darkness. Londoners hailed with joy the first faint indications that the sun was beginning to regain its strength. Donne saw in the coming of Christ into the world the dawn of hope, the promise that what he calls in this sermon "the long and frozen winter nights of sinne, and of the works of darkness" would be dispersed by the eternal Light. His message from the pulpit of St. Paul's was to be that Christ is the source and fountain of life and light. From him proceed the light of nature and the light of reason, the light of grace and the light of glory.[46]

Sermon 7 is a quiet and beautiful discourse on the humanity and the compassion of Jesus. Coleridge, who was a lover but also an outspoken critic of Donne's sermons,[47] singled out a sentence to be found on p. 174 of the present volume as "Worthy almost of Shakespeare!" The sentence is "...that world which findes it selfe truly in an Autumne, in it selfe, findes it selfe in a spring, in our imaginations."

---

[45] Sermon 6, pp. 155–156.

[46] It should be remembered that London is in the latitude of Labrador, and that the sun rises at 8.08 A.M. and sets at 3.45 P.M. on the shortest day.

[47] See a summary of Coleridge's notes on the Sermons in E. M. Simpson's *A Study of the Prose Works of John Donne* (2d ed.; Oxford, Clarendon Press, 1948), pp. 287–290.

The text of the sermon is the shortest verse in the Bible, "Jesus wept," and some time later Donne preached a companion sermon on another text almost as short, "Rejoyce evermore."[48]

No. 8 is the Christmas Day sermon for 1624. It contains one of his most exquisite passages, in which he dilates on his favorite theme, the boundless and ever-present mercy of God:

> God made Sun and Moon to distinguish seasons, and day, and night, and we cannot have the fruits of the earth but in their seasons: But God hath made no decree to distinguish the seasons of his mercies; In paradise, the fruits were ripe, the first minute, and in heaven it is alwaies Autumne, his mercies are ever in their maturity.... He brought light out of darknesse, not out of a lesser light; he can bring thy Summer out of Winter, though thou have no Spring; though thou have been benighted till now, wintred and frozen, clouded and eclypsed, damped and benummed, smothered and stupified till now, now God comes to thee, not as in the dawning of the day, not as in the bud of the spring, but as the Sun at noon to illustrate all shadowes, as the sheaves in harvest, to fill all penuries, all occasions invite his mercies, and all times are his seasons.[49]

This is only a fragment of a long passage which should be read slowly and carefully to relish its full flavor. George Saintsbury singled it out as "a passage than which I hardly know anything more exquisitely rhythmed in the whole range of English from Ælfric to Pater."[50]

Donne achieves some of his effects here by the use of alliteration. In the first sentence quoted we have three alliterative sounds: *s* in "*S*un ... *s*easons ... *s*easons ... *s*easons"; *m* in "*M*oon ... *m*ercies ... *m*inute ... *m*ercies ... *m*aturity"; and *d* in "*d*istinguish ... *d*ay ... *d*ecree ... *d*istinguish." More subtle is the effect produced by the use of heavy consonantal groups and thick vowel sounds in "clouded

---

[48] This sermon is printed in *Sermons*, X, as No. 10. Donne preached a number of sermons on texts which may be said to illustrate the paradoxes of the Christian religion. Thus in *Sermons*, Vol. II, we have one pair of sermons (Nos. 15 and 16) and in Vol. III, another pair (Nos. 3 and 4) which are complementary to one another. Donne was always interested in seeing how he could use one passage of Scripture to illustrate or supplement another.

[49] Sermon 8, p. 182.

[50] *History of English Prose Rhythm* (London, 1912), pp. 162–163.

and eclypsed, damped and benummed, smothered and stupified."
Here the slow heavy syllables suggest the bewilderment of the frozen
soul, contrasted with the sense of life and movement conferred by the
bestowal of God's mercy, suggested by the light anapæstic rhythm
of "not as in the dawning of the day, not as in the bud of the spring,"
a clause which leads up in turn to the full splendor of the climax, "as
the Sun at noon to illustrate [the second syllable is stressed] all
shadows, as the sheaves in harvest, to fill all penuries."

We are not to think of Donne as elaborately working out a series
of rhetorical effects. He was a poet, and whenever he was deeply
moved, as here by his contemplation of God's mercies, he chose with
a poet's instinct the right sounds and rhythms to express the emotions
which he wished to convey.

This magnificence of diction is not sustained throughout the whole
sermon. There are some dull and tedious pages in which Donne
paraphrased and condensed the information which he got from the
massive Latin commentary of Cornelius à Lapide (van den Steen)
on the major prophets. This was published at Antwerp in 1622, and it
followed the same writer's commentaries on the Pentateuch (published in 1616) and on St. Paul's Epistles (published in 1614), of
which Donne also made use.[51]

Sermon 9 is a companion piece to Sermon 7 in its emphasis on the
humanity of Jesus. Here Donne stresses Christ's friendliness with
publicans and sinners, and his readiness to join in the feast which
Matthew made for him. The text enabled Donne to set forth his
intense belief that Christ's religion is meant for bad men and women
who would like to be good.

Shall we wonder that Christ would live with sinners, who was content
to die for sinners? Wonder that he would eat the bread and Wine of

---

[51] Cornelius, a Flemish Jesuit, wrote voluminous commentaries on
almost the whole Bible, but several of these appeared too late for Donne
to have made use of them. I have accumulated proof, however, that Donne
used his works on the Pentateuch and on St. Paul's Epistles. See *Sermons,*
VIII, 393–396, and X, 369–374. Donne mentions him by name in the
margin of the Christmas sermon on Exodus 4.13 (*Sermons,* VIII, 151).
His work was extremely careful and thorough, and it was valued throughout the seventeenth, eighteenth, and nineteenth centuries by Catholics and
Anglicans alike.

sinners, that gave sinners his own flesh to eat, and his own blood to drink? Or if we do wonder at this, (as, indeed, nothing is more wonderful) yet let us not calumniate, let us not mis-interpret any way, that he shall be pleased to take, to derive his mercy to any man: but, (to use *Clement* of *Alexandria*'s comparison) as we tread upon many herbs negligently in the field, but when we see them in an Apothecaries shop, we begin to think that there is some vertue in them; so howsoever we have a perfect hatred, and a religious despite against a sinner, as a sinner; yet if Christ Jesus shall have been pleased to come to his door, and to have stood, and knock'd, and enter'd, and sup'd, and brought his dish, and made himself that dish, and seal'd a reconciliation to that sinner, in admitting him to that Table, to that Communion, let us forget the Name of Publican, the Vices of any particular profession; and forget the name of sinner, the history of any man's former life; and be glad to meet that man now in the arms, and to grow up with that man now in the bowels of Christ Jesus; since Christ doth not now begin to make that man his, but now declares to us, that he hath been his, from all eternity: For in the Book of Life, the name of *Mary Magdalen* was as soon recorded, for all her incontinency, as the name of the blessed Virgin, for all her integrity; and the name of St. *Paul*, who drew his sword against Christ, as soon as St. *Peter*, who drew his in defence of him: for the Book of life was not written successively, word after word, line after line, but delivered as a Print, all together. There the greatest sinners were as soon recorded, as the most righteous; and here Christ comes *to call, not the righteous* at all, *but onely sinners to repentance*.[52]

---

[52] Sermon 9, pp. 207–208. This passage finds a close parallel to the poem *An hymne to the Saints, and to Marquesse Hamylton*, which Donne had written a year earlier, especially in the following lines (*Poems*, ed. Grierson, I, 289–290):

> And if, faire soule, not with first *Innocents*
> Thy station be, but with the *Pænitents*,
> (And, who shall dare to aske then when I am
> Dy'd scarlet in the blood of that pure Lambe,
> Whether that colour, which is scarlet then,
> Were black or white before in eyes of men?)
> When thou rememb'rest what sins thou didst finde
> Amongst those many friends now left behinde,
> And seest such sinners as they are, with thee
> Got thither by repentance, Let it bee
> Thy wish to wish all there, to wish them cleane;
> With *him* a *David*, her a *Magdalen*.

Donne devotes some part of this sermon to a defence of cheerful society and hospitality. This he derived from the circumstances in which Christ spoke the words of the text:

And in the first of these, the Historical and Occasional part, we shall see, first, That Christ by his personal presence justified Feasting, somewhat more then was meerly necessary, for society, and chearful conversation: He justified feasting, and feasting in an Apostles house: though a Churchman, and an Exemplar-man, he was not depriv'd of a plentiful use of Gods creatures, nor of the chearfulness of conversation.[53]

This is in harmony with what we know of Donne's own behavior. Though in his later years he was extremely temperate, he was not austere, and he loved good company and the society of friends, except in such a period of retirement as that after the death of his wife. Walton's testimony of him, given from personal knowledge, was that his company was one of the delights of mankind, and that "his aspect was chearful, and such as gave silent testimony of a clear knowing soul, and of a Conscience at peace with it self." This is confirmed by the funeral elegy which Sidney Godolphin, a minor poet, contributed to the *Poems* of 1635:

> Nor didst thou onely consecrate our teares,
> Give a religious tincture to our feares;
> But even our joyes had learn'd an innocence,
> Thou didst from gladnesse separate offence.[54]

Sermon 10 was preached at the funeral of Sir William Cockayne, an alderman of the City of London. Donne's eulogy of his character and career gave Clement Barksdale one of his *Memorials of Worthy Persons,* published in 1661, and this was reprinted in 1741 in John Wilford's *Memorials and Characters.*[55] But the chief interest of the sermon lies not in this brief eulogy but in Donne's handling of the theme which always moved him profoundly, the certainty of death and the hope of resurrection. The sermon gives us in its text another example of Donne's use of the method of oblique approach which

---

[53] Sermon 9, p. 198.

[54] *Poems,* ed. Grierson, I, 393.

[55] For a less favorable view of Cockayne's career, see Astrid Friis, *Alderman Cockayne's Protest and the Cloth Trade* (Copenhagen and London, 1927).

we have already noted in Sermon 6. Since it was preached at a funeral the audience had already heard the great words of Christ, "I am the resurrection and the life," repeated by the priest as the coffin was carried into the church.[56] According to *John* 11.21-25 they were first uttered as a reply to Martha's reproach, "Lord, if thou hadst been here, my brother had not died." The whole conversation between Jesus and Martha, leading up to this great affirmation, is the theme of Donne's sermon rather than the one verse which he chose as his text. A more ordinary preacher would have announced "I am the resurrection and the life" as his text, but Donne knew that these words had already made their solemn impact when the congregation rose to its feet as the coffin entered the church. He chose his text therefore from the beginning of Christ's conversation with Martha so that he could analyze and dissect Martha's reproach. Thus instead of asserting directly he could suggest by implication that his theme was Christ the Life, just as in his first Christmas sermon he had led his hearers indirectly to the consideration of Christ the True Light. As the symbolism of the Divine Light had dominated the preaching of Donne's first year as Dean of St. Paul's, so in the last two or three years of his ministry the Divine Life, infinite, immortal, is the theme of much of his preaching.[57] Light and life, those two great keywords of this Gospel, are inextricably joined in Donne's mind with the thought of Christ the Sun of Righteousness, who by his rising dispels the darkness of death and brings to men the light of life.[58]

This sermon is a fine one, full of memorable passages. One of these describes the difficulty of concentration in private prayer, and Donne gives us a remarkably vivid picture evidently drawn from his own experience.

---

[56] The rubric at the head of the Office for the Burial of the Dead in the Book of Common Prayer states "The Priest and Clerks meeting the corpse at the entrance of the Church-yard, and going before it, either into the Church, or towards the grave shall say, or sing: "I am the resurrection and the life, saith the Lord . . .""

[57] His Christmas sermon on *John* 10.10, "I am come that they might have life, and that they might have it more abundantly," almost certainly belongs to the end of 1629 (*Sermons,* IX, 12-13). See also VIII, 190-191; IX, 89-90, 127-129, 146-149, 153-154, 187-188, 203-204.

[58] A fuller treatment of this symbolism can be found in *Sermons,* X, 302-306.

I throw my selfe downe in my Chamber, and I call in, and invite God, and his Angels thither, and when they are there, I neglect God and his Angels, for the noise of a Flie, for the ratling of a Coach, for the whining of a doore; I talke on, in the same posture of praying; Eyes lifted up; knees bowed downe; as though I prayed to God; and, if God, or his Angels should aske me, when I thought last of God in that prayer, I cannot tell: Sometimes I finde that I had forgot what I was about, but when I began to forget it, I cannot tell. A memory of yesterdays pleasures, a feare of to morrows dangers, a straw under my knee, a noise in mine eare, a light in mine eye, an any thing, a nothing, a fancy, a Chimera in my braine, troubles me in my prayer. So certainely is there nothing, nothing in spirituall things, perfect in this world.[59]

Much of the sermon deals with that favorite theme of seventeenth-century writers, the imperfection and mutability of earthly things. There is an interesting reference to the "new philosophy" of Copernicus, Kepler, and Galileo, which had fascinated him so much in the earlier years when he was writing *Biathanatos, Ignatius his Conclave,* and the two poetical *Anniversaries:*

I need not call in new Philosophy, that denies a settlednesse, an acquiescence in the very body of the Earth, but makes the Earth to move in that place, where we thought the Sunne had moved; I need not that helpe, that the Earth it selfe is in Motion, to prove this, That nothing upon Earth is permanent; The Assertion will stand of it selfe, till some man assigne me some instance, something that a man may relie upon, and find permanent.[60]

When at last he turned to the consideration of death itself, his prose suddenly caught fire, and he uttered one of his short prose poems in which all the words are charged with poignant associations and a definite rhythm guides the whole movement. He thinks of Goliath as the type of manly strength, of Jezebel the haughty Oriental beauty, of Dives the representative of all rich men who are clothed in purple and fine linen and fare sumptuously every day, and then reflects that strength, beauty, riches, all must come to dust:

When *Goliah* had armed and fortified this body, and *Iezabel* had painted and perfumed this body, And *Dives* had pampered and larded this body, As God said to *Ezekiel*, when he brought him to the *dry bones, Fili*

[59] Sermon 10, pp. 226–227.
[60] Sermon 10, p. 233.

hominis, Sonne of Man, doest thou thinke these bones can live? They said in their hearts to all the world, Can these bodies die? And they are dead. *Iezabels* dust is not Ambar, nor *Goliahs* dust *Terra sigillata,* Medicinall; nor does the Serpent, whose meat they are both, finde any better relish in *Dives* dust, then in *Lazarus.*[61]

Here the words are incomparably enriched by the associations which lie behind the proper names. Ezekiel's vision of the valley of the dry bones, and his cry "Come from the four winds, O breath, and breathe upon these slain, that they may live," Jezebel cruel and brave, who prepared for her horrible death with the courage of a great queen, painting her face and tiring her head, Lazarus the beggar who went from his rags and his filth to Abraham's bosom—all these immortal stories must have risen at once into the minds of Donne's hearers, as he uttered these few sentences. He whose prose is often so copious and redundant here employs a singular economy of words: "They said in their hearts to all the world, Can these bodies die? And they are dead." Is there any other passage in Donne's prose which is so exclusively made up of monosyllables of Anglo-Saxon origin, or any sentence so short and pregnant as "And they are dead"? Coming as the words do, after the first introduction of the foreign names *Goliath, Jezebel, Dives,* and *Ezekiel,* and before their repetition (in a different order, and with the substitution of *Lazarus* for *Ezekiel* in the concluding sentence), they have a peculiar vividness of dramatic effect. Here the poet and preacher are one. It was the poet who brought in amber and that magical and medicinal *Terra sigillata* to suggest something rich and strange about the dust of these who had to die.

After this, Donne relapses for a few sentences into the flattest of pulpit prose. Then in the next paragraph his style rises again at the thought of resurrection. He turns from the Old Testament to Catullus for his associative magic: "The Gentils, and their Poets, describe the sad state of Death so, *Nox una obeunda,* That it is one everlasting Night; To them, a Night; But to a Christian, it is *Dies Mortis,* and *Dies Resurrectionis,* The day of Death, and The day of Resurrection; We die in the light, in the sight of Gods presence, and we rise in the

---

[61] Sermon 10, p. 234.

light, in the sight of his very Essence." Here the line of Catullus with its sad and heavy vowels is contrasted with the deliberate repetition of the long *i* sound in "die," "light," "sight," "rise," "light," "sight." Donne makes his point by a device which he uses very seldom in prose, that of rhyme. Also he uses a very marked anapæstic rhythm to suggest that for the Christian the night of death ends in light, the Light Eternal of the Beatific Vision: "We die in the light, in the sight of Gods presence, and we rise in the light, in the sight of his very Essence." The passage is subtly differentiated from actual verse by the occasional use of nonmetrical weighty syllables, but the effect on the mind and the ear is that of poetry. These two contrasting fragments, the one on death, the other on resurrection, reveal to us how much of the poet still lived in the Dean of St. Paul's.

Note.—A few textual notes to the sermons included in this volume will be found on page 244.

Number 1.

Preached to the Lords upon Easter-day, at the Communion, The King being then dangerously sick at New-Market.

PSAL. 89.48. *WHAT MAN IS HE THAT LIVETH, AND SHALL NOT SEE DEATH?*

AT FIRST, God gave the judgement of death upon man, when he should transgresse, absolutely, *Morte morieris,* Thou shalt surely dye: The woman in her Dialogue with the Serpent, she mollifies it, *Ne fortè moriamur,* perchance, if we eate, we may die; and then the Devill is as peremptory on the other side, *Nequaquam moriemini,* do what you will, surely you shall not die; And now God in this Text comes to his reply, *Quis est homo,* shall they not die? Give me but one instance, but one exception to this rule, *What man is hee that liveth, and shall not see death?* Let no man, no woman, no devill offer a *Ne fortè,* (perchance we may dye) much lesse a *Nequaquam,* (surely we shall not dye) except he be provided of an answer to this question, except he can give an instance against this generall, except he can produce that mans name, and history, that hath lived, and shall not see death. Wee are all conceived in close Prison; in our Mothers wombes, we are close Prisoners all; when we are borne, we are borne but to the liberty of the house; Prisoners still, though within larger walls; and then all our life is but a going out to the place of Execution, to death. Now was there ever any man seen to sleep in the Cart, between New-gate, and Tyborne? between the Prison, and the place of Execution, does any man sleep? And we sleep all the way; from the womb to the grave we are never throughly awake; but passe on with such dreames, and imaginations as these, I may live as well, as another, and why should I dye, rather

[Gen. 3.3, 4]

then another? but awake, and tell me, sayes this Text, *Quis homo?*
who is that other that thou talkest of? *What man is he that liveth,
and shall not see death?*

In these words, we shall first, for our generall humiliation, consider the unanswerablenesse of this question, There is no man that
lives, and shall not see death. Secondly, we shall see, how that modi-
fication of Eve may stand, *forte moriemur*, how there may be a probable answer made to this question, that it is like enough, that there
are some men that live, and shall not see death: And thirdly, we shall
finde that truly spoken, which the Devill spake deceitfully then, we
shall finde the *Nequaquam* verified, we shall finde a direct, and full
answer to this question; we shall finde a man that lives, and shall not
see death, our Lord, and Saviour Christ Jesus, of whom both S. *Augustine,* and S. *Hierome,* doe take this question to be principally
asked, and this Text to be principally intended. Aske me this question then, of all the sons of men, generally guilty of originall sin,
Quis homo, and I am speechlesse, I can make no answer; Aske me
this question of those men, which shall be alive upon earth at the
last day, when Christ comes to judgement, *Quis homo,* and I can
make a probable answer; *forte moriemur,* perchance they shall die;
It is a problematicall matter, and we say nothing too peremptorily.
Aske me this question without relation to originall sin, *Quis homo,*
and then I will answer directly, fully, confidently, *Ecce homo,* there
was a man that lived, and was not subject to death by the law, neither
did he actually die so, but that he fulfilled the rest of this verse; *Eruit
animam de inferno,* by his owne power, he delivered his soule from
the hand of the grave. From the first, this lesson rises, Generall doctrines must be generally delivered, All men must die: From the second, this lesson, Collaterall and unrevealed doctrines must be soberly
delivered, How we shall be changed at the last day, we know not so
clearly: From the third, this lesson arises, Conditionall Doctrines
must be conditionally delivered, If we be dead with him, we shall
be raised with him.

1. Part
Quis homo?

First then, for the generality, Those other degrees of punishment,
which God inflicted upon *Adam,* and *Eve,* and in them upon us,
were as absolutely, and illimitedly pronounced, as this of death, and
yet we see, they are many wayes extended, or contracted; To man it

was said, *In sudore vultus, In the sweat of thy browes, thou shalt eate*   [Gen. 3.19]
thy bread, and how many men never sweat, till they sweat with eat-
ing? To the woman it was said, *Thy desire shall be to thy husband,*   [Gen. 3.16]
and he shall rule over thee: and how many women have no desire
to their husbands, how many over-rule them? Hunger, and thirst,
and wearinesse, and sicknesse are denounced upon all, and yet if you
ask me *Quis homo?* What is that man that hungers and thirsts not,
that labours not, that sickens not? I can tell you of many, that never
felt any of these; but contract the question to that one of death, *Quis
homo?* What man is he that shall not taste death? And I know none.
Whether we consider the Summer Solstice, when the day is sixteen
houres, and the night but eight, or the Winter Solstice, when the
night is sixteen houres, and the day but eight, still all is but twenty
foure houres, and still the evening and the morning make but a day:
The Patriarchs in the old Testament had their Summer day, long
lives; we are in the Winter, short lived; but *Quis homo?* Which of
them, or us come not to our night in death? If we consider violent
deaths, casuall deaths, it is almost a scornfull thing to see, with what
wantonnesse, and sportfulnesse, death playes with us; We have seen
a man Canon proofe in the time of War, and slain with his own
Pistoll in the time of peace: We have seen a man recovered after his
drowning, and live to hang himselfe. But for that one kinde of death,
which is generall, (though nothing be in truth more against nature
then dissolution, and corruption, which is death) we are come to call
that death, naturall death, then which, indeed, nothing is more unnaturall; The generality makes it naturall; *Moses* sayes, that Mans   Psal. 90.10
age is seventy, and eighty is labour and pain; and yet himselfe was
more then eighty, and in a good state, and habitude when he said
so. No length, no strength enables us to answer this *Quis homo?*
What man? &c.
　　Take a flat Map, a Globe *in plano,* and here is East, and there is
West, as far asunder as two points can be put: but reduce this flat
Map to roundnesse, which is the true form, and then East and West
touch one another, and are all one: So consider mans life aright, to
be a Circle, *Pulvis es, & in pulverem reverteris, Dust thou art, and to*   [Gen. 3.19]
dust thou must return; Nudus egressus, Nudus revertar, Naked I   Job 1.[21]
came, and naked I must go; In this, the circle, the two points meet,

the womb and the grave are but one point, they make but one station, there is but a step from that to this. This brought in that custome amongst the Greek Emperours, that ever at the day of their Coronation, they were presented with severall sorts of Marble, that they might then bespeak their Tombe. And this brought in that Custome into the Primitive Church, that they called the Martyrs dayes, wherein they suffered, *Natalitia Martyrum,* their birth dayes; birth, and death is all one.

Their death was a birth to them into another life, into the glory of God; It ended one Circle, and created another; for immortality, and eternity is a Circle too; not a Circle where two points meet, but a Circle made at once; This life is a Circle, made with a Compasse, that passes from point to point; That life is a Circle stamped with a print, an endlesse, and perfect Circle, as soone as it begins. Of this Circle, the Mathematician is our great and good God; The other Circle we make up our selves; we bring the Cradle, and Grave together by a course of nature. Every man does; *Mi Gheber,* sayes the Originall; It is not *Ishe,* which is the first name of man, in the Scriptures, and signifies nothing but a *sound,* a voyce, a word; a Musicall ayre dyes, and evaporates, what wonder if man, that is but *Ishe,* a *sound,* dye too? It is not *Adam,* which is another name of man, and signifies nothing but *red earth;* Let it be earth red with blood, (with that murder which we have done upon our selves) let it be earth red with blushing, (so the word is used in the Originall) with a conscience of our own infirmity, what wonder if man, that is but *Adam,* guilty of this self-murder in himself, guilty of this in-borne frailty in himself, dye too? It is not *Enos,* which is also a third name of man, and signifies nothing but a *wretched and miserable creature;* what wonder if man, that is but earth, that is a burden to his Neighbours, to his friends, to his kindred, to himselfe, to whom all others, and to whom himself desires death, what wonder if he dye? But this question is framed upon none of these names; Not *Ishe,* not *Adam,* not *Enos;* but it is *Mi Gheber, Quis vir;* which is the word alwayes signifying a man accomplished in all excellencies, a man accompanied with all advantages; fame, and good opinion justly conceived, keepes him from being *Ishe,* a meere sound, standing onely upon popular acclamation; Innocency and integrity keepes him from being *Adam,* red earth, from bleeding, or blushing at any thing hee hath done; That holy and Religious Art of Arts, which S. *Paul* professed, *That he knew how to want, and how to abound,* keepes him from being *Enos,* miserable or wretched in any fortune; Hee is *Gheber,* a great Man, and a good Man, a happy Man, and a holy Man, and yet *Mi Gheber, Quis homo,* this man must see death.

[Phil. 4.11, 12]

And therefore we will carry this question a little higher, from *Quis homo,* to *Quis deorum,* Which of the gods have not seene death? Aske it of those, who are Gods by participation of Gods power, of those of whom God saies, *Ego dixi, dii estis,* and God answers for them, and of them, and to them, *You shall dye like men;* Aske it of those gods, who are gods by imputation, whom Creatures have created, whom Men have made gods, the gods of the Heathen, and do we not know, where all these gods dyed? Sometimes divers places dispute, who hath their tombes; but do not they deny their godhead in confessing their tombes? doe they not all answer, that they cannot answer this text, *Mi Gheber, Quis homo,* What man, *Quis deorum,* What god of mans making hath not seen death? As *Iustin Martyr* asks that question, Why should I pray to *Apollo* or *Esculapius* for health, *Qui apud Chironem medicinam didicerunt,* when I know who taught them all that they knew? so why should I looke for Immortality from such or such a god, whose grave I finde for a witnesse, that he himselfe is dead? Nay, carry this question higher then so, from this *Quis homo,* to *quid homo,* what is there in the nature and essence of Man, free from death? The whole man is not, for the dissolution of body and soule is death. The body is not; I shall as soone finde an immortall Rose, an eternall Flower, as an immortall body. And for the Immortality of the Soule, It is safelier said to be immortall, by preservation, then immortall by nature; That God keepes it from dying, then, that it cannot dye. We magnifie God in an humble and faithfull acknowledgment of the immortality of our soules, but if we aske, *quid homo,* what is there in the nature of Man, that should keepe him from death, even in that point, the question is not easily answered.

[Psal. 82.6, 7]

It is every mans case then; every man dyes; and though it may perchance be but a meere Hebraisme to say, that every man shall *see death,* perchance it amounts to no more, but to that phrase, *Gustare*

Videbit

mortem, To taste death, yet thus much may be implied in it too,
That as every man must dye, so every man may see, that he must
dye; as it cannot be avoided, so it may be understood. A beast dyes,
but he does not see death; S. *Basil* sayes, he saw an Oxe weepe for
the death of his yoke-fellow; but S. *Basil* might mistake the occasion
of that Oxes teares. Many men dye too, and yet doe not see death;
The approaches of death amaze them, and stupifie them; they feele
no colluctation with Powers, and Principalities, upon their death bed;
that is true; they feele no terrors in their consciences, no apprehen-
sions of Judgement, upon their death bed; that is true; and this we
call going away like a Lambe. But the Lambe of God had a sorrow-
full sense of death; His soule was heavy unto death, and he had an
apprehension, that his Father had forsaken him; And in this text,
the Chalde Paraphrase expresses it thus, *Videbit Angelum mortis,*
he shall see a Messenger, a forerunner, a power of Death, an executioner of Death, he shall see something with horror, though not such
as shall shake his morall, or his Christian constancy.

So that this *Videbunt, They shall see,* implies also a *Viderunt,* they
have seene, that is, they have used to see death, to observe a death in
the decay of themselves, and of every creature, and of the whole
World. Almost fourteene hundred yeares agoe, S. *Cyprian* writing
against *Demetrianus,* who imputed all the warres, and deaths, and
unseasonablenesses of that time, to the contempt, and irreligion of
the Christians, that they were the cause of all those ils, because they
would not worship their Gods, *Cyprian* imputes all those distempers
to the age of the whole World; *Canos videmus in pueris,* saies hee,
Wee see Children borne gray-headed; *Capilli deficiunt, antequam
crescant,* Their haire is changed, before it be growne. *Nec ætas in
senectute desinit, sed incipit a senectute,* Wee doe not dye with age,
but wee are borne old. Many of us have seene Death in our particular
selves; in many of those steps, in which the morall Man expresses it;
Wee have seene *Mortem infantiæ, pueritiam,* The death of infancy
in youth; and *Pueritiæ, adolescentiam,* and the death of youth in our
middle age; And at last we shall see *Mortem senectutis, mortem
ipsam,* the death of age in death it selfe. But yet after that, a step
farther then that Morall man went, *Mortem mortis in morte Iesu,*
We shall see the death of Death it self in the death of Christ. As we

Basil orat.
de Morte

Cyprian ad
Demetri-
anum

Seneca

could not be cloathed at first, in Paradise, till some Creatures were dead, (for we were cloathed in beasts skins) so we cannot be cloathed in Heaven, but in his garment who dyed for us. [Gen. 3.21]

This *Videbunt,* this future sight of Death implies a *viderunt,* they have seene, they have studied Death in every Booke, in every Creature; and it implies a *Vident,* they doe presently see death in every object, They see the houre-glasse running to the death of the houre; They see the death of some prophane thoughts in themselves, by the entrance of some Religious thought of compunction, and conversion to God; and then they see the death of that Religious thought, by an inundation of new prophane thoughts, that overflow those. As Christ [1 Cor. sayes, that as often as wee eate the Sacramentall Bread, we should 11.24] remember his Death, so as often, as we eate ordinary bread, we may Bern. remember our death; for even hunger and thirst, are diseases; they are *Mors quotidiana,* a daily death, and if they lasted long, would Aug. kill us. In every object and subject, we all have, and doe, and shall see death; not to our comfort as an end of misery, not onely as such a misery in it selfe, as the Philosopher takes it to be, *Mors omnium miseriarum,* That Death is the death of all miserie, because it destroyes and dissolves our beeing; but as it is *Stipendium peccati, The reward of sin;* That as *Solomon* sayes, *Indignatio Regis nuncius mor-* Prov. 16.14 *tis, The wrath of the King, is as a messenger of Death,* so *Mors nuncius indignationis Regis,* We see in Death a testimony, that our Heavenly King is angry; for, but for his indignation against our sinnes, we should not dye. And this death, as it is *Malum,* ill, (for if ye weigh it in the Philosophers balance, it is an annihilation of our present beeing, and if ye weigh it in the Divine Balance, it is a seale of Gods anger against sin) so this death is generall; of this, this question there is no answer, *Quis homo,* What man, &c.

We passe then from the *Morte moriemini,* to the *fortè moriemini,* 2 Part from the generality and the unescapablenesse of death, from this question, as it admits no answer, to the *Fortè moriemini,* perchance we shall dye; that is, to the question as it may admit a probable answer. Of which, we said at first, that in such questions, nothing becomes a Christian better then sobriety; to make a true difference betweene problematicall, and dogmaticall points, betweene upper buildings, and foundations, betweene collaterall doctrines, and Doctrines in the right line: for fundamentall things, *Sine hæsitatione credantur,* They must be beleeved without disputing; there is no more to be done for them, but beleeving; for things that are not so, we are to weigh them in two balances, in the balance of Analogy, and in the balance of scandall: we must hold them so, as may be analogall, proportionable, agreeable to the Articles of our Faith, and we must hold them so, as our brother be not justly offended, nor scandalized by them; wee must weigh them with faith, for our own strength, and we must weigh them with charity, for others weaknesse. Certainly nothing endangers a Church more, then to draw indifferent things to be necessary; I meane of a primary necessity, of a necessity to be beleeved *De fide,* not a secondary necessity, a necessity to be performed and practised for obedience: Without doubt, the Roman Church repents now, and sees now that she should better have preserved her selfe, if they had not defined so many particular things, which were indifferently and problematically disputed before, to bee had necessarily *De fide,* in the Councell of Trent.

Taking then this Text for a probleme, *Quis homo, What man lives, and shall not see Death?* we answer, It may be that those Men, whom Christ shal find upon the earth alive, at his returne to Judge the World, shall dye then, and it may be they shall but be changed, and not dye. That Christ shall judge quick and dead, is a fundamentall thing; we heare it in S. *Peters* Sermon, to *Cornelius* and his company, and we say it every day in the Creed, *Hee shall judge the quick and the dead.* But though we doe not take the quick and the dead, as *Augustine* and *Chrysostome* doe, for the Righteous which lived in faith, and the unrighteous, which were dead in sinne, Though wee doe not take the quick and the dead, as *Ruffinus* and others doe, for the soule and the body, (He shall judge the soule, which was alwaies alive, and he shall the body, which was dead for a time) though we take the words (as becomes us best) literally, yet the letter does not conclude, but that they, whom Christ shall finde alive upon earth, shall have a present and sudden dissolution, and a present and sudden re-union of body and soul again. Saint *Paul* says, *Behold I shew you a mystery;* Therefore it is not a cleare case, and presently, and peremptorily determined; but what is it? *We shall not all sleep, but we shall all be changed.* But whether this sleeping be spoke of

Acts 10.42

August.
Chrys.

1 Cor. 15.51

death it self, and exclude that, that we shall not die, or whether this sleep be spoke of a rest in the grave, and exclude that, we shall not be buried, and remain in death, that may be a mystery still. S. *Paul* sayes too, *The dead in Christ shall rise first; Then we which are alive, and remain, shall be caught up together with them in the clouds, to meet the Lord in the ayre.* But whether that may not still be true, that S. *Augustine* sayes, that there shall be *Mors in raptu,* An instant and sudden dis-union, and re-union of body and soul, which is death, who can tell? So on the other side, when it is said to him, in whom all we were, to *Adam, Pulvis es, Dust thou art, and into dust thou shalt return,* when it is said, *In Adam all die,* when it is said, *Death passed upon all men, for all have sinned,* Why may not all those sentences of Scripture, which imply a necessity of dying, admit that restriction, *Nisi dies judicii naturæ cursum immutet,* We shall all die, except those, in whom the comming of Christ shall change the course of Nature.

1 Thes. 4.[16,] 17

August.

Gen. 3.19
1 Cor. 15.22
Rom. 5.12

Pet. Mar.

Consider the Scriptures then, and we shall be absolutely concluded neither way; Consider Authority, and we shall finde the Fathers for the most part one way, and the Schoole for the most part another; Take later men, and all those in the Romane Church; Then *Cajetan* thinks, that they shall not die, and *Catharin* is so peremptory, that they shall, as that he sayes of the other opinion, *Falsam esse confidenter asserimus, & contra Scripturas satis manifestas, & omnino sine ratione;* It is false, and against Scriptures, and reason, saith he; Take later men, and all those in the reformed Church; and *Calvin* sayes, *Quia aboletur prior natura, censetur species mortis, sed non migrabit anima à corpore:* S. *Paul* calls it death, because it is a destruction of the former Beeing; but it is not truly death, saith *Calvin;* and *Luther* saith, That S. *Pauls* purpose in that place is only to shew the suddennesse of Christs comming to Judgement, *Non autem inficiatur omnes morituros; nam dormire, est sepeliri:* But S. *Paul* doth not deny, but that all shall die; for that sleeping which he speaks of, is buriall; and all shall die, though all shall not be buried, saith *Luther.*

Cajetan
Catherinus

Calvin

Luther

Take then that which is certain; It is certain, a judgement thou must passe: If thy close and cautelous proceeding have saved thee from all informations in the Exchequer, thy clearnesse of thy title from all Courts at Common Law, thy moderation from the Chancery, and Star-Chamber, If heighth of thy place, and Authority, have saved thee, even from the tongues of men, so that ill men dare not slander thy actions, nor good men dare not discover thy actions, no not to thy self, All those judgements, and all the judgements of the world, are but interlocutory judgements; There is a finall judgement, *In judicantes & judicatos,* against Prisoners and Judges too, where all shalbe judged again; *Datum est omne judicium,* All judgement is given to the Son of man, and upon all the sons of men must his judgement passe. A judgement is certain, and the uncertainty of this judgement is certain too; perchance God will put off thy judgement; thou shalt not die yet; but who knows whether God in his mercy, do put off this judgement, till these good motions which his blessed Spirit inspires into thee now, may take roote, and receive growth, and bring forth fruit, or whether he put it off, for a heavier judgement, to let thee see, by thy departing from these good motions, and returning to thy former sins, after a remorse conceived against those sins, that thou art inexcusable even to thy self, and thy condemnation is just, even to thine own conscience. So perchance God will bring this judgement upon thee now; now thou maist die; but whether God will bring that judgement upon thee now, in mercy, whilest his Graces, in his Ordinance of preaching, work some tendernesse in thee, and give thee some preparation, some fitnesse, some courage to say, *Veni Domine Iesu, Come Lord Iesu,* come quickly, come now, or whether he will come now in judgement, because all this can work no tendernesse in thee, who can tell?

    Thou hearest the word of God preached, as thou hearest an Oration, with some gladnesse in thy self, if thou canst heare him, and never be moved by his Oratory; thou thinkest it a degree of wisdome, to be above perswasion; and when thou art told, that he that feares God, feares nothing else, thou thinkest thy self more valiant then so, if thou feare not God neither; Whether or why God defers, or hastens the judgement, we know not; This is certain, this all S. *Pauls* places collineate to, this all the Fathers, and all the Schoole, all the *Cajetans,* and all the *Catharins,* all the *Luthers,* and all the *Calvins* agree in, *A judgement must be,* and it must be *In ictu oculi, In the twinkling of an eye,* and *Fur in nocte, A thiefe in the night.* Make the question, *Quis homo?* What man is he that liveth, and shall not passe this

John 5.[22, 27]

[1 Cor. 15.52]
[1 Thess. 5.2]

judgement? or, what man is he that liveth, and knowes when this judgement shall be? So it is a *Nemo scit,* A question without an answer; but ask it, as in the text, *Quis homo?* Who liveth, and shall not die? so it is a problematicall matter; and in such things as are problematicall, if thou love the peace of Sion, be not too inquisitive to know, nor too vehement, when thou thinkest thou doest know it.

Come then to ask this question, not problematically, (as it is contracted to them that shall live in the last dayes) nor peremptorily of man, (as he is subject to originall sin) but at large, so, as the question may include Christ himself, and then to that *Quis homo? What man is he?* We answer directly, here is the man that shall not see death; And of him principally, and literally, S. *Augustine* (as we said before) takes this question to be framed; *Vt quæras, dictum, non ut desperes,* saith he, this question is moved, to move thee to seek out, and to have thy recourse to that man which is the Lord of Life, not to make thee despaire, that there is no such man, in whose self, and in whom, for all us, there is Redemption from death: For, sayes he, this question is an exception to that which was said before the text; which is, *Wherefore hast thou made all men in vain?* Consider it better, sayes the Holy Ghost, here, and it will not prove so; Man is not made in vain at first, though he do die now; for, *Perditio tua ex te,* This death proceeds from man himself; and *Quare moriemini domus Israel? Why will ye die, O house of Israel?* God made not death, neither hath he pleasure in the destruction of the living; The Wise man sayes it, and the true God sweares it, *As I live saith the Lord, I would not the death of a sinner.* God did not create man in vain then, though he die; not in vain, for since he will needs die, God receives glory even by his death, in the execution of his justice; not in vaine neither, because though he be dead, God hath provided him a Redeemer from death, in his mercy; Man is not created in vain at all; nor all men, so neare vanity as to die; for here is one man, God and Man Christ Jesus, which liveth, and shall not see death. And conformable to S. *Augustines* purpose, speakes S. *Hierome* too, *Scio quòd nullus homo carneus evadet, sed novi Deum sub velamento carnis latentem;* I know there is no man but shall die; but I know where there is a God clothed in mans flesh, and that person cannot die.

3. Part

August.

[Psal. 89.47]

[Ezek. 18.31]
Sap. 1.13

[Ezek. 33.11]

Hieron.

But did not Christ die then? Shall we joyne with any of those
Heretiques, which brought Christ upon the stage to play a part, and
say he was born, or lived, or dyed, *In phantasmate,* In apparance only,
and representation; God forbid; so all men were created in vain indeed, if we had not a regeneration in his true death. Where is the
contract between him, and his Father, that *Oportuit pati, All this
Christ ought to suffer, and so enter into glory:* Is that contract void,
and of none effect? Must he not die? Where is the ratification of that
contract in all the Prophets? Where is *Esays Verè languores nostros
tulit, Surely he hath born our sorrows; and, he made his grave with
the wicked in his death;* Is the ratification of the Prophets cancelled?
Shall he not, must he not die? Where is the consummation, and the
testification of all this? Where is the Gospell, *Consummatum est?
And he bowed his head, and gave up the ghost?* Is that fabulous? Did
he not die? How stands the validity of that contract, Christ must
die; the dignity of those Prophecies, Christ will die; the truth of the
Gospell, Christ did die, with this answer to this question, Here is a
man that liveth and shall not see death? Very well; For though
Christ Jesus did truly die, so as was contracted, so as was prophecied, so as was related, yet hee did not die so, as was intended in this
question, so as other naturall men do die.

For first, Christ dyed because he would dye; other men admitted
to the dignity of Martyrdome, are willing to dye; but they dye by
the torments of the Executioners, they cannot bid their soules goe
out, and say, now I will dye. And this was Christs case: It was not
only, *I lay down my life for my sheep,* but he sayes also, *No man can
take away my soule;* And, *I have power to lay it down;* And *De
facto,* he did lay it down, he did dye, before the torments could have
extorted his soule from him; Many crucified men lived many dayes
upon the Crosse; The thieves were alive, long after Christ was dead;
and therefore Pilate wondred, that he was already dead. His soule
did not leave his body by force, but because he would, and when he
would, and how he would; Thus far then first, this is an answer to
this question, *Quis homo?* Christ did not die naturally, nor violently,
as all others doe, but only voluntarily.

Again, the penalty of death appertaining only to them, who were
derived from *Adam* by carnall, and sinfull generation, Christ Jesus

[Luke
24.26]

Esay, 53.4, 9

[John
19.30]

John 10.15
[also 18]

Mar. 15.44

August.

being conceived miraculously of a Virgin, by the over-shadowing of the Holy Ghost, was not subject to the Law of death; and therefore in his person, it is a true answer to this *Quis homo?* Here is a man, that shall not see death, that is, he need not see death, he hath not incurred Gods displeasure, he is not involved in a general rebellion, and therfore is not involved in the generall mortality, not included in the generall penalty. He needed not have dyed by the rigour of any Law, all we must; he could not dye by the malice, or force of any Executioner, all we must; at least by natures generall Executioners, Age, and Sicknesse; And then, when out of his own pleasure, and to advance our salvation, he would dye, yet he dyed so, as that though there were a dis-union of body and soule, (which is truly death) yet there remained a Nobler, and faster union, then that of body and soule, the Hypostaticall Union of the God-head, not onely to his soule, but to his body too; so that even in his death, both parts were still, not onely inhabited by, but united to the Godhead it selfe; and in respect of that inseparable Union, we may answer to this question, *Quis homo?* Here is a man that shall not see death, that is, he shall see no separation of that, which is incomparably, and incomprehensibly, a better soul then his soule, the God-head shall not be separated from his body.

But, that which is indeed the most direct, and literall answer, to this question, is, That whereas the death in this Text, is intended of such a death, as hath Dominion over us, and from which we have no power to raise our selves, we may truly, and fully answer to his *Quis homo?* here is a man, that shall never see death so, but that he shall even in the jawes, and teeth of death, and in the bowels and wombe of the grave, and in the sink, and furnace of hell it selfe, retaine an Almighty power, and an effectuall purpose, to deliver his soule from death, by a glorious, a victorious, and a Triumphant Resurrection: So it is true, Christ Jesus dyed, else none of us could live; but yet hee dyed not so, as is intended in this question; Not by the necessity of any Law, not by the violence of any Executioner, not by the separation of his best soule, (if we may so call it) the God-head, nor by such a separation of his naturall, and humane soule, as that he would not, or could not, or did not resume it againe.

If then this question had beene asked of Angels at first, *Quis An-*

gelus? what Angel is that, that stands, and shall not fall? though
as many of those Angels, as were disposed to that answer, *Erimus*

[Isa. 14.14]   *similes Altissimo,* We will be like God, and stand of our selves, without any dependance upon him, did fall, yet otherwise they might
have answered the question fairly, All we may stand, if we will; If
this question had been asked of *Adam* in Paradise, *Quis homo?*
though when he harkned to her, who had harkned to that voyce,

[Gen. 3.5]   *Eritis sicut Dii, You shall be as Gods,* he fell too, yet otherwise, he
might have answered the question fairly so, I may live, and not dye,
if I will; so, if this question be asked of us now, as the question implies the generall penalty, as it considers us onely as the sons of
Adam, we have no other answer, but that by *Adam* sin entred upon
all, and death by sin upon all; as it implies the state of them onely,
whom Christ at his second comming shall finde upon earth, wee
have no other answer but a modest, *non liquet,* we are not sure,
whether we shall dye then, or no; wee are onely sure, it shall be so,
as most conduces to our good, and Gods glory; but as the question
implies us to be members of our Head, Christ Jesus, as it was a true
answer in him, it is true in every one of us, adopted in him, Here
is a man that liveth, and shall not see death.

Prov. 18.21   *Death and life are in the power of the tongue,* sayes *Solomon,* in
another sense; and in this sense too, If my tongue, suggested by my
heart, and by my heart rooted in faith, can say, *Non moriar, non
moriar;* If I can say, (and my conscience doe not tell me, that I
belye mine owne state) if I can say, That the blood of my Saviour
runs in my veines, That the breath of his Spirit quickens all my
purposes, that all my deaths have their Resurrection, all my sins
their remorses, all my rebellions their reconciliations, I will harken
no more after this question, as it is intended *de morte naturali,* of a
naturall death, I know I must die that death, what care I? nor *de
morte spirituali,* the death of sin, I know I doe, and shall die so; why

2 Cor.   despaire I? but I will finde out another death, *mortem raptus,* a death
12.[1–4]   of rapture, and of extasie, that death which S. *Paul* died more then
Acts 9   once, The death which S. *Gregory* speaks of, *Divina contemplatio*
Greg.   *quoddam sepulchrum animæ,* The contemplation of God, and heaven,
is a kinde of buriall, and Sepulchre, and rest of the soule; and in this
death of rapture, and extasie, in this death of the Contemplation of

my interest in my Saviour, I shall finde my self, and all my sins enterred, and entombed in his wounds, and like a Lily in Paradise, out
of red earth, I shall see my soule rise out of his blade, in a candor,
and in an innocence, contracted there, acceptable in the sight of his
Father.

Though I have been dead, in the delight of sin, so that that of
S. *Paul, That a Widow that liveth in pleasure, is dead while she*   1 Tim. 5.6
liveth, be true of my soule, that so, *viduatur, gratiâ mortuâ,* when
Christ is dead, not for the soule, but in the soule, that the soule hath
no sense of Christ, *Viduatur anima,* the soul is a Widow, and no
Dowager, she hath lost her husband, and hath nothing from him;
yea though *I have made a Covenant with death, and have been at an*   Esay 28.15
agreement with hell, and in a vain confidence have said to my self,
that when the overflowing scourge shall passe through, it shall not
come to me, yet God shall annull that covenant, he shall bring that
scourge, that is, some medicinall correction upon me, and so give me
a participation of all the stripes of his son; he shall give me a sweat,
that is, some horrour, and religious feare, and so give me a participation of his Agony; he shall give me a diet, perchance want, and
penury, and so a participation of his fasting; and if he draw blood,
if he kill me, all this shall be but *Mors raptus,* a death of rapture
towards him, into a heavenly, and assured Contemplation, that I
have a part in all his passion, yea such an intire interest in his whole
passion, as though all that he did, or suffered, had been done, and
suffered for my soule alone; *Quasi moriens, & ecce vivo:* some shew   2 Cor. 6.9
of death I shall have, for I shall sin; and some shew of death again,
for I shall have a dissolution of this Tabernacle; *Sed ecce vivo,* still
the Lord of life will keep me alive, and that with an *Ecce,* Behold,
I live; that is, he will declare, and manifest my blessed state to me;
I shall not sit in the shadow of death; no nor I shall not sit in darknesse; his gracious purpose shall evermore be upon me, and I shall
ever discerne that gracious purpose of his; I shall not die, nor I shall
not doubt that I shall; If I be dead within doores, (If I have sinned
in my heart) why, *Suscitavit in domo,* Christ gave a Resurrection to   Mat. 9.23
the Rulers daughter within doores, in the house; If I be dead in the   [also 24, 25]
gate, (If I have sinned in the gates of my soule) in mine Eies, or   Luke 7.11
Eares, or Hands, in actuall sins, why, *Suscitavit in porta,* Christ gave   [also 12-15]

a Resurrection to the young man at the gate of *Naim.* If I be dead in the grave, (in customary, and habituall sins) why, *Suscitavit in Sepulchro,* Christ gave a Resurrection to *Lazarus* in the grave too. If God give me *mortem raptus,* a death of rapture, of extasie, of fervent Contemplation of Christ Jesus, a Transfusion, a Transplantation, a Transmigration, a Transmutation into him, (for good digestion brings alwaies assimilation, certainly, if I come to a true meditation upon Christ, I come to a conformity with Christ) this is principally that *Pretiosa mors Sanctorum, Pretious in the sight of the Lord, is the death of his Saints,* by which they are dead and buryed, and risen again in Christ Jesus: pretious is that death, by which we apply that pretious blood to our selves, and grow strong enough by it, to meet *Davids* question, *Quis homo?* what man? with Christs answer, *Ego homo,* I am the man, in whom whosoever abideth, shall not see death.

Number 2.

Preached at S. Pauls.

PSAL. 90.14. *O SATISFIE US EARLY WITH THY MERCY, THAT WE MAY REJOYCE AND BE GLAD ALL OUR DAYES.*

THEY have made a Rule in the Councel of Trent, that no Scripture shall be expounded, but according to the unanime consent of the Fathers: But in this Book of the Psalms, it would trouble them to give many examples of that Rule, that is, of an unanime consent of the Fathers, in the interpretation thereof. In this Psalme, *Bellarmine* in his Exposition of the Psalms, finds himselfe perplexed; He sayes (and sayes truly) *Hieronymus constanter affirmat, Augustinus constanter negat,* S. *Hierome* doth confidently and constantly affirme, and S. *Augustine* with as much confidence, and constancy deny, that this Psalme, and all that follow to the hundredth Psalme, are *Moses* Psalms, and written by him. And this diverse constancy in these two Fathers, S. *Hierome* and S. *Augustine,* shake the constancy of that Canon, which binds to a following of an unanime consent, for that cannot be found. *Bellarmine* expedites himselfe herein, that way, which is indeed their most ordinary way amongst their Expositors, which is, where the Fathers differ, to adhere to S. *Augustine.* So he doth in this point; though most of the Ancients of the Christian Church, most of the Rabbins of the Jews, most of the Writers in the Reformation, take it to be *Moses* Psalme, and that way runs the greatest streame, and nearest to a concurrence. And thus far I have stopped upon this consideration, Whether this be *Moses* Psalme or no, That when it appears to be his Psalme, and that we see, that in the tenth verse of this Psalm, mans life is limited to seventy years, or at most to eighty, and then remember, that *Moses* himselfe, then when he said so, was above eighty, and in a good habitude long after that, we might hereby take occasion to consider, that God does not so limit, and measure himselfe in his blessings to his servants, but that for their good and his glory he enlarges those measures. God hath determined a day, from Sun to Sun, yet when God hath use of a longer day, for his glory, he commands the Sun to stand still, till *Ioshua* have pursued his victory. So God hath given the life of man, into the hand of sicknesse; and yet for all that deadly sicknesse, God enlarges *Hezekiah's* years: *Moses* was more then fourescore, when he told us, that our longest terme was fourescore.

If we require exactly an unanime consent, that all agree in the Author of this Psalme, we can get no farther, then that the holy Ghost is the Author. All agree the words to be Canonicall Scripture, and so from the holy Ghost; and we seek no farther. The words are his, and they offer us these considerations; First, That the whole Psalme being in the Title thereof called a Prayer, *A Prayer of Moses the man of God,* it puts us justly, and pertinently upon the consideration of the many dignities and prerogatives of that part of our worship of God, Prayer; for there we shall see, That though the whole Psalme be not a Prayer, yet because there is a Prayer in the Psalme, that denominates the whole Psalme, the whole Psalme is a Prayer. When the Psalm grows formally to be a Prayer, our Text enters, *O satisfie us early with thy mercy, that we may rejoyce and be glad all our dayes:* And in that there will be two Parts more, The Prayer it selfe, *O satisfie us early with thy mercy,* And the effect thereof, *That we may rejoyce and be glad all our dayes.* So that our Parts are three; First Prayer, Then this Prayer, And lastly the benefit of all Prayer.

1 Part
Prayer

For the first, which is Prayer in generall, I will thrust no farther then the Text leads me in, that is, That Prayer is so essentiall a part of Gods worship, as that all is called Prayer. S. *Hierome* upon this Psalme sayes, *Difficillimum Psalmum aggredior,* I undertake the exposition of a very hard Psalme, and yet, sayes he, I would proceed so in the exposition thereof, *ut interpretatio nostra aliena non egeat interpretatione,* That there should not need another Comment upon my Comment, that when I pretend to interpret the Psalme, they that heare me, should not need another to interpret me: which is a frequent infirmity amongst Expositors of Scriptures, by writing, or preaching, either when men will raise doubts in places of Scripture, which are plaine enough in themselves, (for this creates a jealousie, that if the Scriptures be every where so difficult, they cannot be our evidences, and guides to salvation) Or when men will insist too vehemently, and curiously, and tediously in proving of such things as no man denies; for this also induces a suspition, that that is not so absolutely, so undeniably true, that needs so much art, and curiosity, and vehemence to prove it. I shall therefore avoid these errors; and because I presume you are full of an acknowledgment of the duties, and dignities of Prayer, onely remember you of thus much of the method, or elements of Prayer, That whereas the whole Book of Psalms is called *Sepher Tehillim,* that is, *Liber Laudationum,* The Book of Praise, yet this Psalme, and all that follow to the hundredth Psalme, and divers others besides these, (which make up a faire limme of this body, and a considerable part of the Book) are called Prayers; The Book is Praise, the parts are Prayer. The name changes not the nature; Prayer and Praise is the same thing: The name scarce changes the name; Prayer and Praise is almost the same word; As the duties agree in the heart and mouth of a man, so the names agree in our eares; and not onely in the language of our Translation, but in the language of the holy Ghost himselfe, for that which with us differs but so, Prayer, and Praise, in the Originall differs no more then so, *Tehillim,* and *Tephilloth.*

And this concurrence of these two parts of our devotion, Prayer and Praise, that they accompany one another, nay this co-incidence, that they meet like two waters, and make the streame of devotion the fuller; nay more then that, this identity, that they doe not onely consist together, but constitute one another, is happily expressed in this part of the Prayer, which is our Text; for that which in the Originall language is expressed in the voice of Prayer, *O satisfie us, &c.* in the first Translation, that of the Septuagint, is expressed in the voice of praise, *Saturasti, Thou hast satisfied us;* The Original makes it a Prayer, the Translation a Praise. And not to compare Original with Translation, but Translation with Translation, and both from one man, we have in S. *Hieroms* works two Translations of the Psalmes; one, in which he gives us the Psalmes alone; another, in which he gives them illustrated with his notes and Commentaries. And in one of these Translations he reads this as a Prayer, *Reple nos, O fill us early with thy mercie,* and in the other he reads it as a Praise, *Repleti sumus, Thou hast filled us, &c.* Nay, not to compare Originall with Translation, nor Translation with Translation, but Originall with Originall, the holy Ghost with himselfe, In the Title of this Psalme, (and the Titles of the Psalms are Canonicall Scripture) the holy Ghost calls this Psalme a *Prayer,* and yet enters the Psalme, in the very first verse thereof, with praise and thanksgiving, *Lord, thou hast been our dwelling place in all generations.* And such is the constitution and frame of that Prayer of Prayers, That which is the extraction of all prayers, and draws into a summe all that is in all others, That which is the infusion into all others, sheds and showres whatsoever is acceptable to God, in any other prayer, That Prayer which our Saviour gave us, (for as he meant to give us all for asking, so he meant to give us the words by which we should ask) As that Prayer consists of seven petitions, and seven is infinite, so by being at first begun with glory and acknowledgement of his raigning in heaven, and then shut up in the same manner, with acclamations of power and glory, it is made a circle of praise, and a circle is infinite too, The Prayer, and the Praise is equally infinite. Infinitely poore and needy man, that ever needst infinite things to pray for; Infinitely rich and abundant man, that ever hast infinite blessings to praise God for.

[Isa. 56.7]

Gods house in this world is called the house of Prayer; but in heaven it is the house of Praise: No surprisall with any new necessities there, but one even, incessant, and everlasting tenor of thanksgiving; And it is a blessed inchoation of that state here, here to be continually exercised in the commemoration of Gods former goodnesse towards us. *My voyce shalt thou heare in the morning, O Lord,* sayes *David.* What voice? the voice of his prayer; it is true; *In the morning will I direct my prayer unto thee,* saies *David* there. And not only then, but at noone and at night he vowes that Sacrifice; *Evening and morning, and at noone will I pray, and cry unto thee.* But *Davids* devotion began not, when his prayers began; one part of his devotion was before morning; *At midnight will I rise, to give thanks unto thee O Lord,* sayes he. Doubtlesse when he lay downe and closed his eyes,

Psal. 5.3

Psal. 55.17

Psal. 119.62

he had made up his account with God, and had received his *Quietus est* then: And then the first thing that he does when he wakes againe, is not to importune God for more, but to blesse God for his former blessings. And as this part of his devotion, Praise, began all, so it passes through all, *I will blesse the Lord at all times, and his praise shall be continually in my mouth.* He extends it through all times, and all places, and would faine do so through all persons too, as we see by that adprecation which is so frequent with him, *O that men would therefore praise the Lord, and declare the wondrous workes that he doth for the children of men!*

If we compare these two incomparable duties, Prayer, and Praise, it will stand thus, Our Prayers besiege God, (as *Tertullian* speakes, especially of publique Prayer in the Congregation, *Agmine facto obsidemus Deum*) but our praises prescribe in God, we urge him, and presse him with his ancient mercies, his mercies of old; By Prayer we incline him, we bend him, but by praise we bind him; our thanks for former benefits, is a producing of a specialty, by which he hath contracted with us for more. In Prayer we sue to him, but in our Praise we sue him himselfe; Prayer is as our petition, but Praise is as our Evidence; In that we beg, in this we plead. God hath no law upon himselfe, but yet God himselfe proceeds by precedent: And whensoever we present to him with thanksgiving, what he hath done, he does the same, and more againe. Neither certainly can the Church institute any prayers, more effectuall for the preservation of Religion, or of the State, then the Collects for our deliverances, in the like cases before: And when he heares them, though they have the nature of Praise onely, yet he translates them into Prayers, and when we our selves know not, how much we stand in need of new deliverances, he delivers us from dangers which we never suspected, from Armies and Navies which we never knew were prepared, and from plots and machinations which we never knew were brought into Consultation, and diverts their forces, and dissipates their counsels with an untimely abortion. And farther I extend not this first part of Prayer in generall, in which, to that which you may have heard often, and usefully of the duty and dignity of Prayer, I have only added this, of the method and elements thereof, that prayer consists as much of praise for the past, as of supplication for the future.

Psal. 34.1

[Psal. 107.8]

We passe now to our second Part, To this particular Prayer, and those limmes that make up this body, those pieces that constitute this Part. They are many; as many as words in it: *Satisfie,* and *satisfie Vs,* and doe that *early,* and doe that with that which is *thine,* and let that be *mercy.* So that first it is a prayer for fulnesse and satisfaction, *Satura, satisfie;* And then it is a prayer not onely of appropriation to our selves, *Satisfie me,* But of a charitable dilatation and extension to others, *Satisfie us,* all us, all thy servants, all thy Church; And then thirdly, it is a prayer of dispatch and expedition, *Satura nos mane, Satisfie us early;* and after that, it is a prayer of evidence and manifestation, Satisfie us with that which is, and which we may discerne to be *thine;* And then lastly, it is a prayer of limitation even upon God himselfe, that God will take no other way herein, but the way of *mercy, Satisfie us early with thy mercy.*

And because these are the land-markes that must guide you in this voyage, and the places to which you must resort to assist your memory, be pleased to take another survay and impression of them. I may have an apprehension of a conditionall promise of God, and I may have some faire credulity and testimony of conscience, of an endevour to performe those conditions, and so some inchoations of those promises, but yet this is not a fulnesse, a satisfaction, and this is a prayer for that, *Satura, satisfie:* I may have a full measure in my selfe, finde no want of temporall conveniencies, or spirituall consolation even in inconveniencies, and so hold up a holy alacrity and cheerefulnesse for all concerning my selfe, and yet see God abandon greater persons, and desert some whole Churches, and States, upon whom his glory and Gospel depends much more then upon me, but this is a prayer of charitable extension, *Satura nos,* not *me,* but *us,* all us that professe thee aright: This also I may be sure that God will doe at last, he will rescue his owne honour in rescuing or establishing his Servants, he will bring Israel out of Egypt, and out of Babylon, but yet his Israel may lye long under the scourge and scorne of his and their enemies, 300. yeares before they get out of Egypt, seventy yeares before they get out of Babylon, and so fall into tentations of conceiving a jealousie, and suspition of Gods good purpose towards them, and this is a Prayer of Dispatch and Expedition, *Satura nos mane, Satisfie us early,* O God make speed to save us, O Lord make

[Book of Common Prayer, Morning Prayer]

hast to help us: But he may derive help upon us, by meanes that are
not his, not avowed by him, He may quicken our Counsels by bringing in an *Achitophell,* he may strengthen our Armies by calling in the
Turke, he may establish our peace and friendships, by remitting or
departing with some parts of our Religion; at such a deare price we
may be helped, but these are not his helps, and this is a prayer of
manifestation, that all the way to our end hee will bee pleased to let
us see, that the meanes are from him, *Satura nos tua, Satisfie us* with
that, which is *thine,* and comes from *thee,* and so directs us to *thee:*
All this may be done too, and yet not that done which we pray for
here; God may send that which is his, and yet without present comfort therein; God may multiply corrections, and judgements, and
tribulations upon us, and intend to helpe us that way, by whipping
and beating us into the way, and this is his way; but this is a Prayer
of limitation even upon God himselfe, That our way may be his, and
that his way may be the way of *mercy, Satisfie us early with thy mercy.*

First then, the first word *Satura,* implies a fulnesse, and it implies   *Satura*
a satisfaction, A quietnesse, a contentednesse, an acquiescence in that
fulnesse; *Satisfie* is, let us bee full, and let us feele it, and rest in that
fulnesse. These two make up all Heaven, all the joy, and all the
glory of Heaven, fulnesse and satisfaction in it. And therefore S.
Hierom refers this Prayer of our Text, to the Resurrection, and to that
fulnesse, and that satisfaction which we shall have then, and not till
then. For though we shall have a fulnesse in Heaven, as soone as we
come thither, yet that is not fully a satisfaction, because we shall desire,
and expect a fuller satisfaction in the reunion of body and soule. And
when Heaven it selfe cannot give us this full satisfaction till then, in
what can wee looke for it in this world, where there is no true fulnesse, nor any satisfaction, in that kind of fulnesse which wee seeme
to have? Pleasure and sensuality, and the giving to our selves all that
we desire, cannot give this; you heare God reproaches Israel so, *You*   Ezek.
have multiplied your fornications, & yet are not satisfied. Labor for   16.[29]
profit, or for preferment, cannot doe it; you see God reproaches
Israel for that too, *Ye have sowne much, and bring in little, ye eat,*   Hagg. 1.[6]
but have not enough, ye drinke, but are not filled, ye cloath you, but
are not warme, and he that earneth wages, putteth it into a broken

bag; that is, it runs out as fast as it comes in, he finds nothing at the yeares end, his Midsommer will scarce fetch up Michaelmas, and if he have brought about his yeare, and made up his Circle, yet he hath raised up nothing, nothing appears in his circle. If these things could fill us, yet they could not satisfie us, because they cannot stay with us, or not we with them: *He hath devoured substance, and he shall vomit it.* He devoured it by bribery, and he shall vomit it by a fine; He devoured it by extortion, and he shall vomit it by confiscation; He devoured it in other Courts, and shall vomit it in a Star-chamber. If it stay some time, it shall be with an anguish and vexation; *When he shall be filled with abundance, it shall be a paine to him,* as it is in the same place. Still his riches shall have the nature of a vomit, hard to get downe, and hard to keep in the stomach when it is there; hardly got, hardly kept when they are got. If all these could be overcome, yet it is clogged with a heavy curse, *Wo be unto you that are full, for ye shall be hungry:* Where, if the curse were onely from them, who are poore by their owne sloth, or wastfulnesse, who for the most part delight to curse and maligne the rich, the curse might be contemned by us, and would be throwne back by God into their owne bosomes; but *Os Domini locutum,* The mouth of the Lord hath spoken it, Christ himselfe hath denounced this curse upon worldly men, That they shall be hungry, not onely suffer impairement and diminution, but be reduced to hunger.

There is a spirituall fulnesse in this life, of which S. *Hierom* speakes, *Ebrietas fœlix, satietas salutaris,* A happy excesse, and a wholesome surfet; *quæ quanto copiosiùs sumitur, majorem donat sobrietatem,* In which the more we eate, the more temperate we are, and the more we drinke, the more sober. In which, (as S. *Bernard* also expresses it, in his mellifluence) *Mutuâ, interminabili, inexplicabili generatione,* By a mutuall and reciprocall, by an undeterminable and unexpressible generation of one another, *Desiderium generat satietatem, & satietas parit desiderium,* The desire of spirituall graces begets a satiety, if I would be, I am full of them, And then this satiety begets a farther desire, still we have a new appetite to those spirituall graces: This is a holy ambition, a sacred covetousnesse, and a wholsome Dropsie. *Napthalies* blessing, *O Napthali satisfied with favour,*

Iob. 20.[15]

Luke 6.[25]

Deut. 33.23

and full with the blessing of the Lord; S. Stephens blessing, *Full of faith and of the Holy Ghost;* The blessed Virgins blessing, *Full of Grace; Dorcas* blessing, *Full of good works, and of Almes-deeds;* The blessing of him, who is blessed above all, and who blesseth all, Christ Jesus, ᵃ*Full of wisedome,* ᵇ*Full of the Holy Ghost,* ᶜ*Full of grace and truth.* But so far are all temporall things from giving this fullnesse or satisfaction, as that even in spirituall things, there may be, there is often an error, or mistaking.

Even in spirituall things, there may be a fulnesse, and no satisfaction, And there may be a satisfaction, and no fulnesse; I may have as much knowledge, as is presently necessary for my salvation, and yet have a restlesse and unsatisfied desire, to search into unprofitable curiosities, unrevealed mysteries, and inextricable perplexities: And, on the other side, a man may be satisfied, and thinke he knowes all, when, God knowes, he knowes nothing at all; for, I know nothing, if I know not Christ crucified, And I know not that, if I know not how to apply him to my selfe, Nor doe I know that, if I embrace him not in those meanes, which he hath afforded me in his Church, in his Word, and Sacraments; If I neglect this meanes, this place, these exercises, howsoever I may satisfie my selfe, with an over-valuing mine own knowledge at home, I am so far from fulnesse, as that vanity it selfe is not more empty. In the Wildernesse, every man had one and the same measure of Manna; The same Gomer went through all; for Manna was a Meat, that would melt in their mouths, and of easie digestion. But then for their Quailes, birds of a higher flight, meat of a stronger digestion, it is not said, that every man had an equall number: some might have more, some lesse, and yet all their fulnesse. Catechisticall divinity, and instructions in fundamentall things, is our Manna; Every man is bound to take in his Gomer, his explicite knowledge of Articles absolutely necessary to salvation; The simplest man, as well as the greatest Doctor, is bound to know, that there is one God in three persons, That the second of those, the Sonne of God, tooke our nature, and dyed for mankinde; And that there is a Holy Ghost, which in the Communion of Saints, the Church established by Christ, applies to every particular soule the benefit of Christs universall redemption. But then for our Quails, birds of higher pitch, meat of a stronger digestion, which is the knowledge how to rectifie every stray-

Act. 6.5

[Luke 1.28]

Act. 9.36

ᵃLuk. 2.40
ᵇLuk. 4.1
ᶜJoh. 1.14

[1 Cor. 2.2]

[Exod.
16.16]

ing conscience, how to extricate every entangled, and scrupulous, and perplexed soule, in all emergent doubts, how to defend our Church, and our Religion, from all the mines, and all the batteries of our Adversaries, and to deliver her from all imputations of Heresie, and Schisme, which they impute to us, this knowledge is not equally necessary in all; In many cases a Master of servants, and a Father of children is bound to know more, then those children and servants, and the Pastor of the parish more then parishioners: They may have their fulnesse, though he have more, but he hath not his, except he be able to give them satisfaction.

This fulnesse then is not an equality in the measure; our fulnesse in heaven shall not be so; *Abraham dyed,* says the text, *Plenus dierum, full of yeares;* It is not said so in the text of *Methusalem,* that he dyed full of yeares, and yet he had another manner of Gomer, another measure of life then *Abraham,* for he lived almost eight hundred yeares more then he; But he that is best disposed to die, is fullest of yeares; One man may be fuller at twenty, then another at seaventy. *David* lived not the tithe of *Methusalems* yeares, not ten to his hundred, he lived lesse then *Abraham,* and yet *David* is said to have dyed *Plenus dierum, full of yeares;* he had made himselfe agreeable to God, and so was ripe for him. So *David* is said there to have dyed *full of honor;* God knowes *David* had cast shrowd aspersions upon his own, and others honor; but, as God sayes of Israel, *Because I loved thee, thou wast honorable in my sight;* so because God loved *David,* and he persevered in that love to the end, he dyed full of honor. So also it is said of *David,* that he dyed *full of Riches;* for, though they were very great additions, which *Solomon* made, yet because *David* intended that which he left, for Gods service, and for pious uses, he dyed full of Riches; fulnesse of riches is in the good purpose, and the good employment, not in the possession. In a word, the fulnesse that is inquired after, and required by this prayer, carry it upon temporall, carry it upon spirituall things, is such a proportion of either, as is fit for that calling, in which God hath put us; And then, the satisfaction in this fulnesse is not to hunt and pant after more worldly possessions, by undue meanes, or by macerating labour, as though we could not be good, or could doe no good in the world, except all the goods of the world passed our hands, nor to hunt and

Gen. 25.8
[Gen. 5.27]

1 Chro.
29.28

[Isa. 43.4]

pant after the knowledge of such things, as God by his Scriptures
hath not revealed to his Church, nor to wrangle contentiously and
uncharitably about such points, as doe rather shake others consciences,
then establish our own, as though we could not possibly come to
heaven, except we knew what God meant to doe with us, before he
meant to make us. S. *Paul* expresses fully what this fulnesse is, and
satisfies us in this satisfaction, *Vt sitis pleni in omni voluntate Dei,*
That yee may be filled according to the will of God: What is the will
of God? How shall I know the will of God upon me? God hath
manifested his will in my Calling; and a proportion, competent to this
Calling, is my fulnesse, and should be my satisfaction, that so God
may have *Odorem quietis,* (as it is said in *Noahs* sacrifice, after he
came out of the Arke, *that God smelt a savour of rest*) a sacrifice, in
which he might rest himselfe; for God hath a Sabbath in the Sabbaths
of his servants, a fulnesse in their fulnesse, a satisfaction when they
are satisfied, and is well pleased when they are so.

So then this Prayer is for fulnesse, and fulnesse is a competency in
our calling, And a prayer for satisfaction, and satisfaction is a contentment in that competency; And then this prayer is not onely a
prayer of appropriation to our selves, but of a charitable extention to
others too, *Satura nos, Satisfie us,* All us, all thy Church. Charity
begins in our selves, but it does not end there, but dilates it selfe to
others; The Saints in heaven are full, as full as they can hold, and yet
they pray; Though they want nothing, they pray that God would
powre down upon us graces necessary for our peregrination here,
as he hath done upon them, in their station there. We are full; full
of the Gospel; present peace and plenty in the preaching thereof, and
faire apparances of a perpetuall succession; we are full, and yet we
pray; we pray that God would continue the Gospel where it is, restore
the Gospel where it was, and transfer the Gospel where it hath not
yet been preached. Charity desires not her own, sayes the Apostle;
but much lesse doth charity desire no more then her own, so as not
to desire the good of others too. True love and charity is to doe the
most that we can, all that we can for the good of others; So God himselfe proceeds, when he sayes, *What could I doe, that I have not done?*
And so he seems to have begun at first; when God bestowed upon
man, his first and greatest benefit, his making, it is expressed so,

Colos. 4.12

Gen. 8.21

Nos

[1 Cor. 13.5]

[Isa. 5.4]

[Gen. 1.26]   *Faciamus hominem, Let us,* All us, *make man;* God seems to sum-
mon himselfe, to assemble himselfe, to muster himselfe, all himselfe,
all the persons of the Trinity, to doe what he could in the favour of
man. So also when he is drawne to a necessity of executing judgement, and for his own honor, and consolidation of his servants, puts
himselfe upon a revenge, he proceeds so too; when man had rebelled,
Gen. 11.7   and began to fortifie in Babel, then God sayes, *Venite, Let us,* All
us come together, And *Descendamus, & confundamus, Let us,* all us,
goe down, and confound their language, and their machinations, and
fortifications. God does not give patterns, God does not accept from
us acts of half-devotion, and half-charities; God does all that he can
for us; And therefore when we see others in distresse, whether nationall, or personall calamities, whether Princes be dispossest of their
naturall patrimony, and inheritance, or private persons afflicted with
sicknesse, or penury, or banishment, let us goe Gods way, all the way;
First, *Faciamus hominem ad imaginem nostram,* Let us make that
Man according unto our image, let us consider our selves in him, and
make our case his, and remember how lately he was as well as we,
and how soone we may be as ill as he, and then *Descendamus &
confundamus,* Let us, us, with all the power we have, remove or
slacken those calamities that lie upon them.

This onely is charity, to doe all, all that we can. And something
there is which every man may doe; There are Armies, in the levying
whereof, every man is an absolute Prince, and needs no Commission,
there are Forces, in which every man is his owne Muster-master, The
force which we spoke of before, out of *Tertullian,* the force of prayer;
In publique actions, we obey God, when we obey them to whom
God hath committed the publique; In those things which are in our
own power, the subsidies and contributions of prayer, God looks
that we should second his *Faciamus,* with our *Dicamus,* That since
he must doe all, we would pray him that he would doe it, And his
Descendamus, with our *Ascendamus,* That if we would have him
come down, and fight our battayls, or remove our calamities, we
should first goe up to him, in humble and fervent prayer, That he
would continue the Gospel where it is, and restore it where it was,
and transfer it where it was never as yet heard; Charity is to doe all
to all; and the poorest of us all can doe this to any.

I may then, I must pray for this fulnesse, (and fulnesse is suffi-
ciency) And for this satisfaction, (and satisfaction is contentment)
And that God would extend this, and other his blessings, upon others
too, And if God doe leave us in an Egypt, in a Babylon, without
reliefe, for some time I may proceed to this holy importunity, which
David intimates here, *Satura nos mane,* O Lord, make haste to helpe
us, *Satisfie us early with thy mercy,* and God will doe so. *Weeping
may endure for a night,* sayes *David. David* does not say, It must
indure for a night, that God will by no meanes shorten the time;
perchance God will wipe all teares from thine eyes, at midnight, if
thou pray; Try him that way then. If he doe not, *If weeping doe
indure for a night,* all night, *yet joy commeth in the morning,* saith
David; And then he doth not say, Joy may come in the morning, but
it commeth certainly, infallibly it comes, and comes in the morning.
God is an early riser; *In the Morning-watch, God looked upon the
host of the Egyptians.* Hee looked upon their counsels to see what
they would doe, and upon their forces to see what they could doe. He
is not early up, and never the nearer; *His going forth is prepared as
the Morning,* (there is his generall Providence, in which he visits
every creature) *And hee shall come to us, in the former, and later
raine upon the earth;* Hee makes haste to us in the former, and
seconds his former mercies to us, in more mercies. And as he makes
hast to refresh his servants, so goes he the same pace, to the ruine of
his enemies, *In matutino interficiam, I will early destroy all the
wicked of the land:* It is not a weakning of them, It is a destruction;
It is not of a squadron or regiment, It is all; It is not onely upon the
Land, but the wicked of any Land, he will destroy upon the Sea too.
This is his promise, this is his practise, this is his pace. Thus he did in
Sennacheribs Army, *When they arose early in the Morning, behold
they were all dead carcasses;* They rose early that saw it, but God had
been up earlier, that had done it. And that story, God seemes to have
had care to have recorded almost in all the divisions of the Bible, for
it is in the Historicall part, and it is in the Propheticall part too; and
because God foresaw, that mens curiosities would carry them upon
Apocryphal Books also, it is repeated almost in every Book of that
kinde, in *Ecclesiasticus,* in *Tobit,* in the *Maccabees* in both Books,
That every where our eye might light upon that, and every soule

Mane

Psal. 30.5

Exod. 14.24

Hos. 6.3

Psal. 101.8

2 King.
19.35

might make that Syllogisme, and produce that conclusion to it selfe,
If God bee thus forward, thus early in the wayes of Judgement, much
more is he so in the wayes of mercy; with that he will satisfie us
Mane, early, and as *Tremellius* reads this very Text, *unoquoque
mane,* betimes in the morning, and every morning.

Now if we looke for this early mercy from God, we must rise
betimes too, and meet God early. God hath promised to give *Matu-*
tinam stellam, the Morning-star; but they must be up betimes in the
morning, that will take the Morning-star. He himselfe who is it, hath
told us who is this Morning star; *I Iesus am the bright and Morning*
starre. God will give us Jesus; Him, and all his, all his teares, all his
blood, all his merits; But to whom, and upon what conditions? That
is expressed there, *Vincenti dabo, To him that overcommeth I will*
give the Morning-star. Our life is a warfare, our whole life; It is not
onely with lusts in our youth, and ambitions in our middle yeares,
and indevotions in our age, but with agonies in our body, and tentations in our spirit upon our death-bed, that we are to fight; and he
cannot be said to overcome, that fights not out the whole battell. If
he enter not the field in the morning, that is, apply not himselfe to
Gods service in his youth, If hee continue not to the Evening, If hee
faint in the way, and grow remisse in Gods service, for collaterall
respects, God will overcome his cause, and his glory shall stand fast,
but that man can scarce be said to have overcome.

It is the counsell of the Wise man, *Prevent the Sunne to give thanks*
to God, and at the day-spring pray unto him. You see still, how these
two duties are marshalled, and disposed; First Praise, and then
Prayer, but both early: And it is placed in the Lamentations, as
though it were a lamentable negligence to have omitted it, *It is good*
for a man, that he beare his yoake in his youth. Rise as early as you
can, you cannot be up before God; no, nor before God raise you:
Howsoever you prevent this Sunne, the Sunne of the Firmament,
yet the Sonne of Heaven hath prevented you, for without his preventing Grace you could not stirre. Have any of you slept out their
Morning, resisted his private motions to private Prayer at home,
neglected his callings so? Though a man doe sleepe out his fore-
noone, the Sunne goes on his course, and comes to his Meridionall
splendor, though that man have not looked towards it. That Sonne

Revel. 2.28

Revel. 22.16

Wisd. 16.28

Lament.
3.27

which hath risen to you at home, in those private motions, hath
gone on his course, and hath shined out here, in this house of God,
upon Wednesday, and upon Friday, and upon every day of holy
Convocation; All this, at home, and here, yee have slept out and
neglected. Now, upon the Sabbath, and in these holy Exercises, this
Sonne shines out as at noone, the Grace of God is in the Exaltation,
exhibited in the powerfullest and effectuallest way of his Ordinance,
and if you will but awake now, rise now, meet God now, now at
noone, God will call even this early. Have any of you slept out the
whole day, and are come in that drowsinesse to your evening, to the
closing of your eyes, to the end of your dayes? Yet rise now, and God
shall call even this an early rising; If you can make shift to deceive
your owne soules and say, We never heard God call us; If you neglected your former callings so, as that you have forgot that you have
been called; yet, is there one amongst you, that denies that God calls
him now? If he neglect this calling now, to morrow he may forget that
he was called to day, or remember it with such a terror, as shall blow
a dampe, and a consternation upon his soule, and a lethargy worse
then his former sleepe; but if he will wake now, and rise now, though
this be late in his evening, in his age, yet God shall call this early.
Bee but able to say with *Esay* this night, *My soule hath desired thee*
in the night, and thou maist be bold to say with *David* to morrow
morning, *Satura nos mane, Satisfie us early with thy mercy,* and he
shall doe it.

Isai. 26.9

But yet no prayer of ours, howsoever made in the best disposition,
in the best testimony of a rectified conscience, must limit God his
time, or appoint him, in what morning, or what houre in the morning, God shall come to our deliverance. The Sonne of man was not
the lesse the Sonne of God, nor the lesse a beloved Sonne, though
God hid from him the knowledge of the day of the generall Judgement. Thou art not the lesse the servant of God, nor the lesse rewarded by him, though he keepe from thee the knowledge of thy
deliverance from any particular calamity. All Gods deliverances are
in the morning, because there is a perpetuall night, and an invincible
darknesse upon us, till he deliver us. God is the God of that Climate,
where the night is six Moneths long, as well as of this, where it is but
halfe so many houres. The highest Hill hinders not the roundnesse

[Mar. 13.32]

of the earth, the earth is round for all that hill; The lowest vaults, and mines hinder not the solidnesse of the earth, the earth is solid for all that; Much lesse hath a yeare, or ten yeares, or all our three-score and ten, any proportion at all to eternity; And therefore God comes early in a sort to me, though I lose abundance of my reward by so long lingring, if he come not till hee open me the gate of heaven, by the key of death. There are Indies at my right hand, in the East; but there are Indies at my left hand too, in the West. There are testimonies of Gods love to us, in our East, in our beginnings; but if God continue tribulation upon us to our West, to our ends, and give us the light of his presence then, if he appeare to us at our transmigration, certainly he was favourable to us all our peregrination, and though he shew himselfe late, hee was our friend early. The Prayer is, that he would come early, but it is, if it be rightly formed, upon both these conditions; first, that I rise early to meet him, and then that I magnifie his houre as early, whensoever he shall be pleased to come.

Tuâ

All this I shall doe the better, if I limit my prayer, and my practise, with the next circumstance in *Davids* prayer, *Tuâ, Satisfie us early with* that which is thine, *Thy mercy:* For there are mercies, (in a faire extent and accommodation of the word, that is Refreshings, Eases, Deliverances) that are not his mercies, nor his satisfactions. How many men are satisfied with Riches (I correct my selfe, few are satisfied; but how many have enough to satisfie many?) and yet have never a peny of his mony? Nothing is his, that comes not from him, that comes not by good meanes. How many are there, that are easie to admit scruples, and jealousies, and suspitions in matter of Religion: Easie to think, that that Religion, and that Church, in which they have lived ill, cannot bee a good Religion, nor a true Church; In a troubled, and distempered conscience, they grow easie to admit scruples, and then as over-easie to admit false satisfactions, with a word whispered on one side in a Conventicle, or a word whispered on the other side in a Confession, and yet have never a

[Luke 12.3]

dram of satisfaction from his word, whose word is preached upon the house top, and avowed, and not in corners? How many men are anguished with torturing Diseases, racked with the conscience of ill-spent estates, oppressed with inordinate melancholies, and irreligious dejections of spirit, and then repaire, and satisfie themselves with wine, with women, with fooles, with comedies, with mirth, and musique, and with all *Iobs* miserable comforters, and all this while have no beames of his satisfaction, it is not *Misericordia ejus,* his mercy, his satisfaction? In losses of worldly goods, in sicknesses of children, or servants, or cattell, to receive light or ease from Witches, this is not his mercy. It is not his mercy, except we goe by good wayes to good ends; except our safety be established by allyance with his friends, except our peace may bee had with the perfect continuance of our Religion, there is no safety, there is no peace. But let mee feele the effect of this Prayer, as it is a Prayer of manifestation, Let mee discerne that, that that is done upon mee, is done by the hand of God, and I care not what it be: I had rather have Gods Vinegar, then mans Oyle, Gods Wormewood, then mans Manna, Gods Justice, then any mans Mercy; for, therefore did *Gregory Nyssen* call S. *Basil* in a holy sense, *Ambidextrum,* because he tooke every thing that came, by the right handle, and with the right hand, because he saw it to come from God. Even afflictions are welcome, when we see them to be his: Though the way that he would chuse, and the way that this Prayer intreats, be only mercy, *Satisfie us early with thy mercy.*

[Job 16.2]

That rod and that staffe with which we are at any time corrected, is his. So God cals the Assyrians, *The rod of his anger,* and he sayes, *That the staffe that is in their hand, is his Indignation.* He comes to a sharper execution, from the rod, and the staffe to the sword, and that also is his, *It is my sword, that is put into the hands of the King of Babylon, and he shall stretch out my sword upon the whole land;* God will beat downe, and cut off, and blow up, and blow out at his pleasure; which is expressed in a phrase very remarkeable by *David, He bringeth the winde out of his Treasuries;* And then follow in that place, all the Plagues of Egypt: stormes and tempests, ruines and devastations, are not onely in Gods Armories, but they are in his Treasuries; as hee is the Lord of Hosts, hee fetches his judgements from his Armories, and casts confusion upon his enemies, but as he is the God of mercy, and of plentifull redemption, he fetches these judgements, these corrections out of his treasuries, and they are the Money, the Jewels, by which he redeemes and buyes us againe; God

Misericordia

Esay 10.5

Ezek. 30.24

Psal. 135.7

does nothing, God can doe nothing, no not in the way of ruine and destruction, but there is mercy in it; he cannot open a doore in his Armory, but a window into his Treasury opens too, and he must looke into that.

But then Gods corrections are his Acts, as the Physitian is his Creature, God created him for necessity. When God made man, his first intention was not that man should fall, and so need a Messias, nor that man should fall sick, and so need a Physitian, nor that man should fall into rebellion by sin, and so need his rod, his staffe, his scourge of afflictions, to whip him into the way againe. But yet sayes the Wiseman, *Honour the Physitian for the use you may have of* Ecclus. 38.1 *him; slight him not, because thou hast no need of him yet.* So though Gods corrections were not from a primary, but a secondary intention, yet, when you see those corrections fall upon another, give a good interpretation of them, and beleeve Gods purpose to be not to destroy, but to recover that man: Do not thou make Gods Rheubarbe thy Ratsbane, and poyson thine owne soule with an uncharitable misinterpretation of that correction, which God hath sent to cure his. And then, in thine owne afflictions, flie evermore to this Prayer, *Satisfie us with thy mercy;* first, Satisfie us, make it appeare to us that thine intention is mercy, though thou enwrap it in temporall afflictions, in this darke cloud let us discerne thy Son, and though in an act of displeasure, see that thou art well pleased with us; Satisfie us, that there is mercy in thy judgements, and then satisfie us, that thy mercy is mercy; for such is the stupidity of sinfull man, That as in temporall blessings, we discerne them best by wanting them, so do we the mercies of God too; we call it not a mercy, to have the same blessings still: but, as every man conceives a greater degree of joy, in recovering from a sicknesse, then in his former established health; so without doubt, our Ancestors who indured many yeares Civill and forraine wars, were more affected with their first peace, then we are with our continuall enjoying thereof, And our Fathers more thankfull, for the beginning of Reformation of Religion, then we for so long enjoying the continuance thereof. *Satisfie us with thy mercie,* Let us still be able to see mercy in thy judgements, lest they deject us, and confound us; *Satisfie us with thy mercie,* let us be able to see, that our deliverance is a mercy, and not a naturall thing that might have hapned so, or a necessary thing that must have hapned so, though there had beene no God in Heaven, nor providence upon earth. But especially since the way that thou choosest, is to goe all by mercy, and not to be put to this way of correction, so dispose, so compose our minds, and so transpose all our affections, that we may live upon thy food, and not put thee to thy physick, that we may embrace thee in the light, and not be put to seeke thee in the darke, that wee come to thee in thy Mercy, and not be whipped to thee by thy Corrections. And so we have done also with our second Part, The pieces and petitions that constitute this Prayer, as it is a Prayer for Fulnesse and Satisfaction, a Prayer of Extent and Dilatation, a Prayer of Dispatch and Expedition, and then a Prayer of Evidence and Declaration, and lastly, a Prayer of Limitation even upon God himselfe, *Satisfie,* and *satisfie us,* and *us early,* with that which we may discerne to be *thine,* and let that way be *mercy.*

There remaines yet a third Part, what this Prayer produces, and it is joy, and continual joy, *That we may rejoyce and be glad all our dayes.* The words are the Parts, and we invert not, we trouble not the Order; the Holy Ghost hath laid them fitliest for our use, in the Text it selfe, and so we take them. First then, the gaine is joy. Joy is Gods owne Seale, and his keeper is the Holy Ghost; wee have many sudden ejaculations in the forme of Prayer, sometimes inconsiderately made, and they vanish so; but if I can reflect upon my prayer, ruminate, and returne againe with joy to the same prayer, I have Gods Seale upon it. And therefore it is not so very an idle thing, as some have mis-imagined it, to repeat often the same prayer in the same words; Our Saviour did so; he prayed a third time, and in the same words; This reflecting upon a former prayer, is that that sets to this Seale, this joy, and if I have joy in my prayer, it is granted so far as concernes my good, and Gods glory. It hath beene disputed by many, both of the Gentiles, with whom the Fathers disputed, and of the Schoolemen, who dispute with one another, *An sit gaudium in Deo, de semet,* Whether God rejoyce in himselfe, in contemplation of himselfe, whether God be glad that he is God: But it is disputed by them, onely to establish it, and to illustrate it, for I doe not remember that any one of them denyes it. It is true, that *Plato* dislikes, and justly, that salutation of *Dionysius* the Tyran to God,

3 Part
Gaudium

[Mat. 26.44]

Gaude, & servato vitam Tyranni jucundam; that he should say to God, Live merrily, as merrily as a King, as merrily as I doe, and then you are God enough; to imagine such a joy in God, as is onely a transitory delight in deceivable things, is an impious conceit. But

Plotinus

when, as another Platonique sayes, *Deus est quod ipse semper voluit,* God is that which hee would be, If there be something that God would be, and he be that, If *Plato* should deny, that God joyed in himselfe, we must say of *Plato* as *Lactantius* does, *Deum potius somniaverat, quàm cognoverat, Plato* had rather dreamed that there was a God, then understood what that God was. *Bonum simplex,* sayes S. *Augustine,* To be sincere Goodnesse, Goodnesse it selfe, *Ipsa est delectatio Dei,* This is the joy that God hath in himselfe, of himselfe; And therefore sayes *Philo Iudæus, Hoc necessarium Philosophiæ sodalibus,* This is the tenent of all Philosophers, (And by that title of Philosophers, *Philo* alwaies meanes them that know and study God) *Solum Deum verè festum agere,* That only God can be truly said to keepe holy day, and to rejoyce.

This joy we shall see, when we see him, who is so in it, as that he is this joy it selfe. But here in this world, so far as I can enter into my Masters sight, I can enter into my Masters joy. I can see God in his Creatures, in his Church, in his Word and Sacraments, and Ordinances; Since I am not without this sight, I am not without this joy.

Seneca

Here a man may *Transilire mortalitatem,* sayes that Divine Morall man; I cannot put off mortality, but I can looke upon immortality; I cannot depart from this earth, but I can looke into Heaven. So I cannot possesse that finall and accomplished joy here, but as my body can lay downe a burden or a heavy garment, and joy in that ease, so my soule can put off my body so far, as that the concupiscencies thereof, and the manifold and miserable encumbrances of this world, cannot extinguish this holy joy. And this inchoative joy,

Exultatio

David derives into two branches, *To rejoyce,* and *to be glad.*

The Holy Ghost is an eloquent Author, a vehement, and an abundant Author, but yet not luxuriant; he is far from a penurious, but as far from a superfluous style too. And therefore we doe not take these two words in the Text, *To rejóyce,* and *to be glad,* to signifie meerely one and the same thing, but to be two beames, two branches, two effects, two expressings of this joy. We take them therefore, as they offer themselves in their roots, and first naturall propriety of the words. The first, which we translate *To rejoyce,* is *Ranan;* and *Ranan* denotes the externall declaration of internall joy; for the word signifies *Cantare,* To sing, and that with an extended and loud voyce, for it is the word, which is oftnest used for the musique of the Church, and the singing of Psalmes; which was such a declaration of their zealous alacrity in the primitive Church, as that, when to avoyd discovery in the times of persecution, they were forced to make their meetings in the night, they were also forced to put out their Candles, because by that light in the windowes they were discovered; After that this meeting in the darke occasioned a scandall and ill report upon those Christians, that their meetings were not upon so holy purposes, as they pretended, they discontinued their vigils, and night-meetings, yet their singing of Psalmes, when they did meet, they never discontinued, though that, many times, exposed them to dangers, and to death it selfe, as some of the Authors of the secular story of the Romans have observed and testified unto us. And some ancient Decrees and Constitutions we have, in which such are forbidden to be made Priests, as were not perfect in the Psalmes. And though S. *Hierome* tell us this, with some admiration, and note of singularity, That *Paula* could say the whole book of Psalmes without booke, in Hebrew; yet he presents it as a thing well known to be their ordinary practise; *In villula Christi Bethlem, extra psalmos silentium est,* In the village where I dwell, sayes he, where Christ was borne, in Bethlem, if you cannot sing Psalmes, you must be silent, here you shall heare nothing but Psalmes; for, (as he pursues it) *Arator stivam tenens,* The husbandman that follows the plough, he that sowes, that reapes, that carries home, all begin and proceed in all their labours with singing of Psalmes. Therefore he calls them there, *Cantiones amatorias,* Those that make or entertaine love, that seeke in the holy and honorable way of marriage, to make themselves acceptable and agreeable to one another, by no other good parts, nor conversation, but by singing of Psalmes. So he calls them, *Pastorum sibilum,* and *Arma culturæ,* Our shepheards, sayes S. *Hierome,* here, have no other Eclogues, no other Pastoralls; Our labourers, our children, our servants no other songs, nor Ballads, to recreate themselves withall, then the Psalmes.

And this universall use of the Psalmes, that they served all for all, gives occasion to one Author, in the title of the Booke of Psalmes, to depart from the ordinary reading, which is, *Sepher Tehillim,* The booke of Praise, and to reade it, *Sepher Telim,* which is *Acervorum,* The booke of Heapes, where all assistances to our salvation are heaped and treasured up. And our Countryman *Bede* found another Title, in some Copies of this booke, *Liber Soliloquiorum de Christo,* The Booke of Meditations upon Christ; Because this booke is (as *Gregory Nyssen* calls it) *Clavis David,* that key of *David,* which lets us in to all the mysteries of our Religion; which gave the ground to that which S. *Basil* sayes, that if all the other Books of Scripture could be lost, he would aske no more then the Booke of Psalmes, to catechize children, to edifie Congregations, to convert Gentils, and to convince Heretiques.

But we are launched into too large a Sea, the consideration of this Booke of Psalmes. I meane but this, in this, That if we take that way with God, The way of prayer, prayer so elemented and constituted, as we have said, that consists rather of praise and thanksgiving, then supplication for future benefits, God shall infuse into us, a zeale of expressing our consolation in him, by outward actions, to the establishing of others; we shall not disavow, nor grow slacke in our Religion, nor in any parts thereof; God shall neither take from us, The Candle and the Candlestick, The truth of the Gospel, which is the light, And the cheerfull, and authorized, and countenanced, and rewarded Preaching of the Gospel, which is the Candlestick that exalts the light; nor take from us our zeale to this outward service of God, that we come to an indifferency, whether the service of God be private or publique, sordid or glorious, allowed and suffered, by way of connivency, or commanded and enjoyned by way of authority. God shall give us this *Ranan,* this rejoycing, this externall joy, we shall have the publique preaching of the Gospel continued to us, and we shall shew that we rejoyce in it, by frequenting it, and by instituting our lives according unto it.

Delectabi-
mur

But yet this *Ranan,* this *Rejoycing,* this outward expressing of our inward zeale, may admit interruptions, receive interceptions, intermissions, and discontinuances; for, without doubt, in many places there live many persons, well affected to the truth of Religion, that dare not avow it, expresse it, declare it, especially where that fearfull Vulture, the Inquisition, hovers over them. And therefore the Holy Ghost hath added here another degree of joy, which no law, no severe execution of law, can take from us, in another word of lesse extent, *Shamach,* which is an inward joy, onely in the heart, which we translate here, to be *Glad.* How far we are bound to proceed in outward declarations of Religion, requires a serious and various consideration of Circumstances. You know how far *Daniel* proceeded; The Lords had extorted a Proclamation from the King, That no man should pray to any other God, then the King, for certaine dayes; *Daniel* would not onely not be bound by this Proclamation, and so continue his set and stationary houres of private prayer in his chamber, but he would declare it to all the world; He would set open his chamber windows, that he might be seen to pray; for, though some determine that act of *Daniel,* in setting open his windows at prayer, in this, That because the Jewes were bound by their law, wheresoever they were, in war, in captivity, upon the way, or in their sick beds, to turne towards Jerusalem, and so towards the Temple, whensoever they prayed, according to that stipulation, which had passed between God and *Solomon,* at the Dedication of the Temple, When thy servants pray towards this house, heare them in it; Therefore as *Hezekias,* in his sicke bed, when he turned towards the wall to pray, is justly thought, to have done so, therefore that he might pray towards the Temple, which stood that way; so *Daniel* is thought to have opened his windows to that purpose too, that he might have the more free prospect towards Jerusalem from Babylon; though some, I say, determine *Daniels* act in that, yet it is by more, and more usefully extended, to an expressing of such a zeale, as, in so apparant a dishonor to his God, could not be suffocated nor extinguished with a Proclamation.

In which act of his, which was a direct and evident opposing and affronting of the State, though I dare not joyne with them, who absolutely and peremptorily condemne this act of *Daniel,* because Gods subsequent act in a miraculous deliverance of *Daniel* seems to imply some former particular revelation from God to *Daniel,* that he should proceed in that confident manner, yet dare I much lesse draw this act of *Daniels* into consequence, and propose it for an

Dan. 6.10

[1 Kings 8.30]

[Isa. 38.2]

Example and precedent to private men, least of all, to animate sedi-
tious men, who upon pretence of a necessity, that God must be served
in this, and this, and no other manner, provoke and exasperate the
Magistrate with their schismaticall conventicles and separations. But
howsoever that may stand, and howsoever there may be Circumstances which may prevaile either upon humane infirmity, or upon
a rectified Conscience, or howsoever God in his Judgements, may
cast a cloud upon his own Sunne, and darken the glory of the Gospel,
in some place, for some time, yet, though we lose our *Ranan,* our
publique Rejoycing, we shall never lose our *Shamach,* our inward
gladnesse, that God is our God, and we his servants for all this. God
will never leave his servants without this internall joy, which shall
preserve them from suspicions of Gods power, that he cannot maintaine, or not restore his cause, and from jealousies, that he hath abandoned or deserted them in particular. God shall never give them
over to an indifferency, nor to a stupidity, nor to an absence of tendernesse, and holy affections, that it shall become all one to them, how
Gods cause prospers, or suffers. But if I continue that way, prayer,
and prayer so qualified, if I lose my *Ranan,* my outward declarations
of Rejoycing; If I be tyed to a death-bed in a Consumption, and cannot rejoyce in comming to these publique Congregations, to participate of their prayers, and to impart to them my Meditations; If I be
ruined in my fortune, and cannot rejoyce in an open distribution to
the reliefe of the poore, and a preaching to others, in that way, by
example of doing good works; If at my last minute, I be not able
to edifie my friends, nor Catechize my children, with any thing that
I can doe or say; if I be not able so much, as with hand or eye to make
a signe, though I have lost my *Ranan,* all the Eloquence of outward
declaration, yet God shall never take from me, my *Shamach,* my internall gladnesse and consolation, in his undeceivable and undeceiv-
ing Spirit, that he is mine, and I am his; And this joy, this gladnesse,
in my way, and in my end, shall establish me; for that is that which
is intended in the next, and last word, *Omnibus diebus,* we shall
Rejoyce and be Glad all our dayes.

Omnibus   Nothing but this testimony, *That the Spirit beares witnesse with*
diebus   *my spirit,* that upon my prayer, so conditioned, of praise, and prayer,
[Rom. 8.16]   I shall still prevaile with God, could imprint in me, this *joy, all my*

dayes. The seales of his favour, in outward blessings, fayle me in the dayes of shipwracke, in the dayes of fire, in the dayes of displacing my potent friends, or raysing mine adversaries; In such dayes I cannot rejoyce, and be glad. The seales of his favour, in inward blessings, and holy cheerfulnesse, fayle me in a present remorse after a sinne newly committed. But yet in the strength of a Christian hope, as I can pronounce out of the grounds of Nature, in an Eclipse of the Sunne, that the Sunne shall returne to his splendor againe, I can pronounce out of the grounds of Gods Word, (and Gods Word is much better assurance, then the grounds of Nature, for God can and does shake the grounds of Nature by Miracles, but no Jod of his Word shall ever perish) that I shall returne againe on my hearty penitence, if I delay it not, and rejoyce and be glad all my dayes, that is, what kinde of day soever overtake me. In the dayes of our youth, when the joyes of this world take up all the roome, there shall be roome for this holy Joy, that my recreations were harmelesse, and my conversation innocent; and certainly to be able to say, that in my recreations, in my conversation, I neither ministred occasion of tentation to another, nor exposed my selfe to tentations from another, is a faire beame of this rejoycing in the dayes of my youth. In the dayes of our Age, when we become incapable, insensible of the joyes of this world, yet this holy joy shall season us, not with a sinfull delight in the memory of our former sinnes, but with a re-juveniscence, a new and a fresh youth, in being come so neere to another, to an immortall life. In the dayes of our mirth, and of laughter, this holy joy shall enter; And as the Sunne may say to the starres at Noone, How frivoulous and impertinent a thing is your light now? So this joy shall say *unto laughter, Thou art mad, and unto mirth, what dost thou?* And in the mid-night of sadnesse, and dejection of spirit, this joy shall shine out, and chide away that sadnesse, with *Davids* holy charme, *My soule, why art thou cast downe, why art thou disquieted within me?* In those dayes, which *Iob* speaks of, *Prævenerunt me dies afflictionis meæ, Miseries are come upon me before their time;* My intemperances have hastned age, my riotousnesse hath hastned poverty, my neglecting of due officiousnesse and respect towards great persons hath hastned contempt upon me, Afflictions which I suspected not, thought not of, have prevented my

Eccles. 2.2

Iob 30.27

feares; and then in those dayes, which *Iob* speaks of againe, *Possident me dies afflictionis,* Studied and premeditated plots and practises swallowe mee, possesse me intirely, In all these dayes, I shall not onely have a *Zoar* to flie to, if I can get out of *Sodom,* joy, if I can overcome my sorrow; There shall not be a *Goshen* bordering upon my *Egypt,* joy, if I can passe beyond, or besides my sorrow, but I shall have a *Goshen* in my *Egypt,* nay my very *Egypt* shall be my *Goshen,* I shall not onely have joy, though I have sorrow, but therefore; my very sorrow shall be the occasion of joy; I shall not onely have a Sabbath after my six dayes labor, but *Omnibus diebus,* a Sabbath shall enlighten every day, and inanimate every minute of every day: And as my soule is as well in my foot, as in my hand, though all the waight and oppression lie upon the foot, and all action upon the hand, so these beames of joy shall appeare as well in my pillar of cloud, as in theirs of fire; in my adversity, as well as in their prosperity; And when their Sun shall set at Noone, mine shall rise at midnight; they shall have damps in their glory, and I joyfull exaltations in my dejections.

And to end with the end of all, *In die mortis,* In the day of my death, and that which is beyond the end of all, and without end in it selfe, The day of Judgement, If I have the testimony of a rectified conscience, that I have accustomed my selfe to that accesse to God, by prayer, and such prayer, as though it have had a body of supplication, and desire of future things, yet the soule and spirit of that prayer, that is, my principall intention in that prayer, hath been praise and thanksgiving, If I be involved in S. *Chrysostoms* Patent, *Orantes, non natura, sed dispensatione Angeli fiunt,* That those who pray so, that is, pray by way of praise, (which is the most proper office of Angels) as they shall be better then Angels in the next world, (for they shall be glorifying spirits, as the Angels are, but they shall also be glorified bodies, which the Angels shall never bee) so in this world they shall be as Angels, because they are employed in the office of Angels, to pray by way of praise, If, as S. *Basil* reads those words of that Psalme, not *spiritus meus,* but *respiratio mea laudet Dominum,* Not onely my spirit, but my very breath, not my heart onely, but my tongue, and my hands bee accustomed to glorifie God, *In die mortis,* in the day of my death, when a mist of sorrow, and of sighes shall fill my chamber, and a cloude exhaled and condensed from teares, shall bee the curtaines of my bed, when those that love me, shall be sorry to see mee die, and the devill himselfe that hates me, sorry to see me die so, in the favour of God; And *In die Iudicii,* In the day of Judgement, when as all Time shall cease, so all measures shall cease; The joy, and the sorrow that shall be then, shall be eternall, no end, and infinite, no measure, no limitation, when every circumstance of sinne shall aggravate the condemnation of the unrepentant sinner, and the very substance of my sinne shall bee washed away, in the blood of my Saviour, when I shall see them, who sinned for my sake, perish eternally, because they proceeded in that sinne, and I my selfe, who occasioned their sin received into glory, because God upon my prayer, and repentance had satisfied me early with his mercy, early, that is, before my transmigration, *In omnibus diebus,* In all these dayes, the dayes of youth, and the wantonnesses of that, the dayes of age, and the tastlesnesse of that, the dayes of mirth, and the sportfulnesse of that, and of inordinate melancholy, and the disconsolatenesse of that, the days of such miseries, as astonish us with their suddennesse, and of such as aggravate their owne waight with a heavy expectation; In the day of Death, which pieces up that circle, and in that day which enters another circle that hath no pieces, but is one equall everlastingnesse, the day of Judgement, Either I shall rejoyce, be able to declare my faith, and zeale to the assistance of others, or at least be glad in mine owne heart, in a firme hope of mine owne salvation.

And therefore, beloved, as they, whom lighter affections carry to Shewes, and Masks, and Comedies; As you your selves, whom better dispositions bring to these Exercises, conceive some contentment, and some kinde of Joy, in that you are well and commodiously placed, they to see the Shew, you to heare the Sermon, when the time comes, though your greater Joy bee reserved to the comming of that time; So though the fulnesse of Joy be reserved to the last times in heaven, yet rejoyce and be glad that you are well and commodiously placed in the meane time, and that you sit but in expectation of the fulnesse of those future Joyes: Returne to God, with a joyfull thankfulnesse that he hath placed you in a Church, which withholds nothing from you, that is necessary to salvation, whereas in another Church they lack a great part of the Word, and halfe the Sacrament; And which obtrudes nothing to you, that is not necessary to salvation, whereas in another Church, the Additionall things exceed the Fundamentall; the Occasionall, the Originall; the Collaterall, the Direct; And the Traditions of men, the Commandements of God. Maintaine and hold up this holy alacrity, this religious cheerfulnesse; For inordinate sadnesse is a great degree and evidence of unthankfulnesse, and the departing from Joy in this world, is a departing with one piece of our Evidence, for the Joyes of the world to come.

Number 3.

The First Sermon Preached to King Charles, at Saint James: 3°. April. 1625.

PSALME 11.3. *IF THE FOUNDATIONS BE DESTROYED, WHAT CAN THE RIGHTEOUS DOE?*

WEE ARE still in the season of *Mortification;* in *Lent:* But wee search no longer for *Texts* of *Mortification;* The Almightie hand of *God* hath shed and spred a *Text* of *Mortification* over all the land. The last *Sabboth* day, was his *Sabboth* who entred then into his everlasting *Rest;* Be this our *Sabboth,* to enter into a holy and thankfull acknowledgement of that *Rest,* which *God* affords us, in continuing to us our *Foundations;* for, *If foundations be destroyed, what can the righteous doe?*

I scarse know any word in the Word of *God,* in which the *Originall* is more ambiguous, and consequently the *Translations* more various, and therfore, necessarily also, the *Expositions* more divers, then in these words. There is one thing, in which all agree, that is, the *Argument,* and *purpose,* and *scope* of the *Psalme;* And then, in what sense, the words of the *Text* may conduce to the scope of the *Psalme,* wee rest in this Translation, which our Church hath accepted and authorized, and which agrees with the first Translation knowen to us, by way of Exposition, that is the *Chalde Paraphrase, If Foundations bee destroyed, what can the righteous doe?*

The Church of *God* ever delighted herselfe in a holy officiousnesse in the Commemoration of *Martyrs:* Almost all their solemne, and extraordinarie Meetings, and Congregations, in the Primitive Church, were for that, for the honourable Commemoration of Martyrs: And for that, they came soone to institute and appoynt certaine *Liturgies,* certaine *Offices* (as they called them) certaine *Services* in the Church, which should have reference to that, to the Commemoration of *Martyrs;* as wee have in our *Booke* of *Common Prayer,* certaine *Services* for *Marriage,* for *Buriall,* and for such other holy Celebrations; And in the Office and Service of a *Martyr,* the Church did use this *Psalme;* This *Psalme,* which is in generall, a Protestation of *David,* That though hee were so vehemently pursued by *Saul,* as that all that wished him well, sayd to his Soule, *Flie as a Bird to the Mountaine,* as it is in the first verse; Though hee saw, *That the wicked had bent their Bowes, and made ready their Arrowes, upon the string, that they might privily shoot at the upright in heart,* as it is in the second verse: Though he take it almost as granted, that *Foundations are destroyed,* (*And then, what can the righteous doe?*) as it is in the third verse which is our *Text,* yet in this distresse he findes what to doe. For as hee begunne in the first verse, *In thee Lord, put I my trust:* So after he had passed the enumeration of his dangers, in the second and third verses, in the fourth he pursues it as he begun, *The Lord is in his holy Temple, the Lords Throane is in Heaven.* And in the fifth hee fixes it thus, *The Lord tryeth the Righteous,* (he may suffer much to be done for their triall) *but the wicked, and him that loveth violence, his soule hateth.* This then is the *Syllogisme,* this is the *Argumentation* of the righteous Man; In Collaterall things, in Circumstantiall things, in things that are not fundamentall, a righteous Man, a constant Man should not bee shaked at all, not at all Scandalized; Thats true; But then, (in a second place) sometimes it comes to that, *That Foundations are destroyd, and what can the Righteous doe then?* Why even then, this is a question, not of desperation, that nothing can bee done, but of Consultation with God, what should be done. I know, sayes *David,* I should not be, and thou knowest, O God, I have not beene mov'd with ordinary trialls; not though my Friends have dis-avowed mee, and bid *mee flye to the Mountaine as a Bird,* not though mine enemies prepare, and *prepare Arrowes,* and shoote, and *shoote privily,* (bestowe their labour, and their cost, and their witts, to ruine mee) yet these have not moov'd mee, because I had fixed my selfe upon certaine *Foundations,* Confidences, and Assurances of Deliverance from thee. But if, O Lord, I see these foundations destroyed, if thou put mee into mine Enemies hand, if thou make them thy Sword, if their furie draw that Sword, and then, thy Almightie Arme, sinewed even with thine owne indignation, strike with that sword, what can I, how righteous soever I were, doe? So then, for the *Explication,* and *Application* of these words, there will need no more, but to spread them by way of *Paraphrase* upon these three considerations: First, That the righteous is bolde as a *Lyon,* not easily shaked; But then, *Foundations* themselves may bee destroyed, and so hee may bee shaked; If hee bee, yet hee knowes what to doe, or where to aske Counsell, for these are not wordes of *Desperation,* but of *Consultation, If Foundations bee destroyed, &c.*

Divisio

First then, wee fixe our selves upon this consideration, that the Prophet in proposing this thus, *If Foundations bee destroyed,* intimates pregnantly, that except there bee danger of destroying *Foundations,* it is the part of the righteous Man, the godly man to bee quiet. *Studie to bee quiet,* sayes the *Apostle; Studie,* that is an action of the Minde; and then, *Operam detis,* sayes the *Vulgate Edition, Labour to bee quiet,* and *Labour* is an action of the bodie: Indeed it is the proper businesse of the *Minde* and *Bodie* too, of *Thoughts* and *Actions* too, to bee quiet: And yet, alas, how many breake their sleepe in the night, about things that disquiet them in the day too, and trouble themselves in the day, about things that disquiet them all night too? Wee disquiet our selves too much, in beeing over tender, over sensible of imaginarie injuries. *Transeant iniuriæ,* sayes the Morall man; *Let many injuries passe over;* for, *Plærasque non accipit, qui nescit; Hee that knowes not of an injurie, or takes no knowledge of it, for the most part, hath no injurie. Qui inquirunt, quid in se dictum est,* sayes hee, They that are too inquisitive, what other men say of them, they disquiet themselves; for that which others would but *whisper,* they *publish.* And therefore that which hee addes there, for *Morall,* and *Civill* matters, holds in a good proportion, in things of a more *Divine* Nature, in such parts of the religious worship and service of *God,* as concerne not *Foundations, Non expedit omnia videre, non omnia audire;* we must not too jealously suspect, not too bitterly condemne, not too peremptorily conclude, that what soever is not done, as wee would have it done, or as wee have seene it done in former times, is not well done: for there is a large Latitude, and, by necessitie of Circumstances, much may bee admitted, and yet no *Foundations destroyed;* and till *Foundations bee destroyed, the righteous should bee quiet.*

1. *Part*

1 Thess. 4.11

Seneca

Now this should not prepare, this should not incline any man, to such an indifferencie, as that it should bee all one to him, what became of all things; all one, whether wee had one, or two, or tenne, or no Religion; or that hee should not bee awake, and active, and diligent, in assisting trueth, and resisting all approaches of Errour. For, *God* hath sayd of all, into whose hand hee hath committed power, *You are Gods.* Now, they are not *Gods,* but *Idoles,* if, as the *Prophet* sayes,

Psal. 115.6

They have Eyes and see not, Eares and heare not, Hands and strike not; nay, (as hee addes there) *if they have Noses and smell not;* if they smell not out a mischievous practise, before it come to execution. For,

Iob 34.21

Gods eyes are upon the wayes of man, and hee sees all his goings: Those, who are in the number of them, of whome *God* hath said, they are *Gods,* must have their eyes upon the *wayes* of men, and not upon their *Ends* onely; upon the *pathes* of mischiefe, and not upon the *bed* of mischiefe onely; upon the *Actors* of mischiefe, and not upon the *Act* onely. *Gods eye sees our wayes,* sayes *David* too; that is, hee can see

Iere. 32.19

them, when hee will; but there is more in the other *Prophet, Gods eyes are open upon all our wayes;* always open, and hee cannot chuse but see: So that, a wilfull shutting of the eye, a winking, a connivencie,

Abac. 1.13

is not an assimilation to *God.* And then, *Gods eyes are purer, then to beholde evill, and they cannot looke upon iniquitie:* So that in an indifferencie, whether Times, or Persons bee good or badd, there is not

Hebr. 4.13

this assimilation to *God.* Againe, *All things are naked and open to the eyes of God:* So that in the disguising, and palliating, and extenuating the faults of men, there is not this assimilation to *God.* Thus farre they falsifie *Gods* Word, who hath sayd, *They are Gods;* for *they are Idoles, and not Gods, if they have eyes, and see not.* So is it also in the con-

Psal. 94.9

sideration of the *Eare* too: for, as *David* sayes, *Shall not hee that planted the Eare, heare?* So wee may say, Shall hee upon whom *God* hath planted an Eare, bee deafe? *Gods* eares are so open, so tender, so

Psal. 39.12

sensible of any motion, as that *David* formes one Prayer thus, *Auribus percipe lachrimas meas,* O Lord, heare my teares; hee puts the office of the *Eye* too, upon the *Eare.* And then, if the *Magistrate* stop his Eares with *Wooll,* (with staple bribes, profitable bribes) and with *Cyvet* in his wooll, (perfumes of pleasure and preferment in his bribes) hee falsifies *Gods* Word, who hath said, they are *Gods,* for *they are Idoles, and not Gods, if they have eares, and heare not.* And so it is also of the hand too; In all that *Iob* suffered, he sayes no more, but that *the Hand of God had touched him;* but *touched* him, in respect of that hee could have done: for, when *Iob* sayes to men, *Why persecute you mee, as God?* hee meanes, as *God* could doe, so vehemently, so ruinously, so destructively, so irreparably. There is no *phrase* oftner in the *Scriptures,* then that *God* delivered his people, in the *hand* of *Moses,* and the *hand* of *David,* and the *hand* of the *Prophets:* all their Ministeriall office is called the *Hand:* and therfore, as *David* prayes to *God, That hee would pull his hand out of his bosome, and strike:* so must wee ever exhort the *Magistrate,* That hee would plucke his hand out of his pocket, and forget what is there, and execute the Lawes committed to him. For, as wee, at last, shall commend our Spirits, into the hands of *God, God* hath commended our Spirits, not onely our civill peace, but our Religion too, into the *hand* of the *Magistrate.* And therefore, when the *Apostle* sayes, *Studie to bee quiet,* it is not quiet in the blindnesse of the *Eye,* nor quiet in the *Deafenesse* of the *Eare,* nor quiet in the *Lamenesse* of the *Hand;* the just discharge of the dueties of our severall places, is no *disquieting* to any man. But when *private* men will spend all their thoughts upon their *Superiours* actions, this must necessarily disquiet them; for they are off of their owne *Center,* and they are *extra Sphæram Activitatis,* out of their owne *Distance,* and *Compasse,* and they cannot possibly discerne the *Ende,* to which their *Superiours* goe. And to such a jealous man, when his jealousie is not a tendernesse towards his owne actions, which is a holy and a wholesome jealousie, but a suspition of his *Superiours* actions, to this Man, every *Wheele* is a *Drumme,* and every *Drumme* a *Thunder,* and every *Thunder-clapp* a dissolution of the whole frame of the World: If there fall a broken tyle from the house, hee thinkes *Foundations are destroyed;* if a crazie woman, or a disobedient childe, or a needie servant fall from our *Religion,* from our *Church,* hee thinkes the whole *Church* must necessarily fall, when all this while there are no *Foundations destroyed;* and *till foundations bee destroyed, the righteous should be quiet.*

Hence have wee just occasion, first to *condole* amongst *our selves,* who, for matters of *Foundations* professe one and the same *Religion,* and then to complaine of our *Adversaries,* who are of another. First, that amongst our selves, for matters not *Doctrinall,* or if *Doctrinall,*

Iob 19.22

yet not *Fundamentall,* onely because wee are sub-divided in divers *Names,* there should bee such Exasperations, such Exacerbations, such Vociferations, such Ejulations, such Defamations of one another, as if all *Foundations* were destroyed. Who would not tremble, to heare those *Infernall* words, spoken by men, to men, of one and the same Religion fundamentally, as *Indiabolificata, Perdiabolificata,* and *Superdiabolificata,* that the *Devill,* and all the *Devills* in Hell, and worse then the *Devill* is in their *Doctrine,* and in their *Divinitie,* when, *God* in heaven knowes, if their owne uncharitablenesse did not exclude him, there were roome enough for the *Holy Ghost,* on both, and on either side, in those *Fundamentall* things, which are unanimely professed by both: And yet every *Mart,* wee see more Bookes written by these men against one another, then by them both, for *Christ.*

But yet though this *Torrent* of uncharitablenesse amongst them, bee too violent, yet it is within some bankes; though it bee a *Sea,* and too tempestuous, it is limitted within some bounds; The poynts are certaine, knowen, limitted, and doe not grow upon us every yeare, and day. But the uncharitablenesse of the *Church* of *Rome* towards us all, is not a *Torrent,* nor it is not a *Sea,* but a *generall Flood,* an universall *Deluge,* that swallowes all the world, but that *Church,* and *Churchyard,* that *Towne,* and *Suburbes,* themselves, and those that depend upon them; and will not allowe possibilitie of Salvation to the whole *Arke,* the whole *Christian Church,* but to one *Cabin* in that *Arke,* the *Church* of *Rome;* and then denie us this Salvation, not for any *Positive Errour,* that ever they charged us to affirme; not because wee affirme any thing, that they denie, but because wee denie some things, which they in their afternoone are come to affirme.

If they were *Iusti,* Righteous, right and just dealing men, they would not raise such dustes, and then blind mens eyes with this dust of their own raysing, in things that concerne no *Foundations.* It is true, that all *Heresie* does concerne *Foundations:* there is no *Heresie* to bee called little: Great *Heresies* proceeded from things, in apparance, small at first, and seem'd to looke but towards small matters. There were great *Heresies,* that were but *Verball, Heresies* in some Word. That great Storme, that shaked the *State,* and the *Church,* in the *Councell* of *Ephesus,* and came to Factions, and Commotions in the *Secular* part, and to Exautorations, and Excommunications amongst the *Bishops*, so farre, as that the *Emperour* came to declare both sides to bee *Heretiques;* All this was for an Errour in a *Word*, in the word *Deipara*, whether the *Blessed Virgine Marie* were to bee called the *Mother of God*, or no. There have beene *Verball Heresies*, and *Heresies* that were but *Syllabicall;* little *Præpositions* made *Heresies;* not onely *State-præpositions*, Precedencies, and Prerogatives of *Church* above *Church*, occasioned great *Schismes*, but *Literall Præpositions*, *Præpositions* in *Grammar*, occasioned great *Heresies*. That great *Heresie* of the *Acephali*, against which *Damascene* bendes himselfe in his Booke, *De Natura Composita*, was grounded in the *Præposition*, *In;* They would confesse *Ex*, but not *In*, That *Christ* was made *of* two Natures, but that hee did not consist *in* two Natures. And wee all know, what differences have beene raysed in the *Church*, in that one poynt of the *Sacrament*, by these three Prepositions, *Trans*, *Con*, and *Sub*. There have beene great *Heresies*, but *Verball*, but *Syllabicall;* and as great, but *Litterall;* The greatest *Heresie* that ever was, that of the *Arrians*, was but in one Letter. So then, in *Heresie*, there is nothing to bee called little, nothing to bee suffered. It was excellently sayde of *Heretiques*, (though by one, who, though not then declared, was then an *Heretique* in his heart,) *Condolere Hereticis crimen est;* It is a fault, not onely to bee too indulgent to an *Heretique*, but to bee too compassionate of an *Heretique*, too sorrie for an *Heretique*. It is a fault to say, Alas, let him alone, hee is but an *Heretique;* but, to say, Alas, hope well of him, till you bee better sure, that hee is an Heretique, is charitably spoken. *God* knowes, the sharpe and sowre Name of *Heretique*, was too soone let loose, and too fast spread in many places of the world. Wee see, that in some of the first *Catalogues*, that were made of *Heretiques*, men were Registred for *Heretiques*, that had but expounded a place of *Scripture*, otherwise then that place had beene formerly expounded, though there were no harme, in that newe Exposition. And then, when once that infamous Name of *Heretique* was fastened upon a man, nothing was too heavie for, any thing was beleeved of that man. And from thence it is, without question, that wee finde so many so absurd, so senselesse Opinions imputed to those men, who were then called *Heretiques*, as could not, in trueth, with any possibilitie, fall into the imagination or fancie of any man, much lesse bee *Doctrinally*, or *Dogmatically* delivered. And then, upon this,

Nestorius

there issued *Lawes*, from particular *States*, against particular *Heresies*, that troubled those *States* then, as namely, against the *Arrians*, or *Macedonians*, and such; and in a short time, these *Lawes* came to bee extended, to all such *Opinions*, as the passion of succeeding times, called *Heresie*. And at last, the *Romane Church* having constituted that *Monopolie*, That Shee onely should declare what should bee *Heresie*, and having declared that to bee *Heresie*, which opposed, or retarded the dignitie of *that Church*, now they call in *Brachium Spirituale*, All those Sentences of *Fathers*, or *Councells* that mention *Heresie*, and they call in *Brachium Sæculare*, all those *Lawes* which punish *Heresie*, and whereas these *Fathers*, and *Councells*, and *States*, intended by *Heresie*, Opinions that destroyed *Foundations*, they bend all these against every poynt, which may endammage, not the *Church* of *God*, but the *Church* of *Rome*; nor the *Church* of *Rome*, but the *Court* of *Rome*; nor the *Court* of *Rome*, but the *Kitchin* of *Rome*; not for the *Heart*, but for the *Bellie*; not the *Religion*, but the *Policie*; not the *Altar*, but the *Exchequer* of *Rome*.

But the Righteous lookes to *Foundations*, before hee will be scandalized himselfe, or condemne another. When they call Saint *Peter* their first *Pope*, and being remembred, how hee denied his *Master*, say then, that was but an Acte of *Infirmitie*, not of *Infidelitie*, and there were no *Foundations* destroyed in that; wee presse not that evidence against *Saint Peter*, wee forbeare, and wee are quiet. When wee charge some of *Saint Peters* imaginary Successors, some of their *Popes*, with actuall, and personall *Sacrificing* to *Idoles*, some with *subscribing* to formall *Heresies*, with their owne hand, many with so enormous an ill life, as that their owne Authors will say, that for many yeares together, there lived not one *Pope*, of whose Salvation, any hope could bee conceived; and they answere to all this, that all these were but *Personall* faults, and destroyed no *Foundations;* wee can bee content to bury their faultes with their persons, and wee are quiet. When wee remember them, how many of the *Fathers* excused *officious Lyes*, and thought some kinde of *Lying* to bee no *Sinne*, how very many of them hearded in the *heresie* of the *Millenarians*, That the *Saints* of *God* should enjoy a thousand yeares of temporall felicity in this world, after their *Resurrection*, before they ascended into Heaven; And that they say to all this, The *Fathers* said these things before the *Church* had decreed any thing to the contrary, and till that, it was lawfull for any man to say, or thinke what hee would, wee do not load the memory of those blessed *Fathers* with any heavier pressings, but wee are quiet. Yet wee cannot chuse but tell them, that tell us this, that they have taken a hard way, to make that saying true, that all things are growen deare in our times; for they have made *Salvation* deare; Threescore yeares agoe, a man might have beene sav'd at halfe the price hee can now: Threescore yeares agoe, he might have beene saved for beleeving the *Apostles Creed;* now it will cost him the *Trent Creed* too. Evermore they will presse for all, and yeeld nothing; and there is indeed their *Specification,* there's their *Character,* that's their *Catholique,* their *Vniversall;* To *have all;* As, in *Athanasius* his time, when the *Emperour* pressed him to affoord the *Arrians* one *Church* in *Alexandria,* where hee was *Bishop,* and hee asked but one *Church* in *Antioch,* where the *Arrians* prevayled, not doubting but hee should draw more to the true *Church* in *Antioch,* then they should corrupt in *Alexandria,* yet this would not bee granted; It would not be granted at *Rome,* if we should aske a *Church* for a *Church.* In a word, wee charge them with *uncharitablenesse,* (and *Charitie* is without all Controversie, a *Foundation* of *Religion*) that they will so peremptorily exclude us from Heaven, for matters that doe not appertaine to *Foundations.* For, if they will call all *Foundations,* that that *Church hath,* or *doth,* or *shall* decree, wee must learne our *Catechisme* upon our *Death-bedd,* and inquire for the Articles of our Faith, when wee are going out of the world, for they may have decreed something that Morning. No one *Author* of theirs denied *Pope Ioane,* till they discerned the *Consequence,* That by confessing a *Woman Pope,* they should disparage that *Succession* of *Bishops,* which they pretend, And this *Succession* must bee *Foundation.* No Author of our side denied *Saint Peters* beeing at *Rome,* till wee discerned the *Consequence,* That upon his *personall* being there, they grounded a *Primacie* in that *Sea,* And this *Primacie* must bee *Foundation.* Much might bee admitted in cases of *Indifferencie,* even in the *Nature of the things,* Much in cases of *Necessitie,* for the *importance of Circumstances,* much in cases of *Conveniency,* for the suppling of boysterous, and for the becalming of tempestuous humours; but when every thing must be called *Foundation,* we shall never knowe where to stop, where to consist. If wee should beleeve their *Sacrificium incruentum*, their unbloody Sacrifice in the *Masse*, if wee did not beleeve their *Sacrificium Cruentum* too, that there was a power in that *Church*, to sacrifice the Blood of *Kings*, wee should bee sayde to bee defective in a *fundamentall Article*. If wee should admitt their *Metaphysiques*, their transcendent *Transubstantiation*, and admitt their *Chimiques*, their *Purgatorie* Fires, and their *Mythologie*, and *Poetrie*, their apparitions of *Soules* and *Spirits*, they would binde us to their *Mathematiques* too, and they would not let us bee saved, except wee would reforme our *Almanackes* to their *tenne dayes*, and reforme our *Clockes* to their *foure and twentie*: for who can tell when there is an ende of *Articles of Faith*, in an *Arbitrarie*, and in an *Occasionall Religion?* When then this *Prophet* sayes, *If Foundations bee destroyed, what can the righteous doe*, hee meanes, that till that, the righteous should bee *quiet*: Except it were in *fundamentall Articles* of Faith, our selves should not bee so bitter towards one another, our Adversarie should not bee so uncharitable against us all. And farther wee need not extend this first Consideration.

2. *Part*

The second is, to Survay some such *Foundations*, as fall within the frayltie, and suspition, and possibilitie of this Text, that they may bee destroyed: for when the Prophet sayes, *If they bee*, they may bee. Now *Fundamentum proprie de ædificijs dicitur*, sayes the *Lawe*: when wee speake of *Foundations*, wee intend a *house*: and heere, wee extend this *House* to foure Considerations; for in foure *Houses* have every one of us a dwelling. For, first, *Ecclesia Domus*, the *Church* is a *House*, it is *Gods house;* and in that House, wee are *of the houshold of the faithfull*, if (as it is testified of *Moses*) *wee bee faithfull in all his House, as Servants.* You see there is a faithfulnesse required in every man, in *all the house of God*, not in any one roome; a disposition required to doe good to the whole *Church* of *God* every where, and not onely at *home*. Secondly, *Respublica Domus*, The *Commonwealth*, the *State*, the *Kingdome* is a *House;* and this is that which is called so often, *Domus Israel*, *The house of Israel*, the State, the Government of the *Iewes*: And in this *House*, God dwells, as well as in the other; In the *State*, as well as in the *Church*: For, these words, *The Lord hath chosen Sion*, *hee hath desired it for a habitation*, are spoken of the whole Bodie, *Church*, and *State*. Thirdly,

Hebr. 3.5

Psa. 132.13

there is *Domus Habitationis, Domus quæ Domicilium,* a House to
dwell in, and to dwell with, a *Family:* and in this House *God* dwells
too; for, as *David* sayes of the *Building,* wee may say of the *Dwelling,*
Except the Lord build the House, they labour in vaine: So except   Psal. 127.1
the Lord dwell in the House, it is a desolate Habitation. And then
lastly, there is *Domus quæ Dominus,* a house which is the *Master* of
the *House;* for as every Man is a little World, so every man is his
owne House, and dwels in himselfe: And in this *House God* dwells
too; for the *Apostle* seemes so much to delight himselfe in that *Meta-*
phore, as that hee repeats it almost in all his *Epistles, Habitat in nobis,*
That the Holy Ghost dwells in us. Now, of all these foure *Houses,*
that *house* which hath no walles, but is spread over the face of the
whole Earth, the *Church,* And that *House,* which with us, hath no
other walls, but the *Sea,* the *State,* the *Kingdome,* And that *house*
which is walled with *drie Earth,* our dwelling house, our family, and
this *house* which is wall'd with *wet Earth,* this loame of flesh, our
selfe, Of all these foure houses, those three, of which, and in which
we are, and this fourth, which wee our selfe are, *God* is the *Founda-*
tion, and so *foundations* cannot be destroyed; But, as, though the
common foundation of all buildings bee the *Earth,* yet wee make
particular foundations for particular buildings, of Stone, or Brick,
or Piles, as the Soyle requires; so shall wee also heere consider such
particular Foundations of these foure houses, as may fall within the
frailtie, and suspition, within the possibilitie, and danger of the Text,
of being *destroyed.*

Of the first *House* then, which is the *Church,* the foundation is   *Ecclesia*
Christ, Other foundation can no man lay, then that which is layd,   *Domus*
which is Iesus Christ. Non propterea dicimus, sayes Saint *Augustine,*   1 Cor. 3.11
Wee doe not say that our *Church* is *Catholique* therefore, because   De unitate
Optatus sayes so, and because *Ambrose* sayes so, (and yet *Optatus,*   Eccles. C. 16
and *Ambrose,* the *Fathers,* are good Witnesses) neither do we say
it, (sayes he) *Quia Collegarum nostrorum Conciliis prædicta est,*
Because some *Synodes* and *Councells* of men of our owne Religion
have said it is *Catholique* (And yet a *Harmony of Confessions* is good
Evidence,) *Nec quia tanta fiunt in ea mirabilia,* sayes hee, wee call
it not *Catholique,* because so many *Myracles* are wrought in it, (for
wee oppose *Gods* many miraculous Deliverances of this *State* and

Church, to all their *imaginary miracles* of *Rome*) *Non ideo manifestatur Catholica,* sayes still that *Father,* All this does not make our
Church *Catholique,* nay, *non manifestatur,* all this does not declare
it to bee *Catholique,* all these are no infallible marks thereof, but onely
this one, sayes hee, *Quia ipse Dominus Iesus, &c.* because the *Lord
Iesus* himselfe is the *Foundation* of this Church. But may not this be
subject to reasoning, to various Disputation, Whether wee have that

De Moribus
Eccles. Cat.
C.25

foundation, or no? It may; but that will goe farre in the clearing
thereof, which the same Father sayes in another Booke, *Nihil in Ecclesia catholica salubrius fit, quam ut Rationem præcedat Autoritas:*
Nothing is safer for the finding of the *Catholique* Church, then to
preferre *Authoritie* before my *Reason,* to submit and capivate my
Reason to *Authoritie.* This the *Romane Church* pretends to embrace;
but *Apishly;* like an *Ape,* it kills with embracing, for it evacuates the
right *Authoritie;* The *Authority* that they obtrude, is the *Decretals*
of their owne *Bishops,* The *authoritie,* which *Saint Augustine* literally and expressely declares himselfe to meane, is the *authoritie* of the
Scriptures.

    Christ then, that is, the *Doctrine of Christ,* is the *foundation* of this

2 Chro. 3.3

first *House,* the *Church. Hæc sunt fundamenta quæ jecit Salomon,*
sayes the *vulgate Edition,* These are the *foundations* that *Salomon*
layde; and then our *Translation* hath it, *These are the things in which
Salomon was instructed;* One calls it *Foundations,* the other *Instructions;* All's one; The *Instructions* of *Christ,* the *Doctrine* of *Christ,*
the *Word,* the *Scriptures* of *Christ,* are the *Foundation* of this *House.*

Ephes. 2.20

For, when the Apostle sayes, *Christ Iesus himselfe is the chiefe corner
Stone,* yet hee adds there, *Yee are built upon the Prophets and Apostles:* for the *Prophets* and *Apostles,* had their part in the *foundation;*
in the *laying,* though not in the *beeing* of the *Foundation. The wall*

Apoc. 21.14

of the citie, sayes Saint *Iohn, had twelve Foundations, and in them,
the Names of the twelve Apostles:* But still, in that place, they are
Apostles of the Lambe, still they have relation to *Christ:* For, they,
who by inspiration of the *Holy Ghost,* writt of *Christ,* and so made
up the Bodie of the Scriptures, have their parts too, in this *Foundation.* Besides these, it is sayd, in the building of the *Materiall Temple,*

1 Reg. 5.17

*The King commaunded, and they brought great Stones, and costly
Stones, and hewed Stones, to lay the foundations of the House:* The

care of the *King*, the labours of men conduce to the *foundation*. And besides this, in that place of the *Revelation*, The *foundation* of the Wall, is sayde to bee *garnished with all manner of precious stones; Garnished*, but not *made* of that kinde of precious stones. So then *Salomons* hewed Stones, and costly stones, may, in a faire accommodation, bee understood to bee the *Determinations*, and *Resolutions, Canons*, and *Decrees* of generall *Councels:* And Saint *Iohns* garnishment of precious stones, may, in a faire accommodation, bee understood to bee the Learned and Laborious, the zealous and the pious *Commentaries* and *Expositions* of the *Fathers;* For *Councells* and *Fathers* assist the *Foundation;* But the *foundation* it selfe is Christ himselfe in his *Word;* his *Scriptures*. And then, certainely they love the *House* best, that love the *foundation* best: not they, that impute to the *Scriptures* such an *Obscuritie*, as should make them *in-intelligible* to us, or such a defect as should make them *insufficient* in themselves. To denie us the use of *Scriptures* in our vulgar Translations, and yet to denie us the use of them, in the *Originall* Tongues too, To tell us we must not trie *Controversies* by our *English*, or our *Latine Bibles*, nor by the *Hebrew Bibles* neither, To put such a Majestie upon the *Scriptures*, as that a Lay man may not touch them, and yet to put such a diminution upon them, as that the writings of men shall bee equall to them; this is a wrinching, a shrinking, a sinking, an undermining, a destroying of *Foundations*, of the *foundation* of this first *House*, which is the *Church*, the *Scriptures*.

Enter wee now into a Survay of the second *House*, The *State*, the *Kingdome*, the *Common-wealth;* and of this *House*, the *foundation* is the *Law*. And therefore Saint *Hierome* referres this Text, in a litterall and primary signification to that, to the *Law:* for so, in his *Commentaries* upon the *Psalmes*, he translates this Text, *Si dissipatæ Leges*, Hee makes the evacuating of the *Law*, this destroying of *foundations. Lex communis Reipub. sponsio*, sayes the *Law* it selfe: The *Law* is the mutuall, the reciprocall Suretie betweene the *State* and the *Subject*. The *Lawe* is my *Suretie* to the *State*, that I shall pay my Obedience, And the *Lawe* is the States *Suretie* to mee, that I shall enjoy my Protection. And therefore, therein did the *Iewes* justly exalt themselves above all other Nations, That *God was come so much nearer to them then to other Nations, by how much they had*

Respub. Domus

[Deut. 4.7 and 8]

Lawes and Ordinances more righteous then other Nations had. Now, as it is sayd of the *Foundations* of the other *House,* the *Temple, The King commaunded in the laying thereof,* the *King* had his hand in the *Church,* so is it also in this *House,* the *State,* the *Common-wealth,* the *King* hath his hand *in,* and *upon* the *foundation* here also, which is the *Lawe:* so farre, as that every *forbearing* of a *Lawe,* is not an *Evacuating* of the *Law;* every *Pardon,* whether a *Post-pardon,* by way of mercy, after a Lawe is broken, or a *Præ-pardon,* by way of *Dispensation,* in wisedome before a Lawe bee broken, is not a *Destroying of this foundation.* For, when such things as these are done, *Non astu Mentientis, sed affectu compatientis,* not upon colourable disguises, nor private respects, but truely for the *Generall good,* all these *Pardons,* and *Dispensations* conduce and concurre to the *Office,* and contract the *Nature* of the *Foundation* it selfe, which is, that the whole Bodie may bee the better supported. But where there is an inducing of a *super-Soveraigne,* and a *super-Supremacie,* and a *Sea* above our *foure Seas,* and a *Horne* above our *Head,* and a *forraine Power* above our *Native* and *naturall Power,* where there are dogmaticall, Positive Assertions, that men borne of us, and living with us, and by us, are yet none of us, no *Subjects,* owe no *Allegeance,* this is a wrinching, a shrinking, a sinking, an undermining, a destroying of *Foundations,* the *Foundation* of this second *House,* which is the *State,* the *Law.*

Ivo

Domus Domicilium

The third *House* that falles into our present Survay, is *Domus quæ Domicilium, Domus habitationis,* our *Dwelling house,* or *Family,* and of this *house,* the foundation is *Peace:* for *Peace* compacts all the peeces of a *family* together; Husband and Wife, in Love and in Obedience, Father and Sonne, in Care and in Obedience, Master and Servant, in Discipline and in Obedience: Still *Obedience* is one Ingredient in all *Peace;* there is no *Peace* where there is no *Obedience.* Now every smoke does not argue the house to bee on fire; Every domestique offence taken or given, does not destroy this *Foundation,* this *Peace,* within doores. There may bee a *Thunder* from above, and there may bee an *Earth-quake* from below, and yet the *foundation* of the House safe: From above there may bee a defect in the *Superiour,* in the Husband, the Father, the Master; and from below, in the Wife, the Sonne, the Servant; There may bee a *Iealousie* in the Husband, a *Morositie* in the Father, an *Imperiousnesse* in the Master; And there may bee an *inobsequiousnesse* and an *indiligence* in the Wife, there may bee *levitie* and *inconsideration* in the Sonne, and there may bee *unreadinesse, unseasonablenesse* in a Servant, and yet *Foundations* stand, and *Peace* maintayned, though not by an exquisite performing of all duties, yet by a mutuall support of one anothers infirmities. This destroyes no *Foundation;* But if there bee a windowe opened in the house, to let in a *Iesuiticall firebrand,* that shall whisper, though not proclaime, deliver with a *non Dominus sed Ego,* that though it bee not a declared *Tenet* of the *Church,* yet hee thinkes, that in case of *Heresie,* Civill and Naturall, and Matrimoniall duties cease, no Civill, no Naturall, no Matrimoniall Tribute due to an *Heretique;* Or if there bee such a fire kindled within doores, that the Husbands jealousie come to a *Substraction* of necessary meanes at home, or to *Defamation* abroad, or the Wives levitie induce just *Imputation* at home, or *scandall* abroad, If the Fathers wastfulnesse amount to a *Disinheriting,* because hee leaves nothing to bee inherited, Or the Sonnes incorrigiblenesse occasion a just *disinheriting,* though there bee enough, If the Master make *Slaves* of Servants, and macerate them, or the Servants make *prize* of the Master, and prey upon him, in these cases, and such as these, there is a wrinching, a shrinking, a sinking, an undermining, a destroying of *Foundations,* the *Foundation* of this third *House,* which is the *family, Peace.*

There remains yet another *House,* a fourth House, a poore and wretched *Cottage;* worse then our *Statute Cottages;* for to them the *Statute* layes out certaine *Acres;* but for these *Cottages,* wee measure not by *Acres,* but by *Feete;* and five or sixe foote serves any *Cottager:* so much as makes a *Grave,* makes up the best of our *Glebe,* that are of the *Inferiour,* and the best of their *Temporalties,* that are of the *Superiour Cleargie,* and the best of their *Demeanes* that are in the greatest *Soveraigntie* in this world: for this *house* is but *our selfe,* and the *foundation* of this *House* is *Conscience.* For, this proceeding with a good *Conscience* in every particular action, is that, which the *Apostle* calles, *The laying up in store for our selves, a good foundation, against the time to come:* The *House* comes not till the time to come, but the *Foundation* must bee layde heere. *Abraham looked for a Citie;* that was a *future* expectation; but, sayes that Text, it was a *Citie that hath a foundation;* the *foundation* was layd alreadie, even in this life, in

Domus
Dominus

I Tim. 6.19

Heb. 11.10

a good *Conscience:* For no interest, no mansion shall that Man have in the upper-roomes of that *Ierusalem,* that hath not layd the *foundation* in a good *Conscience* heere. But what is *Conscience?* *Conscience* hath but these two *Elements, Knowledge,* and *Practise;* for *Conscientia presumit Scientiam;* Hee that does any thing with a good *Conscience,* knowes that hee should doe it, and why hee does it: Hee that does *good* ignorantly, stupidly, inconsiderately, implicitely, does *good,* but hee does that good *ill. Conscience* is, *Syllogismus practicus;* upon certaine premisses, well debated, I conclude, that I should doe it, and then I doe it. Now for the destroying of this *foundation,* there are *sinnes,* which by *Gods* ordinary grace exhibited in his *Church,* proove but *Alarums,* but *Sentinells* to the *Conscience:* The very sinne, or something that does naturally accompany that sinne, *Povertie,* or *Sickenesse,* or *Infamie,* calls upon a man, and awakens him to a remorse of the sinne. Which made Saint *Augustine* say, *That a man got by some sinnes;* some sinnes helpe him in the way of repentance for sinne; and these sinnes doe not *destroy the foundation.* But there are sinnes, which in their nature preclude repentance, and batter the *Conscience,* devastate, depopulate, exterminate, annihilate the *Conscience,* and leave no sense at all, or but a sense of *Desperation,* And

Sap. 17.11

then, the case being reduc'd to that, *That wickednes condemned by her owne wickednes, becomes very timerous,* (so as the *Conscience* growes afrayd, that the promises of the *Gospell* belong not to her) And (as it is added there) *beeing pressed with Conscience, alwayes forecasteth grievous things,* that whatsoever *God* layes upon him heere, all that is but his *earnest* of future worse torments, when it

Ver. 12

comes to such a *Feare,* as (as it is added in the next verse) *Betrayes the succours that Reason offers him,* That whereas in reason a man might argue, *God* hath pardoned greater sinnes, and greater sinners, yet hee can finde no hope for himselfe; this is a shrinking, a sinking, an undermining, a destroying of this *Foundation* of this fourth *House,* the *Conscience:* And farther wee proceed not in this *Survay.*

3. *Part*

Wee are now upon that which we proposed for our last Consideration; Till *foundations* are shaked, the righteous stirres not; In some cases some *foundations* may be shaked; if they be, *what can the righteous doe?* The *holy Ghost* never askes the question, what the *unrighteous,* the wicked can doe: They doe well enough, best of all, in such cases: Demolitions and Ruines are their raisings; Troubles are their peace, Tempests are their calmes, Fires and combustions are their refreshings, Massacres are their harvest, and Destruction is their Vintage; All their Rivers runne in Eddies, and all their Centers are in wheeles, and in perpetuall motions; the wicked do well enough, best of all then; *but what shall the righteous do?* The first entrance of the *Psalme* in the first verse, seemes to give an answere; *The righteous may flie to the Mountaine as a Bird;* he may *retire,* withdraw himselfe. But then the generall *scope* of the *Psalme,* gives a *Reply* to the *Answere;* for all *Expositors* take the whole *Psalme* to bee an answere from *David,* and given with some indignation against them, who perswaded him to flie, or retire himselfe. Not that *David* would constitute a *Rule* in his *Example,* that it was unlawfull to flie in a time of danger or persecution, (for it would not bee hard to observe at least nine or ten severall flights of *David*) but that in some cases such circumstances of *Time,* and *Place,* and *Person,* may accompany and invest the action, as that it may bee inconvenient for *that Man,* at *that Time,* to retire himselfe. As oft, as the retyring amounts to the *forsaking of a Calling,* it will become a very disputable thing, how farre a retyring may bee lawfull. Saint *Peters* vehement zeale in disswading *Christ* from going up to *Ierusalem,* in a time of danger, was so farre from retarding *Christ* in that purpose, as that it drew a more bitter increpation from *Christ* upon *Peter,* then at any other time. Mat. 16.21

So then, in the *Text,* we have a *Rule* implyed, *Something is left to the righteous to doe, though some Foundations bee destroyed;* for the words are words of *Consultation,* and *consultation* with *God;* when Man can afford no Counsayle, *God* can, and will direct those that are his, the righteous, what to doe. The words give us the *Rule,* and *Christ* gives us the *Example* in himselfe. First, hee continues his *Innocencie,* and *avowes* that; the destroying of *Foundations,* does not destroy his *Foundation, Innocence:* still hee is able to confound his adversaries, with that, *Which of you can convince mee of sinne?* And then, hee Ioh. 8.46
[Mat. 26.39] *prayes* for the remooving of the persecution, *Transeat Calix,* let this Cup passe. When that might not bee, hee *prayes* even for them, who inflicted this persecution, *Pater ignosce,* Father forgive them; And [Luke
23.34] when all is done, hee *suffers* all that can bee done unto him: And hee calls his whole Passion, *Horam suam,* it spent *nights* and *dayes;* his whole life was a continuall Passion; yet how long soever, he calls it but an *Houre,* and how much soever it were *their* act, the act of their malignitie that did it, yet hee calls it *his,* because it was the act of his owne *Predestination* as *God,* upon himselfe as *Man;* And hee calles it by a more acceptable Name then that, hee calles his Passion *Calicem suum,* his Cup, because hee brought not onely a patience to it, but a delight and a joy in it; for, *for the joy that was set before him, hee endured the Crosse.* All this then the righteous can doe, though *Foundations bee destroyed;* Hee can *withdrawe* himselfe, if the duties of his place make not his residence necessarie; If it doe, hee can *pray;* and then hee can *suffer;* and then hee can *rejoyce* in his sufferings; and hee can make that *protestation, Our God is able to deliver us, and hee will deliver us; but if not, wee will serve no other Gods.* For, the righteous hath evermore this refuge, this assurance, that though some *Foundations* bee destroyed, all cannot bee: for first, *The foundation of God stands sure, and hee knowes who are his;* Hee is safe in *God;* and then he is safe in his owne *Conscience,* for, *The Righteous is an everlasting foundation;* not onely that he *hath* one, but *is* one; and not a temporary, but an everlasting *Foundation:* So that *foundations* can never bee so destroyed, but that hee is safe in *God,* and safe in *himselfe.*

For such things then, as concerne the *foundation* of the first *House,* the *Church,* Bee not apt to call *Super-Edifications, Foundations;* Collaterall Divinitie, Fundamentall Divinitie; Problematicall, Disputable, Controvertible poynts, poynts Essentiall, and Articles of Faith. Call not *Super-Edifications, Foundations,* nor call not the *furniture* of the *House, Foundations;* Call not *Ceremoniall,* and *Rituall* things, *Essentiall* parts of Religion, and of the worship of *God,* otherwise then as they imply *Disobedience;* for *Obedience* to lawfull Authoritie, is alwayes an *Essentiall*·part of Religion. Doe not *Anti-date* Miserie; doe not *Prophesie* Ruine; doe not *Concurre* with Mischiefe, nor *Contribute* to Mischiefe so farre, as to *over-feare* it before, nor to misinterpret their *wayes,* whose *Ends* you cannot knowe; And doe not call the cracking of a pane of glasse, a *Destroying of foundations.* But every man doing the particular duties of his distinct Calling, for the preservation of *Foundations, Praying,* and *Preaching,* and *Doing,* and *Counsailing,* and *Contributing* too, *Foundations* beeing never destroyed, the Righteous shall doe still, as they have done, enjoy *God*

Hebr. 12.2

Dan. 3.17

2 Tim. 2.19

Pro. 10.25

Domus Ecclesia

manifested in *Christ,* and *Christ* applyed in the *Scriptures,* which is the *foundation* of the first *House,* the *Church.*

For things concerning the *Foundation* of the second *House,* the *Commonwealth,* which is the *Lawe,* Dispute not *Lawes,* but obey them when they are made; In those *Councells,* where *Lawes* are made, or reformed, dispute; but there also, without particular interest, without private affection, without personall relations. Call not every entrance of such a *Iudge,* as thou thinkest insufficient, a *corrupt* entrance; nor every *Iudgement,* which hee enters, and thou understandest not, or likest not, a *corrupt* Judgement. As in *Naturall* things, it is a weakenesse to thinke, that every thing that I knowe not how it is done, is done by *Witch-craft,* So is it also in *Civill* things, if I know not why it is done, to thinke it is done for *Money.* Let the *Law* bee sacred to thee, and the Dispensers of the *Law,* reverend; Keepe the *Lawe,* and the *Lawe* shall keepe thee; And so *Foundations* being never destroyed, the Righteous shall doe still, as they have done, enjoy their Possessions, and Honours, and themselves, by the overshadowing of the *Lawe,* which is the *Foundation* of the second *House,* the *State.*

For those things which concerne the *Foundations* of the third *House,* the *Family,* Call not light faults by heavie Names; Call not all sociablenesse, and Conversation, Disloyaltie in thy Wife; Nor all levitie, or pleasurablenesse, Incorrigiblenesse in thy Sonne; nor all negligence, or forgetfulnesse, Perfidiousnesse in thy Servant; Nor let every light disorder within doores, shut thee out of doores, or make thee a stranger in thine owne House. In a smoakie roome, it may bee enough to open a Windowe, without leaving the place; In Domestique unkindnesses, and discontents, it may bee wholesomer to give them a Concoction at home in a discreete patience, or to give them a vent at home, in a moderate rebuke, then to thinke to ease them, or put them off, with false divertions abroad. As *States* subsist in part, by keeping their weakenesses from being knowen, so is it the quiet of *Families,* to have their *Chauncerie,* and their *Parliament* within doores, and to compose and determine all emergent differences there: for so also, *Foundations* beeing kept undestroyed, the righteous shall doe, as they should doe, enjoy a *Religious* Unitie, and a *Civill* Unitie, the same Soule towards *God,* the same heart towards one another, in a holy, and in a happy *Peace,* and *Peace* is the *foundation* of this third *House,* The *Family.*

Respub.
Domus

Domus
Domicilium

Lastly, for those things which concerne the *Foundations* of the fourth *House, Our selves,* Mis-interprete not *Gods* former Corrections upon thee, how long, how sharpe soever: Call not his Phisicke, poyson, nor his Fish, Scorpions, nor his Bread, Stone: Accuse not *God,* for that hee hath done, nor suspect not *God,* for that hee may doe, as though *God* had made thee, onely because hee lacked a man, to damne. In all

[Ioh. 6.68]

scruples of *Conscience,* say with Saint *Peter, Domine quo vadam, Lord, whither shall I goe, thou hast the Word of eternall life,* And *God* will not leave thee in the darke: In all oppression from potent Ad-

[Ps. 51.4]

versaries, say with *David, Tibi soli peccavi: Against thee, O Lord, onely have I sinned,* And *God* will not make the malice of another man his Executioner upon thee. Crie to him; and if hee have not heard thee, crie lowder, and crie oftner; The first way that *God* admitted thee to him was by *Water,* the water of *Baptisme;* Goe still the same

[Isa. 38.5.
The Vulgate has
lacrymas]

way to him, by *Water,* by repentant *Teares:* And remember still, that when *Ezechias* wept, *Vidit lachrymam, God saw his Teare,* His Teare in the *Singular: God* sawe his first teare, every severall teare: If thou thinke *God* have not done so by thee, Continue thy teares, till thou finde hee doe. The first way that *Christ* came to thee, was in *Blood;* when hee submitted himselfe to the *Lawe,* in *Circumcision;* And the last thing that hee bequeathed to thee, was his *Blood,* in the Institution of the Blessed *Sacrament;* Refuse not to goe to him, the same way too, if his glorie require that *Sacrifice.* If thou pray, and hast an apprehension that thou hearest *God* say, hee will not heare thy prayers, doe not beleeve that it is hee that speakes; If thou canst not chuse but beleeve that it is hee, let mee say, in a pious sense, doe not beleeve him: *God* would not bee beleeved, in denouncing of Judgements, so absolutely, so peremptorily, as to bee thought to speake unconditionally, illimitedly: *God* tooke it well at *Davids* hands, that when the *Prophet* had

[2 Sam.
12.14]

Psal. 61.4
62.7 [Vulg.
reading]

tolde him, *The childe shall surely die,* yet hee beleeved not the *Prophet* so peremptorily, but that hee proceeded in Prayer to *God,* for the life of the childe. Say with *David, Thou hast beene a strong Tower to mee; I will abide in thy Tabernacle, Et non Emigrabo,* I will never goe out, I know thou hast a *Church,* I know I am in it, and I will never depart from it; and so *Foundations* beeing never destroyed, the righteous shall doe, as the righteous have alwayes done, enjoy the *Evidence,* and the *Verdict,* and the *Iudgement,* and the *Possession* of a good *Con-*

science, which is the *Foundation* of this fourth *House.* First, governe this first *House, Thy selfe,* well; and as *Christ* sayde, hee shall say againe, *Thou hast beene faithfull in a little, take more;* Hee shall enlarge thee in the next House, Thy *Family,* and the next, The *State,* and the other, The *Church,* till hee say to thee, as hee did to *Ierusalem,* after all his other Blessings, *Et prosperata es in Regnum, Now I have brought thee up to a Kingdome,* A Kingdome, where not onely no *Foundations* can bee destroyed, but no stone shaked; and where the Righteous know alwayes what to doe, to glorifie *God,* in that incessant Acclamation, *Salvation to our God, who sits upon the Throne, and to the Lambe;* And to this *Lambe of God,* who hath taken away the *sinnes* of the world, and but changed the *Sunnes* of the world, who hath complicated two wondrous workes in one, To make *our Sunne* to set at Noone, and to make *our Sunne* to rise at Noone too, That hath given him *Glorie,* and not taken away our *Peace,* That hath exalted him to Upper-roomes, and not shaked any *Foundations* of ours, To this *Lambe of God,* the glorious *Sonne of God,* and the most Almightie *Father,* and the *Blessed Spirit* of Comfort, three Persons and one *God,* bee ascribed by us, and the whole *Church,* the *Triumphant Church,* where the *Father* of blessed *Memorie* raignes *with God,* and the *Militant Church,* where the *Sonne* of blessed *Assurance* raignes *for God,* All Power, Praise, Might, Majestie, Glory, and Dominion, now, and for ever.

Amen.
FINIS.

[Luke
19.17]

[Ezek.
16.13]

[Apoc. 7.10]

Number 4.

The second of my Prebend Sermons upon my five Psalmes. Preached at S. Pauls, Ianuary 29. 1625. [1625/6]

PSAL. 63.7. *BECAUSE THOU HAST BEEN MY HELPE, THEREFORE IN THE SHADOW OF THY WINGS WILL I REJOYCE.*

Wisd. 16.20

THE PSALMES are the Manna of the Church. As Manna tasted to every man like that that he liked best, so doe the Psalmes minister Instruction, and satisfaction, to every man, in every emergency and occasion. *David* was not onely a cleare Prophet of Christ himselfe, but a Prophet of every particular Christian; He foretels what I, what any shall doe, and suffer, and say. And as the whole booke of Psalmes is *Oleum effusum,* (as the Spouse speaks of the name of Christ) an Oyntment powred out upon all sorts of sores, A Searcloth that souples all bruises, A Balme that searches all wounds; so are there some certaine Psalmes, that are Imperiall Psalmes, that command over all affections, and spread themselves over all occasions, Catholique, universall Psalmes, that apply themselves to all necessities. This is one of those; for, of those Constitutions which are called Apostolicall, one is, That the Church should meet every day, to sing this Psalme. And accordingly, S. *Chrysostome* testifies, That it was decreed, and ordained by the Primitive Fathers, that no day should passe without the publique singing of this Psalme. Under both these obligations, (those ancient Constitutions, called the Apostles, and those ancient Decrees made by the primitive Fathers) belongs to me, who have my part in the service of Gods Church, the especiall medi-

Cant. 1.3

Constitut.
Apostol.

Chrysost.

tation, and recommendation of this Psalme. And under a third obligation too, That it is one of those five psalmes, the daily rehearsing whereof, is injoyned to me, by the Constitutions of this Church, as five other are to every other person of our body. As the whole booke is Manna, so these five Psalmes are my Gomer, which I am to fill and empty every day of this Manna.

Now as the spirit and soule of the whole booke of Psalmes is contracted into this psalme, so is the spirit and soule of this whole psalme contracted into this verse. The key of the psalme, (as S. *Hierome* calls the Titles of the psalmes) tells us, that *David* uttered this psalme, *when he was in the wildernesse of Iudah;* There we see the present occasion that moved him; And we see what was passed between God and him before, in the first clause of our Text; (*Because thou hast been my helpe*) And then we see what was to come, by the rest, (*Therefore in the shadow of thy wings will I rejoyce.*) So that we have here the whole compasse of Time, Past, Present, and Future; and these three parts of Time, shall be at this time, the three parts of this Exercise; first, what *Davids* distresse put him upon for the present; and that lyes in the Context; secondly, how *David* built his assurance upon that which was past; (*Because thou hast been my help*) And thirdly, what he established to himselfe for the future, (*Therefore in the shadow of thy wings will I rejoyce.*) First, His distresse in the Wildernesse, his present estate carried him upon the memory of that which God had done for him before, And the Remembrance of that carried him upon that, of which he assured himselfe after. Fixe upon God any where, and you shall finde him a Circle; He is with you now, when you fix upon him; He was with you before, for he brought you to this fixation; and he will be with you hereafter, for *He is yesterday, and to day, and the same for ever.*

For *Davids* present condition, who was now in a banishment, in a persecution in the Wildernesse of Judah, (which is our first part) we shall onely insist upon that, (which is indeed spread over all the psalme to the Text, and ratified in the Text) That in all those temporall calamities *David* was onely sensible of his spirituall losse; It grieved him not that he was kept from *Sauls* Court, but that he was kept from Gods Church. For when he sayes, by way of lamentation, *That he was in a dry and thirsty land, where no water was,* he ex-

Divisio

Hieron.

Heb. 13.8

Ver. 1

presses what penury, what barrennesse, what drought and what thirst

he meant; *To see thy power, and thy glory, so as I have seene thee in*

the Sanctuary. For there, *my soule shall be satisfied as with marrow,*

and with fatnesse, and there, *my mouth shall praise thee with joyfull lips.* And in some few considerations conducing to this, That spirituall losses are incomparably heavier then temporall, and that therefore, The Restitution to our spirituall happinesse, or the continuation of it, is rather to be made the subject of our prayers to God, in all pressures and distresses, then of temporall, we shall determine that first part. And for the particular branches of both the other parts, (The Remembring of Gods benefits past, And the building of an assurance for the future, upon that Remembrance) it may be fitter to open them to you, anon when we come to handle them, then now. Proceed we now to our first part, The comparing of temporall and spirituall afflictions.

In the way of this Comparison, falls first the Consideration of the universality of afflictions in generall, and the inevitablenesse thereof. It is a blessed Metaphore, that the Holy Ghost hath put into the mouth of the Apostle, *Pondus Gloriæ,* That our *afflictions* are but *light,* because there is an *exceeding,* and an *eternall waight of glory* attending them. If it were not for that exceeding waight of glory, no other waight in this world could turne the scale, or waigh downe those infinite waights of afflictions that oppresse us here. There is not onely

Pestis valde gravis, (*the pestilence grows heavy upon the Land*) but there is *Musca valde gravis,* God calls in but the fly, to vexe Egypt, and even the fly is a heavy burden unto them. It is not onely *Iob* that complains, *That he was a burden to himselfe,* but even *Absaloms* haire was a burden to him, till it was polled. It is not onely *Ieremy* that complains, *Aggravavit compedes,* That God had made their fetters and their chains heavy to them, but the workmen in harvest

complaine, That God had made a faire day heavy unto them, (*We have borne the heat, and the burden of the day.*) *Sand is heavy,* sayes *Solomon;* And how many suffer so? under a sand-hill of crosses, daily, hourely afflictions, that are heavy by their number, if not by their single waight? And *a stone is heavy;* (sayes he in the same place) And how many suffer so? How many, without any former preparatory crosse, or comminatory, or commonitory crosse, even in the midst of prosperity, and security, fall under some one stone, some grind-stone, some mil-stone, some one insupportable crosse that ruines them? But then, (sayes *Solomon* there) *A fooles anger is heavier then both;* And how many children, and servants, and wives suffer under the anger, and morosity, and peevishnesse, and jealousie of foolish Masters, and Parents, and Husbands, though they must not say so? *David* and *Solomon* have cryed out, That all this world is *vanity,* and *levity;* And (God knowes) all is waight, and burden, and heavinesse, and oppression; And if there were not a waight of future glory to counterpoyse it, we should all sinke into nothing.

I aske not *Mary Magdalen,* whether lightnesse were not a burden; (for sin is certainly, sensibly a burden) But I aske *Susanna* whether even chast beauty were not a burden to her; And I aske *Ioseph* whether personall comelinesse were not a burden to him. I aske not *Dives,* who perished in the next world, the question; but I aske them who are made examples of *Solomons* Rule, of that *sore evill,* (as he calls it) *Riches kept to the owners thereof for their hurt,* whether Riches be not a burden. Eccles. 5.13

All our life is a continuall burden, yet we must not groane; A continuall squeasing, yet we must not pant; And as in the tendernesse of our childhood, we suffer, and yet are whipt if we cry, so we are complained of, if we complaine, and made delinquents if we call the times ill. And that which addes waight to waight, and multiplies the sadnesse of this consideration, is this, That still the best men have had most laid upon them. As soone as I heare God say, that he hath found *an upright man, that feares God, and eschews evill,* in the next lines I finde a Commission to Satan, to bring in Sabeans and Chaldeans upon his cattell, and servants, and fire and tempest upon his children, and loathsome diseases upon himselfe. As soone as I heare God say, That he hath found *a man according to his own heart,* I see his sonnes ravish his daughters, and then murder one another, and then rebell against the Father, and put him into straites for his life. As soone as I heare God testifie of Christ at his Baptisme, *This is my beloved Sonne in whom I am well pleased,* I finde that Sonne of his *led up by the Spirit, to be tempted of the Devill.* And after I heare God ratifie the same testimony againe, at his Transfiguration, (*This is my beloved Sonne, in whom I am well pleased*) I finde that beloved Sonne of his,

[Job 1. 1]

[1 Sam. 13.14]

Mat. 3.17

Matt. 4.1

Matt. 17.5

deserted, abandoned, and given over to Scribes, and Pharisees, and Publicans, and Herodians, and Priests, and Souldiers, and people, and Judges, and witnesses, and executioners, and he that was called the beloved Sonne of God, and made partaker of the glory of heaven, in this world, in his Transfiguration, is made now the Sewer of all the corruption, of all the sinnes of this world, as no Sonne of God, but a meere man, as no man, but a contemptible worme. As though the greatest weaknesse in this world, were man, and the greatest fault in man were to be good, man is more miserable then other creatures, and good men more miserable then any other men.

Afflictio
spiritualis

But then there is *Pondus Gloriæ, An exceeding waight of eternall glory,* and that turnes the scale; for as it makes all worldly prosperity as dung, so it makes all worldly adversity as feathers. And so it had need; for in the scale against it, there are not onely put temporall afflictions, but spirituall too; And to these two kinds, we may accommodate those words, *He that fals upon this stone,* (upon temporall afflictions) may be bruised, broken, *But he upon whom that stone falls,* (spirituall afflictions) *is in danger to be ground to powder.* And then, the great, and yet ordinary danger is, That these spirituall afflictions grow out of temporall; Murmuring, and diffidence in God, and obduration, out of worldly calamities; And so against nature, the fruit is greater and heavier then the Tree, spirituall heavier then temporall afflictions.

Matt. 21.44

Plin. l. 27.11
Litho-
spermus

They who write of Naturall story, propose that Plant for the greatest wonder in nature, which being no firmer then a bull-rush, or a reed, produces and beares for the fruit thereof no other but an intire, and very hard stone. That temporall affliction should produce spirituall stoninesse, and obduration, is unnaturall, yet ordinary. Therefore doth God propose it, as one of those greatest blessings, which he multiplies upon his people, *I will take away your stony hearts, and give you hearts of flesh;* And, Lord let mee have a fleshly heart in any sense, rather then a stony heart. Wee finde mention amongst the observers of rarities in Nature, of hairy hearts, hearts of men, that have beene overgrowne with haire; but of petrified hearts, hearts of men growne into stone, we read not; for this petrefaction of the heart, this stupefaction of a man, is the last blow of Gods hand upon the heart of man in this world. Those great afflictions which are powred out of the Vials

Ezek. 11.19
and 36.26
Plin. and
Plutar.

Revel. 16

of the seven Angels upon the world, are still accompanied with that
heavy effect, that that affliction hardned them. *They were scorched*
with heats and plagues, by the fourth Angel, and it followes, *They*
blasphemed the name of God, and repented not, to give him glory.   ver. 9
Darknesse was induced upon them by the fift Angel, and it followes,
They blasphemed the God of heaven, and repented not of their deeds.   ver. 11
And from the seventh Angel there fell hailestones of the waight of
talents, (perchance foure pound waight) upon men; And yet these   ver. 21
men had so much life left, as to *blaspheme God,* out of that respect,
which alone should have brought them to glorifie God, *Because the*
plague thereof was exceeding great. And when a great plague brings
them to blaspheme, how great shall that second plague be, that comes
upon them for blaspheming?

Let me wither and weare out mine age in a discomfortable, in an
unwholesome, in a penurious prison, and so pay my debts with my
bones, and recompence the wastfulnesse of my youth, with the beg-
gery of mine age; Let me wither in a spittle under sharpe, and foule,
and infamous diseases, and so recompence the wantonnesse of my
youth, with that loathsomnesse in mine age; yet, if God with-draw
not his spirituall blessings, his Grace, his Patience, If I can call my
suffering his Doing, my passion his Action, All this that is temporall,
is but a caterpiller got into one corner of my garden, but a mill-dew
fallen upon one acre of my Corne; The body of all, the substance of
all is safe, as long as the soule is safe. But when I shall trust to that,
which wee call a good spirit, and God shall deject, and empoverish,
and evacuate that spirit, when I shall rely upon a morall constancy,
and God shall shake, and enfeeble, and enervate, destroy and de-
molish that constancy; when I shall think to refresh my selfe in the
serenity and sweet ayre of a good conscience, and God shall call up
the damps and vapours of hell it selfe, and spread a cloud of diffidence,
and an impenetrable crust of desperation upon my conscience; when
health shall flie from me, and I shall lay hold upon riches to succour
me, and comfort me in my sicknesse, and riches shall flie from me, and
I shall snatch after favour, and good opinion, to comfort me in my
poverty; when even this good opinion shall leave me, and calumnies
and misinformations shall prevaile against me; when I shall need
peace, because there is none but thou, O Lord, that should stand for

me, and then shall finde, that all the wounds that I have, come from thy hand, all the arrowes that stick in me, from thy quiver; when I shall see, that because I have given my selfe to my corrupt nature, thou hast changed thine; and because I am all evill towards thee, therefore thou hast given over being good towards me; When it comes to this height, that the fever is not in the humors, but in the spirits, that mine enemy is not an imaginary enemy, fortune, nor a transitory enemy, malice in great persons, but a reall, and an irresistible, and an inexorable, and an everlasting enemy, The Lord of Hosts himselfe, The Almighty God himselfe, the Almighty God himselfe onely knowes the waight of this affliction, and except hee put in that *pondus gloriæ,* that exceeding waight of an eternall glory, with his owne hand, into the other scale, we are waighed downe, we are swallowed up, irreparably, irrevocably, irrecoverably, irremediably.

This is the fearefull depth, this is spirituall misery, to be thus fallen from God. But was this *Davids* case? was he fallen thus farre, into a diffidence in God? No. But the danger, the precipice, the slippery sliding into that bottomlesse depth, is, to be excluded from the meanes of comming to God, or staying with God; And this is that that *David* laments here, That by being banished, and driven into the wildernesse of Judah, hee had not accesse to the Sanctuary of the Lord, to sacrifice his part in the praise, and to receive his part in the prayers of the Congregation; for Angels passe not to ends, but by wayes and meanes, nor men to the glory of the triumphant Church, but by participation of the Communion of the Militant. To this note *David* sets his Harpe, in many, many Psalms: Sometimes, that God had suffered his enemies to possesse his Tabernacle, (*Hee forsooke the Tabernacle of Shiloh, Hee delivered his strength into captivity, and his glory into the enemies hands*) But most commonly he complaines, that God disabled him from comming to the Sanctuary. In which one thing he had summed up all his desires, all his prayers, (*One thing have I desired of the Lord, that will I looke after; That I may dwell in the house of the Lord, all the dayes of my life, to behold the beauty of the Lord, and to enquire in his Temple*) His vehement desire of this, he expresses againe, (*My soule thirsteth for God, for the living God; when shall I come and appeare before God?*) He expresses a holy jealousie, a religious envy, even to the sparrows and swallows, (yea, *the sparrow*

Psal. 78.60

Psal. 27.4

Psal. 42.2

Psal. 84.3

hath found a house, and the swallow a nest for her selfe, and where
she may lay her yong, Even thine Altars, O Lord of Hosts, my King
and my God.) Thou art my King, and my God, and yet excludest me
from that, which thou affordest to sparrows, *And are not we of more*   Luk. 12.7
value then many sparrows?

And as though *David* felt some false ease, some half-tentation, some
whispering that way, That God is *in the wildernesse of Iudah,* in
every place, as well as in his *Sanctuary,* there is in the Originall in that   Psal. 84.3
place, a patheticall, a vehement, a broken expressing expressed, *O*
thine Altars; It is true, (sayes *David*) thou art here in the wildernesse,
and I may see thee here, and serve thee here, but, *O thine Altars, O*
Lord of hosts, my King and my God. When *David* could not come
in person to that place, yet he bent towards the Temple, (*In thy feare*   Psal. 5.7
will I worship towards thy holy Temple.) Which was also *Daniels*   Dan. 6.10
devotion; when he prayed, *his Chamber windowes were open towards*
Ierusalem; And so is *Hezekias* turning to the wall to weepe, and to   Esa. 38.2
pray in his sick bed, understood to be to that purpose, to conforme,
and compose himselfe towards the Temple. In the place consecrated
for that use, God by *Moses* fixes the service, and fixes the Reward;   Deut. 31.11
And towards that place, (when they could not come to it) doth
Solomon direct their devotion in the Consecration of the Temple,
(*when they are in the warres, when they are in Captivity, and pray*
towards this house, doe thou heare them.) For, as in private prayer,   1 King. 8.44
when (according to Christs command) we are shut in our chamber,
there is exercised *Modestia fidei,* The modesty and bashfulnesse of our
faith, not pressing upon God in his house: so in the publique prayers
of the Congregation, there is exercised the fervor, and holy courage
of our faith, for *Agmine facto obsidemus Deum,* It is a Mustering of   Tertull.
our forces, and a besieging of God. Therefore does *David* so much
magnifie their blessednesse, that are in this house of God; (*Blessed*
are they that dwell in thy house, for they will be still praising thee)   [Psal. 84.4]
Those that looke towards it, may praise thee sometimes, but those
men who dwell in the Church, and whose whole service lyes in the
Church, have certainly an advantage of all other men (who are necessarily withdrawne by worldly businesses) in making themselves acceptable to almighty God, if they doe their duties, and observe their
Church-services aright.

Man being therefore thus subject naturally to manifold calamities, and spirituall calamities being incomparably heavier then temporall, and the greatest danger of falling into such spirituall calamities being in our absence from Gods Church, where onely the outward meanes of happinesse are ministred unto us, certainely there is much tendernesse and deliberation to be used, before the Church doores be shut against any man. If I would not direct a prayer to God, to excommunicate any man from the Triumphant Church, (which were to damne him) I would not oyle the key, I would not make the way too slippery for excommunications in the Militant Church; For, that is to endanger him. I know how distastfull a sin to God, contumacy, and contempt, and disobedience to Order and Authority is; And I know, (and all men, that choose not ignorance, may know) that our Excommunications (though calumniators impute them to small things, because, many times, the first complaint is of some small matter) never issue but upon contumacies, contempts, disobediences to the Church. But they are reall contumacies, not interpretative, apparant contumacies, not presumptive, that excommunicate a man in Heaven; And much circumspection is required, and (I am far from doubting it) exercised in those cases upon earth; for, though every Excommunication upon earth be not sealed in Heaven, though it damne not the man, yet it dammes up that mans way, by shutting him out of that Church, through which he must goe to the other; which being so great a danger, let every man take heed of Excommunicating himselfe. The imperswasible Recusant does so; The negligent Libertin does so; The fantastique Separatist does so; The halfe-present man, he, whose body is here, and minde away, does so; And he, whose body is but halfe here, his limbes are here upon a cushion, but his eyes, his eares are not here, does so: All these are selfe-Excommunicators, and keepe themselves from hence. Onely he enjoyes that blessing, the want whereof *David* deplores, that is here intirely, and is glad he is here, and glad to finde this kinde of service here, that he does, and wishes no other.

And so we have done with our first Part, *Davids* aspect, his present condition, and his danger of falling into spirituall miseries, because his persecution, and banishment amounted to an Excommunication, to an excluding of him from the service of God, in the Church. And we passe, in our Order proposed at first, to the second, his retrospect, the Consideration, what God had done for him before, *Because thou hast beene my helpe.* Through this second part, we shall passe by these three steps. First, 2 Part That it behoves us, in all our purposes, and actions, to propose to our selves a copy to write by, a patterne to worke by, a rule, or an example to proceed by, Because it hath beene thus heretofore, sayes *David*, I will resolve upon this course for the future. And secondly, That the copy, the patterne, the precedent which we are to propose to our selves, is, The observation of Gods former wayes and proceedings upon us, Because God hath already gone this way, this way I will awaite his going still. And then, thirdly and lastly, in this second part, The way that God had formerly gone with *David*, which was, That he had been his helpe, (*Because thou hast beene my helpe.*)

First then, from the meanest artificer, through the wisest Philoso- *Ideæ* pher, to God himselfe, all that is well done, or wisely undertaken, is undertaken and done according to pre-conceptions, fore-imaginations, designes, and patterns proposed to our selves beforehand. A Carpenter builds not a house, but that he first sets up a frame in his owne minde, what kinde of house he will build. The little great Philosopher *Epictetus*, would undertake no action, but he would first propose to himselfe, what *Socrates*, or *Plato*, what a wise man would do in that case, and according to that, he would proceed. Of God himselfe, it is safely resolved in the Schoole, that he never did any thing in any part of time, of which he had not an eternall pre-conception, an eternall Idea, in himselfe before. Of which Ideaes, that is, pre-conceptions, pre-determinations in God, S. *Augustine* pronounces, *Tanta vis in Ideis* August. *constituitur,* There is so much truth, and so much power in these Ideaes, as that without acknowledging them, no man can acknowledge God, for he does not allow God Counsaile, and Wisdome, and deliberation in his Actions, but sets God on worke, before he have thought what he will doe. And therefore he, and others of the Fathers read that place, (which we read otherwise) *Quod factum est, in ipso* Ioh. 1.3, 4 *vita erat;* that is, in all their Expositions, whatsoever is made, in time, was alive in God, before it was made, that is, in that eternall Idea, and patterne which was in him. So also doe divers of those Fathers read those words to the Hebrews, (which we read, *The things that are* Heb. 11.3

seene, are not made of things that doe appeare) Ex invisibilibus visi-
bilia facta sunt, Things formerly invisible, were made visible; that is,
we see them not till now, till they are made, but they had an invisible
being, in that Idea, in that pre-notion, in that purpose of God before,
for ever before. Of all things in Heaven, and earth, but of himselfe,
God had an Idea, a patterne in himselfe, before he made it.

And therefore let him be our patterne for that, to worke after pat-
ternes; To propose to our selves Rules and Examples for all our actions; and the more, the more immediately, the more directly our
actions concerne the service of God. If I aske God, by what Idea he
[Gen. 1.26]
made me, God produces his *Faciamus hominem ad Imaginem*
nostram, That there was a concurrence of the whole Trinity, to make
me in *Adam,* according to that Image which they were, and according
to that Idea, which they had pre-determined. If I pretend to serve God,
and he aske me for my Idea, How I meane to serve him, shall I bee
able to produce none? If he aske me an Idea of my Religion, and my
opinions, shall I not be able to say, It is that which thy word, and thy
Catholique Church hath imprinted in me? If he aske me an Idea
of my prayers, shall I not be able to say, It is that which my particular
necessities, that which the forme prescribed by thy Son, that which
the care, and piety of the Church, in conceiving fit prayers, hath imprinted in me? If he aske me an Idea of my Sermons, shall I not be
able to say, It is that which the Analogy of Faith, the edification of
the Congregation, the zeale of thy worke, the meditations of my heart
have imprinted in me? But if I come to pray or to preach without this
kind of Idea, if I come to extemporall prayer, and extemporall preaching, I shall come to an extemporall faith, and extemporall religion;
and then I must looke for an extemporall Heaven, a Heaven to be
made for me; for to that Heaven which belongs to the Catholique
Church, I shall never come, except I go by the way of the Catholique
Church, by former Idea's, former examples, former patterns, To beleeve according to ancient beliefes, to pray according to ancient formes,
to preach according to former meditations. God does nothing, man
does nothing well, without these Idea's, these retrospects, this recourse to pre-conceptions, pre-deliberations.

Via Domini   Something then I must propose to my selfe, to be the rule, and the
reason of my present and future actions; which was our first branch

in this second Part; And then the second is, That I can propose nothing more availably, then the contemplation of the history of Gods
former proceeding with me; which is *Davids* way here, Because this
was Gods way before, I will looke for God in this way still. That
language in which God spake to man, the Hebrew, hath no present
tense; They forme not their verbs as our Westerne Languages do, in
the present, *I heare,* or *I see,* or *I reade,* But they begin at that which is
past, *I have seene* and *heard,* and *read.* God carries us in his Language,
in his speaking, upon that which is past, upon that which he hath
done already; I cannot have better security for present, nor future,
then Gods former mercies exhibited to me. *Quis non gaudeat,* sayes
S. *Augustine,* Who does not triumph with joy, when hee considers
what God hath done? *Quis non & ea, quæ nondum venerunt, ventura
sperat, propter illa, quæ jam tanta impleta sunt?* Who can doubt of
the performance of all, that sees the greatest part of a Prophesie performed? If I have found that true that God hath said, of the person
of Antichrist, why should I doubt of that which he sayes of the ruine
of Antichrist? *Credamus modicum quod restat,* sayes the same Father,
It is much that wee have seene done, and it is but little that God hath
reserved to our faith, to beleeve that it shall be done.

There is no State, no Church, no Man, that hath not this tie upon
God, that hath not God in these bands, That God by having done
much for them already, hath bound himselfe to doe more. Men proceed in their former wayes, sometimes, lest they should confesse an
error, and acknowledge that they had beene in a wrong way. God is
obnoxious to no error, and therefore he does still, as he did before.
Every one of you can say now to God, Lord, Thou broughtest me
hither, therefore enable me to heare; Lord, Thou doest that, therefore
make me understand; And that, therefore let me beleeve; And that
too, therefore strengthen me to the practise; And all that, therefore
continue me to a perseverance. Carry it up to the first sense and apprehension that ever thou hadst of Gods working upon thee, either in
thy selfe, when thou camest first to the use of reason, or in others in
thy behalfe, in thy baptisme, yet when thou thinkest thou art at the
first, God had done something for thee before all that; before that,
hee had elected thee, in that election which S. *Augustine* speaks of,
Habet electos, quos creaturus est eligendos, God hath elected certaine

August.

August.

men, whom he intends to create, that he may elect them; that is, that he may declare his Election upon them. God had thee, before he made thee; He loved thee first, and then created thee, that thou loving him, he might continue his love to thee. The surest way, and the nearest way to lay hold upon God, is the consideration of that which he had done already. So *David* does; And that which he takes knowledge of, in particular, in Gods former proceedings towards him, is, Because God had been his helpe, which is our last branch in this part, *Because thou hast beene my helpe.*

From this one word, That God hath been my *Helpe,* I make account that we have both these notions; first, That God hath not left me to my selfe, He hath come to my succour, He hath helped me; And then, That God hath not left out my selfe; He hath been my Helpe, but he hath left some thing for me to doe with him, and by his helpe. My security for the future, in this consideration of that which is past, lyes not onely in this, That God hath delivered me, but in this also, that he hath delivered me by way of a Helpe, and Helpe alwayes presumes an endevour and co-operation in him that is helped. God did not elect me as a helper, nor create me, nor redeeme me, nor convert me, by way of helping me; for he alone did all, and he had no use at all of me. God infuses his first grace, the first way, meerly as a Giver; intirely, all himselfe; but his subsequent graces, as a helper; therefore we call them Auxiliant graces, Helping graces; and we alwayes receive them, when we endevour to make use of his

former grace. *Lord, I beleeve,* (sayes the Man in the Gospel to Christ) *Helpe mine unbeliefe.* If there had not been unbeliefe, weaknesse, unperfectnesse in that faith, there had needed no helpe; but if there had not been a Beliefe, a faith, it had not been capable of helpe and assistance, but it must have been an intire act, without any concurrence on the mans part.

So that if I have truly the testimony of a rectified Conscience, That God hath helped me, it is in both respects; first, That he hath never forsaken me, and then, That he hath never suffered me to forsake my selfe; He hath blessed me with that grace, that I trust in no helpe but his, and with this grace too, That I cannot looke for his helpe, except I helpe my selfe also. God did not helpe heaven and earth to proceed out of nothing in the Creation, for they had no possibility of any disposition towards it; for they had no beeing: But God did helpe the earth to produce grasse, and herbes; for, for that, God had infused a seminall disposition into the earth, which, for all that, it could not have perfected without his farther helpe. As in the making of Woman, there is the very word of our Text, *Gnazar,* God made him a *Helper,* one that was to doe much for him, but not without him. So that then, if I will make Gods former working upon me, an argument of his future gracious purposes, as I must acknowledge that God hath done much for me, so I must finde, that I have done what I could, by the benefit of that grace with him; for God promises to be but a helper. *Lord open thou my lips,* sayes *David;* that is Gods worke intirely; And then, *My mouth, My mouth shall shew forth thy praise;* there enters *David* into the worke with God. And then, sayes God to him, *Dilata os tuum, Open thy mouth,* (It is now made *Thy mouth,* and therefore doe thou open it) *and I will fill it;* All inchoations and consummations, beginnings and perfectings are of God, of God alone; but in the way there is a concurrence on our part, (by a successive continuation of Gods grace) in which God proceeds as a Helper; and I put him to more then that, if I doe nothing. But if I pray for his helpe, and apprehend and husband his graces well, when they come, then he is truly, properly my helper; and upon that security, that testimony of a rectified Conscience, I can proceed to *Davids* confidence for the future, *Because thou hast been my Helpe, therefore in the shadow of thy wings will I rejoyce;* which is our third, and last generall part.

    In this last part, which is, (after *Davids* aspect, and consideration of his present condition, which was, in the effect, an Exclusion from Gods Temple, And his retrospect, his consideration of Gods former mercies to him, That he had been his Helpe) his prospect, his confidence for the future, we shall stay a little upon these two steps; first, That that which he promises himselfe, is not an immunity from all powerfull enemies, nor a sword of revenge upon those enemies; It is not that he shall have no adversary, nor that that adversary shall be able to doe him no harme, but that he should have a refreshing, a respiration, *In velamento alarum,* under the shadow of Gods wings. And then, (in the second place) That this way which God shall be pleased to take, this manner, this measure of refreshing, which God

Psal. 51.15

Psal. 81.10

Divisio.
3 Part

shall vouchsafe to afford, (though it amount not to a full deliverance) must produce a joy, a rejoycing in us; we must not onely not decline to a murmuring, that we have no more, no nor rest upon a patience for that which remains, but we must ascend to a holy joy, as if all were done and accomplished, *In the shadow of thy wings will I rejoyce.*

Vmbra Alarum   First then, lest any man in his dejection of spirit, or of fortune, should stray into a jealousie or suspition of Gods power to deliver him, As God hath spangled the firmament with starres, so hath he his Scriptures with names, and Metaphors, and denotations of power. Sometimes he shines out in the name of a *Sword,* and of a *Target,* and of a *Wall,* and of a *Tower,* and of a *Rocke,* and of a *Hill;* And sometimes in that glorious and manifold constellation of all together, *Dominus exercituum, The Lord of Hosts.* God, as God, is never represented to us, with Defensive Armes; He needs them not. When the Poets present their great Heroes, and their Worthies, they alwayes insist upon their Armes, they spend much of their invention upon the description of their Armes; both because the greatest valour and strength needs Armes, (*Goliah* himselfe was armed) and because to expose ones selfe to danger unarmed, is not valour, but rashnesse. But God is invulnerable in himselfe, and is never represented armed; you finde no shirts of mayle, no Helmets, no Cuirasses in Gods Armory.

Esay. 59.17   In that one place of *Esay,* where it may seeme to be otherwise, where God is said *to have put on righteousnesse as a breastplate, and a Helmet of Salvation upon his head;* in that prophecy God is Christ, and is therefore in that place, called *the Redeemer.* Christ needed defensive armes, God does not. Gods word does; His Scriptures doe; And therefore S. *Hierome* hath armed them, and set before every booke his *Prologum galeatum,* that prologue that armes and defends every booke from calumny. But though God need not, nor receive not defensive armes for himselfe, yet God is to us a Helmet, a Breastplate, a strong tower, a rocke, every thing that may give us assurance and defence; and as often as he will, he can refresh that Proclamation,

Psal. 105.15   *Nolite tangere Christos meos,* Our enemies shall not so much as touch us.

But here, by occasion of his Metaphore in this Text, (*Sub umbra alarum, In the shadow of thy wings*) we doe not so much consider an absolute immunity, That we shall not be touched, as a refreshing and consolation, when we are touched, though we be pinched and wounded. The Names of God, which are most frequent in the Scriptures, are these three, *Elohim,* and *Adonai,* and *Iehovah;* and to assure us of his Power to deliver us, two of these three are Names of Power. *Elohim* is *Deus fortis,* The mighty, The powerfull God: And (which deserves a particular consideration) *Elohim* is a plurall Name; It is not *Deus fortis,* but *Dii fortes,* powerfull Gods. God is all kinde of Gods; All kinds, which either Idolaters and Gentils can imagine, (as Riches, or Justice, or Wisdome, or Valour, or such) and all kinds which God himself hath called gods, (as Princes, and Magistrates, and Prelates, and all that assist and helpe one another) God is *Elohim,* All these Gods, and all these in their height and best of their power; for *Elohim,* is *Dii fortes,* Gods in the plurall, and those plurall gods in their exaltation.

The second Name of God, is a Name of power too, *Adonai.* For, *Adonai* is *Dominus,* The Lord, such a Lord, as is Lord and Proprietary of all his creatures, and all creatures are his creatures; And then, *Dominium est potestas tum utendi, tum abutendi,* sayes the law; To be absolute Lord of any thing, gives that Lord a power to doe what he will with that thing. God, as he is *Adonai, The Lord,* may give and take, quicken and kill, build and throw downe, where and whom he will. So then two of Gods three Names are Names of absolute power, to imprint, and re-imprint an assurance in us, that hee can absolutely deliver us, and fully revenge us, if he will. But then, his third Name, and that Name which hee chooses to himselfe, and in the signification of which Name, hee employes *Moses,* for the reliefe of his people under Pharaoh, that Name *Iehovah,* is not a Name of Power, but onely of Essence, of Being, of Subsistence, and yet in the vertue of that Name, God relieved his people. And if, in my afflictions, God vouchsafe to visit mee in that Name, to preserve me in my being, in my subsistence in him, that I be not shaked out of him, disinherited in him, excommunicate from him, devested of him, annihilated towards him, let him, at his good pleasure, reserve his *Elohim,* and his *Adonai,* the exercises and declarations of his mighty Power, to those great publike causes, that more concerne his Glory, then any thing that can befall me; But if he impart his *Iehovah,* enlarge himselfe so far towards me, as that I may live, and move, and have my beeing in him, though I be not instantly delivered, nor mine enemies absolutely destroyed, yet this is as much as I should promise my selfe, this is as much as the Holy Ghost intends in this Metaphor, *Sub umbra alarum, Vnder the shadow of thy wings,* that is a Refreshing, a Respiration, a Conservation, a Consolation in all afflictions that are inflicted upon me.

Yet, is not this Metaphor of *Wings* without a denotation of Power. As no Act of Gods, though it seeme to imply but spirituall comfort, is without a denotation of power, (for it is the power of God that comforts me; To overcome that sadnesse of soule, and that dejection of spirit, which the Adversary by temporall afflictions would induce upon me, is an act of his Power) So this Metaphor, *The shadow of his wings,* (which in this place expresses no more, then consolation and refreshing in misery, and not a powerfull deliverance out of it) is so often in the Scriptures made a denotation of Power too, as that we can doubt of no act of power, if we have this shadow of his wings. For, in this Metaphor of *Wings,* doth the Holy Ghost expresse the *Maritime* power, the power of some Nations at Sea, in Navies, (*Woe to the land shadowing with wings;*) that is, that hovers over the world, and intimidates it with her sailes and ships. In this Metaphor doth God remember his people, of his powerfull deliverance of them, (*You have seene what I did unto the Egyptians, and how I bare you on Eagles wings, and brought you to my selfe.*) In this Metaphor doth God threaten his and their enemies, what hee can doe, (*The noise of the wings of his Cherubims, are as the noise of great waters, and of an Army.*) So also, what hee will doe, (*Hee shall spread his wings over Bozrah, and at that day shall the hearts of the mighty men of Edom, be as the heart of a woman in her pangs.*) So that, if I have the shadow of his wings, I have the earnest of the power of them too; If I have refreshing, and respiration from them, I am able to say, (as those three Confessors did to *Nebuchadnezzar*) *My God is able to deliver me,* I am sure he hath power; *And my God will deliver me,* when it conduces to his glory, I know he will; *But, if he doe not, bee it knowne unto thee, O King, we will not serve thy Gods;* Be it knowne unto thee, O Satan, how long soever God deferre my deliverance, I will not seeke false comforts, the miserable comforts of

Esay. 18.1

Exod. 19.4

Ezek. 1.24

Ier. 49.22

Dan. 3.17

this world. I will not, for I need not; for I can subsist under this shadow of these Wings, though I have no more.

The Mercy-seat it selfe was covered with the Cherubims Wings; and who would have more then Mercy? and a Mercy-seat; that is, established, resident Mercy, permanent and perpetuall Mercy; present and familiar Mercy; a Mercy-seat. Our Saviour Christ intends as much as would have served their turne, if they had laid hold upon it, when hee sayes, *That hee would have gathered Ierusalem, as a henne gathers her chickens under her wings.* And though the other Prophets doe (as ye have heard) mingle the signification of Power, and actuall deliverance, in this Metaphor of Wings, yet our Prophet, whom wee have now in especiall consideration, *David,* never doth so; but in every place where hee uses this Metaphor of Wings (which are in five or sixe severall Psalmes) still hee rests and determines in that sense, which is his meaning here; That though God doe not actually deliver us, nor actually destroy our enemies, yet if hee refresh us in the shadow of his Wings, if he maintaine our subsistence (which is a religious Constancy) in him, this should not onely establish our patience, (for that is but halfe the worke) but it should also produce a joy, and rise to an exultation, which is our last circumstance, *Therefore in the shadow of thy wings, I will rejoice.*

I would always raise your hearts, and dilate your hearts, to a holy Joy, to a joy in the Holy Ghost. There may be a just feare, that men doe not grieve enough for their sinnes; but there may bee a just jealousie, and suspition too, that they may fall into inordinate griefe, and diffidence of Gods mercy; And God hath reserved us to such times, as being the later times, give us even the dregs and lees of misery to drinke. For, God hath not onely let loose into the world a new spirituall disease; which is, an equality, and an indifferency, which religion our children, or our servants, or our companions professe; (I would not keepe company with a man that thought me a knave, or a traitor; with him that thought I loved not my Prince, or were a faithlesse man, not to be beleeved, I would not associate my selfe; And yet I will make him my bosome companion, that thinks I doe not love God, that thinks I cannot be saved) but God hath accompanied, and complicated almost all our bodily diseases of these times, with an extraordinary sadnesse, a predominant melancholy,

Exod. 25.20

Matt. 23.37

Gaudium

a faintnesse of heart, a chearlesnesse, a joylesnesse of spirit, and therefore I returne often to this endeavor of raising your hearts, dilating your hearts with a holy Joy, Joy in the holy Ghost, for *Vnder the shadow of his wings,* you may, you should, *rejoyce.*

If you looke upon this world in a Map, you find two Hemisphears, two half worlds. If you crush heaven into a Map, you may find two Hemisphears too, two half heavens; Halfe will be Joy, and halfe will be Glory; for in these two, the joy of heaven, and the glory of heaven, is all heaven often represented unto us. And as of those two Hemisphears of the world, the first hath been knowne long before, but the other, (that of America, which is the richer in treasure) God reserved for later Discoveries; So though he reserve that Hemisphear of heaven, which is the Glory thereof, to the Resurrection, yet the other Hemisphear, the Joy of heaven, God opens to our Discovery, and delivers for our habitation even whilst we dwell in this world. As God hath cast upon the unrepentant sinner two deaths, a temporall, and a spirituall death, so hath he breathed into us two lives; for so, as the word for death is doubled, *Morte morieris, Thou shalt die the death,* so is the word for life expressed in the plurall, *Chaiim, vitarum, God breathed into his nostrils the breath of lives,* of divers lives. Though our naturall life were no life, but rather a continuall dying, yet we have two lives besides that, an eternall life reserved for heaven, but yet a heavenly life too, a spirituall life, even in this world; And as God doth thus inflict two deaths, and infuse two lives, so doth he also passe two Judgements upon man, or rather repeats the same Judgement twice. For, that which Christ shall say to thy soule then at the last Judgement, *Enter into thy Masters joy,* Hee sayes to thy conscience now, *Enter into thy Masters joy.* The everlastingnesse of the joy is the blessednesse of the next life, but the entring, the inchoation is afforded here. For that which Christ shall say then to us, *Venite benedicti, Come ye blessed,* are words intended to persons that are comming, that are upon the way, though not at home; Here in this world he bids us *Come,* there in the next, he shall bid us *Welcome.* The Angels of heaven have joy in thy conversion, and canst thou bee without that joy in thy selfe? If thou desire revenge upon thine enemies, as they are Gods enemies, That God would bee pleased to remove, and root out all such as oppose him, that Affection apper-

Gen. 2.17

Matt. 25.23

Verse 34

Luk. 15.10

taines to Glory; Let that alone till thou come to the Hemisphear of Glory; There joyne with those Martyrs under the Altar, *Vsquequo Domine,* How long O Lord, dost thou deferre Judgement? and thou shalt have thine answere there for that. Whilst thou art here, here joyne with *David,* and the other Saints of God, in that holy increpation of a dangerous sadnesse, *Why art thou cast downe O my soule? why art thou disquieted in mee?* That soule that is dissected and anatomized to God, in a sincere confession, washed in the teares of true contrition, embalmed in the blood of reconciliation, the blood of Christ Jesus, can assigne no reason, can give no just answer to that Interrogatory, *Why art thou cast downe O my soule? why art thou disquieted in me?* No man is so little, as that he can be lost under these wings, no man so great, as that they cannot reach to him; *Semper ille major est, quantumcumque creverimus,* To what temporall, to what spirituall greatnesse soever wee grow, still pray wee him to shadow us under his Wings; for the poore need those wings against oppression, and the rich against envy. The Holy Ghost, who is a Dove, shadowed the whole world under his wings; *Incubabat aquis,* He hovered over the waters, he sate upon the waters, and he hatched all that was produced, and all that was produced so, was good. Be thou a Mother where the Holy Ghost would be a Father; Conceive by him; and be content that he produce joy in thy heart here. First thinke, that as a man must have some land, or els he cannot be in wardship, so a man must have some of the love of God, or els he could not fall under Gods correction; God would not give him his physick, God would not study his cure, if he cared not for him. And then thinke also, that if God afford thee the shadow of his wings, that is, Consolation, respiration, refreshing, though not a present, and plenary deliverance, in thy afflictions, not to thanke God, is a murmuring, and not to rejoyce in Gods wayes, is an unthankfulnesse. Howling is the noyse of hell, singing the voyce of heaven; Sadnesse the damp of Hell, Rejoycing the serenity of Heaven. And he that hath not this joy here, lacks one of the best pieces of his evidence for the joyes of heaven; and hath neglected or refused that Earnest, by which God uses to binde his bargaine, that true joy in this world shall flow into the joy of Heaven, as a River flowes into the Sea; This joy shall not be put out in death, and a new joy kindled in me in Heaven; But

Revel. 6.10

Psal. 42.5

August.

[Gen. 1.2]

as my soule, as soone as it is out of my body, is in Heaven, and does not stay for the possession of Heaven, nor for the fruition of the sight of God, till it be ascended through ayre, and fire, and Moone, and Sun, and Planets, and Firmament, to that place which we conceive to be Heaven, but without the thousandth part of a minutes stop, as soone as it issues, is in a glorious light, which is Heaven, (for all the way to Heaven is Heaven; And as those Angels, which came from Heaven hither, bring Heaven with them, and are in Heaven here, So that soule that goes to Heaven, meets Heaven here; and as those Angels doe not devest Heaven by comming, so these soules invest Heaven, in their going.) As my soule shall not goe towards Heaven, but goe by Heaven to Heaven, to the Heaven of Heavens, So the true joy of a good soule in this world is the very joy of Heaven; and we goe thither, not that being without joy, we might have joy infused into us, but that as Christ sayes, *Our joy might be full,* perfected, sealed with an everlastingnesse; for, as he promises, *That no man shall take our joy from us,* so neither shall Death it selfe take it away, nor so much as interrupt it, or discontinue it, But as in the face of Death, when he layes hold upon me, and in the face of the Devill, when he attempts me, I shall see the face of God, (for, every thing shall be a glasse, to reflect God upon me) so in the agonies of Death, in the anguish of that dissolution, in the sorrowes of that valediction, in the irreversiblenesse of that transmigration, I shall have a joy, which shall no more evaporate, then my soule shall evaporate, A joy, that shall passe up, and put on a more glorious garment above, and be joy super-invested in glory. *Amen.*

Iohn 16.24
22

Number 5.

Preached to the Nobility.

LUKE 23.34. *FATHER FORGIVE THEM, FOR THEY KNOW NOT WHAT THEY DO.*

THE WORD of God is either the co-eternall and co-essentiall Sonne, our Saviour, which tooke flesh (*Verbum Caro factum est*) or it is the spirit of his mouth, by which we live, and *not by bread onely*. And so, in a large acceptation, every truth is the word of God; for truth is uniforme, and irrepugnant, and indivisible, as God. *Omne verum est omni vero consentiens.* More strictly the word of God, is that which God hath uttered, either in writing, as twice in the Tables to *Moses;* or by ministery of Angels, or Prophets, in words; or by the unborne, in action, as in *John Baptists* exultation within his mother; or by new-borne, from the mouths of babes and sucklings; or by things unreasonable, as in *Balaams* Asse; or insensible, as in the whole booke of such creatures, *The heavens declare the glory of God, &c.* But nothing is more properly the word of God to us, then that which God himself speakes in those Organs and Instruments, which himself hath assumed for his chiefest worke, our redemption. For in creation God spoke, but in redemption he did; and more, he suffered. And of that kinde are these words. God in his chosen man-hood saith, *Father, forgive them, for they know not what they do.*

These words shall be fitliest considered, like a goodly palace, if we rest a little, as in an outward Court, upon consideration of prayer in generall; and then draw neare the view of the Palace, in a second Court, considering this speciall prayer in generall, as the face of the whole palace. Thirdly, we will passe thorow the chiefest rooms of the palace it self; and then insist upon foure steps: 1. Of whom he

[Joh. 1.14]
[Deut. 8.3; Mat. 4.4]

[Psal. 19.1]

begs, (*Father.*) 2. What he asks, (*forgive them.*) 3. That he prays
upon reason, (*for.*) 4. What the reason is, (*they know not.*) And
lastly, going into the backside of all, we will cast the objections: as
why onely *Luke* remembers this prayer: and why this prayer, (as it
seemes by the punishment continuing upon the Jews to this day) was
not obtained at Gods hands.

Of Prayer

[Mat. 7.7]

[Luk. 19.46]

So therefore prayer is our first entry, for when it is said, *Ask and
it shall be given,* it is also said, *Knock and it shall be opened,* showing
that by prayer our entrance is. And not the entry onely, but the whole
house: *My house is the house of prayer.* Of all the conduits and con-
veyances of Gods graces to us, none hath been so little subject to
cavillations, as this of prayer. The Sacraments have fallen into the
hands of flatterers and robbers. Some have attributed too much to
them, some detracted. Some have painted them, some have with-
drawn their naturall complexion. It hath been disputed, whether they
be, how many they be, what they be, and what they do. The preaching
of the word hath been made a servant of ambitions, and a shop of
many mens new-fangled wares. Almost every meanes between God
and man, suffers some adulteratings and disguises: But prayer least:
And it hath most wayes and addresses. It may be mentall, for we may
thinke prayers. It may be vocall, for we may speake prayers. It may

[Gen. 18.20]

[Tobit 12.9]

[1.12]

be actuall, for we do prayers. For deeds have voyce; the vices of
Sodome did cry, and the Almes of *Toby.* And if it were proper for St.
John, in the first of the *Revelations* to turne back to see a voyce, it is
more likely God will looke down, to heare a worke. So then to do the
office of your vocation sincerely, is to pray. How much the favourites
of Princes, and great personages labour, that they may be thought to
have been in private conference with the Prince. And though they
be forced to wait upon his purposes, and talk of what he will, how
fain they would be thought to have solicited their own, or their
Dependants businesse. With the Prince of Princes, this every man
may doe truly; and the sooner, the more begger he is: for no man is
heard here, but *in formâ pauperis.*

Here we may talk long, welcomely, of our own affaires, and be
sure to speed. You cannot whisper so low alone in your Chamber, but
he heares you, nor sing so lowd in the Congregation, but he distinguishes you. He grudges not to be chidden and disputed with, by

Job. *The Arrows of the Almighty are in me, and the venim thereof*   [6.4, 12]
hath drunk up my spirit. Is my strength, the strength of stones, or is
my flesh of brasse, &c. Not to be directed and counselled by *Jonas:*
who was angry and sayd; Did not I say, when I was in my Country,   [4.2, 9]
thou wouldest deale thus? And when the Lord sayd, *Doest thou well*
to be angry? He replyed, *I doe well to be angry to the death.* Nor
almost to be threatned and neglected by *Moses: Doe this, or blot my*   [Exod.
name out of thy book. It is an Honour to be able to say to servants,   32.32]
Doe this: But to say to God, *Domine fac hoc,* and prevail, is more;
And yet more easie. God is replenishingly every where: but most
contractedly, and workingly in the Temple. Since then every rectified
man, is the temple of the Holy Ghost, when he prays; it is the Holy
Ghost it selfe that prays; and what can be denyed, where the Asker
gives? He plays with us, as children, shewes us pleasing things, that
we may cry for them, and have them. Before we call, he answers, and
when we speak, he heares: so *Esay* 65.24. Physicians observe some
symptomes so violent, that they must neglect the disease for a time,
and labour to cure the accident; as burning fevers, in Dysenteries. So
in the sinfull consumption of the soule, a stupidity and indisposition
to prayer, must first be cured. For, *Ye lust, and have not, because ye*
aske not, Jam. 4.2. The adulterous Mother of the three great brothers,
Gratian, Lombard, and *Comestor,* being warned by her Confessour,
to be sorry for her fact, sayd, she could not, because her fault had so
much profited the Church. At least, sayd he, be sorry that thou canst
not be sorry. So whosoever thou be, that canst not readily pray, at
least pray, that thou mayst pray. For, as in bodily, so in spirituall
diseases, it is a desperate state, to be speechlesse.

It were unmannerlinesse to hold you longer in the Entry. One turne   Of this
in the inner Court, of this speciall prayer in generall, and so enter the   Prayer
Palace. This is not a prayer for his own ease, as that in his Agony
seemes. It hath none of those infirmities, which curious schismatikes
finde in that. No suspicion of ignorance, as there, (*If it be possible.*)   [Mat. 26.39]
No tergiversation nor abandoning the noble worke which he had
begunne, as there, (*Let this cup passe.*) It is not an exemplar, or
forme, for us to imitate precisely, (otherwise then in the Doctrine) as
that Prayer, *Mat.* 6. which we call the Lords Prayer, not because he
sayd it, for he could never say, *forgive us our trespasses,* but because

he commanded us to say it. For though by *Matthew*, which saith, *After this manner pray*, we seem not bound to the words, yet *Luke* sayth, *When you pray*, say, *Our Father which art, &c.* But this is a prayer of God, to God. Not as the Talmudist Jews faine God to pray to himselfe, *Sit voluntas mea, ut misericordia mea superet iram meam;* But as when forain merchandise is mis-ported, the Prince may permit, or inhibit his Subjects to buy it, or not to buy it. Our blessed Saviour arriving in this world fraited with salvation, a thing which this world never had power to have without him, except in that short time, between mans Creation and fall, he by this prayer begs, that even to these despisers of it, it may be communicable, and that their ignorance of the value of it, may not deprive them of it. Teaching that by example here, which he gave in precept before, *Mat.* 5.44. *Pray for them which persecute you, that you may be the children of your Father which is in heaven.* Therefore, doing so now, he might well say, *Father, forgive them,* which is the first room in this glorious Palace. And in this contemplation, O my unworthy soule, thou art presently in the presence. No passing of guards, nor ushers. No examination of thy degree or habit. The Prince is not asleep, nor private, nor weary of giving, nor refers to others. He puts thee not to prevaile by Angels nor Archangels. But lest any thing might hinder thee, from coming into his presence, his presence comes into thee. And lest Majesty should dazell thee, thou art to speake but to thy Father. Of which word, *Abba*, the root is, *To will;* from which root, the fruit also must be willingnesse, and propensenesse to grant. God is the Father of Christ, by that mysticall and eternall unexpressible generation, which never began nor ended. Of which incomprehensible mystery, *Moses* and the ancient Prophets spake so little, and so indirectly, that till the dawning of the day of Christ, after *Esdras* time, those places seem not to be intended of the Trinity. Nay, a good while after Christ, they were but tenderly applyed to that sense. And at this day, the most of the writers in the reformed Churches, considering that we need not such farre fetcht, and such forced helps, and withall, weighing how well the Jews of these times are provided with other expositions of those places, are very sparing in using them, but content themselves modestly herein, with the testimonies of the New Testament. Truly, this mystery is rather the object of faith then rea-

[11.2]

Father

son; and it is enough that we believe Christ to have ever been the Son of God, by such generation, and our selves his sonnes by adoption. So that God is Father to all; but yet so, that though Christ say, *Iohn* 10. [29, 30] *My Father is greater then all,* he addes, *I and my Father are all one,* to shew his eternall interest: and *Iohn* 20. Hee seemes to put a difference, *I goe to my Father, and your Father, my God, and your God.* [17] The Roman stories have, that when *Claudius* saw it conduce to his ends, to get the tribuneship, of which he was incapable, because a Patrician, he suffered himself to be adopted. But against this Adoption, two exceptions were found; one, that he was adopted by a man of lower ranke, a Plebeian; which was unnaturall; and by a younger man then himselfe, which took away the presentation of a Father. But our Adoption is regular. For first, we are made the sonnes of the Most High, and this alsoe by the ancient of daies. There was no one word, by which he could so nobly have maintained his Dignity, kept his station, justified his cause, and withall expressed his humility and charity, as this, Father. They crucifyed him, for saying himself to be the Sonne of God. And in the midst of torment, he both professes the same still, and lets them see, that they have no other way of forgivenesse, but that he is the Sonne of that Father. For no man cometh to [Joh. 14.6] the Father but by the Son.

And at this voice (Father) O most blessed Saviour, thy Father,   Forgive
which is so fully thine, that for thy sake, he is ours too, which is so   them
wholly thine, that he is thy selfe, which is all mercy, yet will not spare thee, all justice, yet will not destroy us. And that glorious Army of Angels, which hitherto by their own integrity maintained their first and pure condition, and by this worke of thine, now neare the *Consummatum est,* attend a confirmation, and infallibility of ever   [Joh. 19.30] remaining so; And that faithfull company of departed Saints, to whom thy merit must open a more inward and familiar room in thy Fathers Kingdome, stand all attentive, to heare what thou wilt aske of this Father. And what shall they heare? what doest thou aske? *Forgive them,* forgive them? Must murderers be forgiven? Must the offended aske it? And must a Father grant it? And must he be solicited, and remembred by the name of Father to doe it? Was not thy passion enough, but thou must have compassion? And is thy mercy so violent, that thou wilt have a fellow-feeling of their im-

minent afflictions, before they have any feeling? The Angels might expect a present employment for their destruction: the Saints might be out of feare, that they should be assumed or mingled in their fellowship. But thou wilt have them pardoned. And yet doest not out of thine own fulnesse pardon them, as thou didst the theef upon the Crosse, because he did already confesse thee; but thou tellest them, that they may be forgiven, but at thy request, and if they acknowledge their Advocate to be the Son of God. *Father, forgive them.* I that cannot revenge thy quarrell, cannot forgive them. I that could not be saved, but by their offence, cannot forgive them. And must a Father, Almighty, and well pleased in thee, forgive them? Thou art more charitable towards them, then by thy direction wee may be to our selvs. We must pray for our selvs limitedly, forgive us, as we forgive. But thou wilt have their forgivenes illimited and unconditioned. Thou seemest not so much as to presume a repentance; which is so essentiall, and necessary in all transgressions, as where by mans fault the actions of God are diverted from his appointed ends, God himself is content to repent the doing of them. As he repented first the making of man, and then the making of a King. But God will have them within the armes of his generall pardon. And we are all delivered from our Debts; for God hath given his word, his co-essentiall word, for us all. And though, (as in other prodigall debts, the Interest exceed the Principall) our Actuall sinnes exceed our Originall, yet God by giving his word for us, hath acquitted all.

[Gen. 6.6]

[1 Sam. 15.11]

But the Affections of our Saviour are not inordinate, nor irregular. He hath a *For*, for his Prayer: *Forgive them, for, &c.* And where he hath not this *For*, as in his Praier in his agony, he quickly interrupts the violence of his request, with a But, *Father, let this cup passe;* but *not my will:* In that form of Prayer which himself taught us, he hath appointed a *for*, on Gods part, which is ever the same unchangeable: *For thine is the Kingdome;* Therefore supplications belong to thee: *The power, Thou openest thy hand and fillest every living thing: The Glory,* for thy Name is glorified in thy grants. But because on our part, the occasions are variable, he hath left our *for*, to our religious discretion. For, when it is said, James 4. *You lust and have not, because you aske not;* it followeth presently, *You aske and misse, because you aske amisse.* It is not a fit *for*, for every private man, to

For

[Psa. 145.16]

[ver. 2]
[ver. 3]

aske much means, for he would doe much good. I must not pray, Lord put into my hands the strength of Christian Kings, for out of my zeale, I will imploy thy benefits to thine advantage, thy Souldiers against thine enemies, and be a bank against that Deluge, wherewith thine enemy the Turk threatens to overflow thy people. I must not pray, Lord fill my heart with knowledge and understanding, for I would compose the Schismes in thy Church, and reduce thy garment to the first continuall and seemlesse integrity; and redresse the deafnesses and oppressions of Judges, and Officers. But he gave us a convenient scantling for our *fors,* who prayed, Give me enough, for I may else despair, give me not too much, for so I may presume. Of Schoolmen, some affirm Prayer to be an act of our will; for we would have that which we aske. Others, of our understanding; for by it we ascend to God, and better our knowledge, which is the proper aliment and food of our understanding; so, that is a perplexed case. But all agree, that it is an act of our Reason, and therefore must be reasonable. For onely reasonable things can pray; for the beasts and Ravens, Psalme 147.9. are not said to pray for food, but *to cry.* Two things are required to make a Prayer. 1. *Pius affectus,* which was not in the Devills request, Matth. 8.31. *Let us goe into the Swine;* nor Job 1.11. *Stretch out thy hand, and touch all he hath;* and, *stretch out thy hand, and touch his bones;* and therefore these were not Prayers. And it must be *Rerum decentium:* for our government in that point, this may inform us. Things absolutely good, as Remission of sinnes, we may absolutely beg: and, to escape things absolutely ill, as sinne. But mean and indifferent things, qualified by the circumstances, we must aske conditionally and referringly to the givers will. For 2 Cor. 12.8. when *Paul* begged *stimulum Carnis* to be taken from him, it was not granted, but he had this answer, *My grace is sufficient for thee.*

Let us now (not in curiosity, but for instruction) consider the reason: *They know not what they doe.* First, if Ignorance excuse: And then, if they were ignorant.

Hast thou, O God, filled all thy Scriptures, both of thy *Recorders* and *Notaries,* which have penned the *History of thy love, to thy People;* and of thy *Secretaries* the Prophets, admitted to the foreknowledge of thy purposes, and instructed in thy Cabinet; hast thou filled these with prayses and perswasions of wisedome and knowl-

[Prov. 30.8, 9]

[Job 2.5]

They know not
Ignorance

edge, and must these persecutors be pardoned for their ignorance? Hast thou bid *Esay* to say, 27.11. *It is a people of no understanding, therefore he that made them, shall not have compassion of them.* And *Hosea* 4.6. *My people are destroyed for lack of knowledge;* and now dost thou say, Forgive them because they know not? Shall ignorance, which is often the cause of sinne, often a sinne it self, often the punishment of sinne, and ever an infirmity and disease contracted by the first great sinne, advantage them? *Who can understand his faults?* saith the man according to thy heart, *Psalme* 19.12. *Lord cleanse me from my secret faults:* He durst not make his ignorance the reason of his prayer, but prayed against ignorance. But thy Mercy is as the Sea: both before it was the Sea, for it overspreads the whole world; and since it was called into limits: for it is not the lesse infinite for that. And as by the Sea, the most remote and distant Nations enjoy one another, by traffique and commerce, East and West becoming neighbours: so by mercy, the most different things are united and reconciled; Sinners have Heaven; Traytors are in the Princes bosome; and ignorant persons are in the spring of wisdome, being forgiven, not onely though they be ignorant, but because they are ignorant. But all ignorance is not excusable; nor any lesse excusable, then not to know, what ignorance is not to be excused. Therefore, there is an ignorance which they call *Nescientiam,* a not knowing of things not appertaining to us. This we had had, though *Adam* had stood; and the Angels have it, for they know not the latter day, and therefore for this, we are not chargeable. They call the other privation, which if it proceed meerly from our owne sluggishnesse, in not searching the meanes made for our instruction, is ever inexcusable. If from God, who for his owne just ends hath cast clouds over those lights which should guide us, it is often excusable. For 1 *Tim.* 1.13. *Paul* saith, *I was a blasphemer, and a persecutor, and an oppressor, but I was received to mercy, for I did it ignorantly, through unbelief.* So, though we are all bound to believe, and therefore faults done by unbeliefe cannot escape the name and nature of sinne, yet since beliefe is the immediate gift of God, faults done by unbeliefe, without malicious concurrences and circumstances, obtaine mercy and pardon from that abundant fountaine of grace, Christ Jesus. And therefore it was a just reason, *Forgive them, for they know not.* If they knew not, which is evident, both by this speech from truth it self, and by 1 *Cor.* 2.8. *Had they known it, they would not have crucified the Lord of glory;* and *Acts* 3.17. *I know that through ignorance ye did it.* And though after so many powerfull miracles, this ignorance were vincible, God having revealed enough to convert them, yet there seemes to be enough on their parts, to make it a perplexed case, and to excuse, though not a malitious persecuting, yet a not consenting to his Doctrine. For they had a Law, *Whosoever shall make himself the sonne*   [Joh. 19.7] *of God, let him dye:* And they spoke out of their Lawes, when they said, *We have no other King but Cæsar.* There were therefore some   [Joh. 19.15] among them reasonably, and zealously ignorant. And for those, the Sonne ever-welcome, and well-heard, begged of his Father, ever accessible, and exorable, a pardon ever ready and naturall.

We have now passed through all those roomes which we unlockt and opened at first. And now may that point, Why this prayer is remembred onely by one Evangelist, and why by *Luke,* be modestly inquired: For we are all admitted and welcommed into the acquaintance of the Scriptures, upon such conditions as travellers are into other Countries: if we come as praisers and admirers of their Commodities and Government, not as spies into the mysteries of their State, nor searchers, nor calumniators of their weaknesses. For though the Scriptures, like a strong rectified State, be not endangered by such a curious malice of any, yet he which brings that, deserves no admittance. When those great Commissioners which are called the Septuagint, sent from *Hierusalem,* to translate the Hebrew Scriptures into Greeke, had perfected their work, it was, and is an argument of Divine assistance, that writing severally, they differed not. The same may prove even to weake and faithlesse men, that the holy Ghost super-intended the foure Evangelists, because they differ not; as they which have written their harmonies, make it evident: But to us, faith teacheth the other way. And we conclude not, because they agree, the holy Ghost directed; for heathen Writers and Malefactors in examinations do so; but because the holy Ghost directed, we know they agree, and differ not. For as an honest man, ever of the same thoughts, differs not from himself, though he do not ever say the same things, if he say not contraries; so the foure Evangelists observe the uniformity and samenesse of their guide, though all did not say all the same things, since none contradicts any. And as, when my soule, which enables all my limbs to their functions, disposes my legs to go, my whole body is truly said to go, because none stayes behinde; so when the holy Spirit, which had made himself as a common soule to their foure soules, directed one of them to say any thing, all are well understood to have said it. And therefore when to that place in *Matth.* 27.9. where that Evangelist cites the Prophet *Jeremy,* for words spoken by *Zachary,* many medicines are applyed by the Fathers; as, That many copies have no name, That *Jeremy* might be binominous, and have both names, a thing frequent in the Bible, That it might be the error of a transcriber, That there was extant an *Apocryph* booke of *Jeremy,* in which these words were, and sometimes things of such

[2 Tim. 3.8]

books were vouched, as *Jannes* and *Jambres* by *Paul;* St. *Augustine* insists upon, and teaches rather this, That it is more wonderfull, that all the Prophets spake by one Spirit, and so agreed, then if any one of them had spoken all those things; And therefore he adds, *Singula sunt omnium, & omnia sunt singulorum,* All say what any of them say; And in this sense most congruously is that of St. *Hierome* applyable, that the foure Evangelists are *Quadriga Divina,* That as the foure Chariot wheeles, though they looke to the foure corners of the world, yet they move to one end and one way, so the Evangelists have both one scope, and one way.

Yet not so precisely, but that they differ in words: For as their generall intention, common to them all begat that consent, so a private reason peculiar to each of them, for the writing of their Histories at that time, made those diversities which seem to be. For *Matthew,* after he had preached to the Jewes, and was to be transplanted into another vineyard, the Gentiles, left them written in their owne tongue, for permanency, which he had before preached unto them transitorily by word. *Mark,* when the Gospell fructified in the West, and the Church enlarged her self, and grew a great body, and therefore required more food, out of *Peters* Dictates, and by his approbation published his Evangile. Not an Epitome of *Matthewes,* as Saint *Jerome* (I know not why) imagines, but a just and intire History of our blessed Saviour. And as *Matthewes* reason was to supply a want in the Eastern Church, *Markes* in the Western; so on the other side *Lukes* was to cut off an excesse and superfluitie: for then many had undertaken this Story, and dangerously inserted and mingled uncertainties and obnoxious improbabilities: and he was more curious and more particular then the rest, both because he was more learned, and because he was so individuall a companion of the most learned Saint *Paul,* and did so much write *Pauls* words, that *Eusebius* thereupon mistaketh the words 2 *Tim.* 2.8. *Christ is raised according to my Gospell,* to prove that *Paul* was author of this Gospell attributed to *Luke. John* the Minion of *Christ* upon earth, and survivor of the Apostles, (whose books rather seem fallen from Heaven, and writ with the hand which ingraved the stone Tables, then a mans work) because the heresies of *Ebion* and *Cerinthus* were rooted, who upon this true ground, then evident and fresh, that Christ had spoke many things which none of the other three Evangelists had Recorded, uttered many things as his, which he never spoke: *John* I say, more diligently then the rest handleth his Divinity, and his Sermons, things specially brought into question by them. So therefore all writ one thing, yet all have some things particular. And *Luke* most, for he writ last of three, and largeliest for himselfe, *Act.* 1.1 saith, *I have made the former Treatise of all that Jesus began to doe and teach, untill the Day that he was taken up;* which speech, lest the words in the last of *John, If all were written which Jesus did, the world could not contain the Bookes,* should condemne, *Ambrose* and *Chrysostome* interpret well out of the words themselves, *Scripsit de omnibus, non omnia,* He writ of all, but not all: for it must have the same limitation, which *Paul* giveth his words, who saith, *Acts* 20. in one verse, *I have kept nothing back, but have shewed you all the counsell of God;* and in another, *I kept back nothing that was profitable.* It is another peculiar singularity of *Lukes,* that he addresseth his History to one man, *Theophilus.* For it is but weakely surmised, that he chose that name, for all *lovers of God,* because the interpretation of the word suffereth it, since he addeth *most noble Theophilus.* But the work doth not the lesse belong to the whole Church, for that, no more then his Masters Epistles doe though they be directed to particulars.

It is also a singularitie in him to write upon that reason, because divers have written. In humane knowledge, to abridge or suck, and then suppresse other Authors, is not ever honest nor profitable: We see after that vast enterprise of *Justinian,* who distilled all the Law

[27]
[20]

into one vessell, and made one Booke of 2000, suppressing all the rest, *Alciate* wisheth he had let them alone, and thinketh the Doctors of our times, would better have drawn usefull things from those volumes, then his *Trebonian* and *Dorothee* did. And *Aristotle* after, by the immense liberality of *Alexander,* he had ingrossed all Authors, is said to have defaced all, that he might be in stead of all: And therefore, since they cannot rise against him, he imputes to them errours which they held not: vouches onely such objections from them, as he is able to answer; and propounds all good things in his own name, which he ought to them. But in this History of *Lukes,* it is otherwise: He had no authority to suppresse them, nor doth he reprehend or calumniate them, but writes the truth simply, and leaves it to outweare falshood: and so it hath: *Moses* rod hath devoured the Conjurers rods, and *Lukes* Story still retains the majestie of the maker, and theirs are not.

[Exod. 7.12]

Other singularities in *Luke,* of form or matter, I omit, and end with one like this in our Text. As in the apprehending of our blessed Saviour, all the Evangelists record, that *Peter* cut off *Malchus* eare, but onely *Luke* remembers the healing of it again: (I think) because that act of curing, was most present and obvious to his consideration, who was a Physician: so he was therefore most apt, to remember this Prayer of Christ, which is the Physick and *Balsamum* of our Soule, and must be applied to us all, (for we doe all Crucifie him, and we know not what we do.) And therefore Saint *Hierome* gave a right Character of him, in his Epistle to *Paulinus, Fuit Medicus, & pariter omnia verba illius, Animæ languentis sunt Medicinæ,* As he was a Physitian, so all his words are Physick for a languishing soule.

[Mat. 26.51;
Mark 14.47;
Luke 22.50–
51;
Joh. 18.10]

Now let us dispatch the last consideration, of the effect of this Prayer. Did Christ intend the forgivenesse of the Jewes, whose utter ruine God (that is, himselfe) had fore-decreed? And which he foresaw, and bewaild even then hanging upon the Crosse? For those Divines which reverently forbeare to interpret the words *Lord, Lord, why hast thou forsaken me?* of a suffering hell in his soule, or of a departing of the Father from him; (for *Joh.* 16. it is, *I am not alone, for the Father is with me*) offer no exposition of those words more convenient, then that the foresight of the Jewes imminent calamities, expressed and drew those words from him: *In their Afflictions, were*

[Mat. 27.46]

[v. 32]

all kindes, and all degrees of Miserie. So that as one writer of the
Roman story saith elegantly, *He that considereth the Acts of Rome,
considereth not the Acts of one People, but of Mankinde:* I may truly
say of the Jewes Afflictions, he that knoweth them, is ignorant of
nothing that this world can threaten. For to that which the present
authority of the Romanes inflicted upon them, our Schools have
added upon their posterities; that they are as slaves to Christians,
and their goods subject to spoile, if the Lawes of the Princes where
they live, did not out of indulgency defend them. Did he then aske,
and was not heard? God forbid. A man is heard, when that is given
which his will desired; and our will is ever understood to be a will
rectified, and concurrent with God. This is *Voluntas,* a discoursed
and examined will. That which is upon the first sight of the object,
is *Velleitas,* a willingnesse, which we resist not, onely because we
thought not of it. And such a willingnesse had Christ, when suddenly
he wished that the cup might passe: but quickly conformed his will
to his Fathers. But in this Prayer his will was present, therefore
fulfilled. Briefly then, in this Prayer he commended not all the Jewes,
for he knew the chief to sin knowingly, and so out of the reach of
his reason, (*for they know not.*) Nor any, except they repented after:
for it is not ignorance, but repentance, which deriveth to us the
benefit of Gods pardon. For he that sinnes of Ignorance, may be
pardoned if he repent; but he that sinnes against his Conscience, and
is thereby impenitible, cannot be pardoned. And this is all, which I
will say of these words, *Father forgive them, for they know not what
they do.*

*O eternall God, look down from thy Throne to thy footstoole:
from thy blessed Company of Angels and Saints, to us, by our own
faults made more wretched and contemptible, then the wormes which
shall eat us, or the dust which we were, and shall be. O Lord, under
the weight of thy Justice we cannot stand. Nor had any other title to
thy mercie, but the Name of Father, and that we have forfeited. That
name of Sonnes of God, thou gavest to us, all at once in Adam; and
he gave it away from us all by his sinne. And thou hast given it again
to every one of us, in our regeneration by Baptisme, and we have lost
it again by our transgressions. And yet thou wert not weary of being*

mercifull, but diddest choose one of us, to be a fit and worthy ransome for us all; and by the death of thy Christ, our Jesus, gavest us again the title and priviledge of thy Sonnes; but with conditions, which though easie, we have broke, and with a yoke, which though light, and sweet, we have cast off. How shall we then dare to call thee Father? Or to beg that thou wilt make one triall more of us? These hearts are accustomed to rebellions, and hopelesse. But, O God, create in us new hearts, hearts capable of the love and feare, due to a Father. And then we shall dare to say, Father, *and to say,* Father forgive us. *Forgive us O Father, and all which are engaged, and accountable to thee for us: forgive our Parents, and those which undertooke for us in Baptisme. Forgive the civill Magistrate, and the Minister. Forgive them their negligences, and us our stubbornnesses. And give us the grace that we may ever sincerely say, both this Prayer of Example and Counsell,* Forgive our enemies, *and that other of Precept,* Our Father which art in Heaven, *&c.*

Number 6.

Preached at Saint Pauls upon
Christmasse day, 1621.

JOHN 1.8. *HE WAS NOT THAT LIGHT, BUT WAS*
SENT TO BEAR WITNESSE OF THAT LIGHT.

IT IS AN injury common to all the Evangelists, (as *Irenæus* notes)
that all their *Gospels* were severally refused by one Sect of *Here-*
ticks or other. But it was proper to Saint *John* alone, to be refused
by a Sect, that admitted *all the* other three Evangelists, (as *Epi-*
phanius remembers) and refused onely Saint *John*. These were the
Alogiani, a limme and branch of the *Arians*, who being unable to
looke upon the glorious Splendour, the divine Glory, attributed by
Saint *John* to this *Logos*, (which gave them their name of *Alogiani*)
this *Word*, this *Christ*, not comprehending this *Mystery*, That *this*
Word was so with God, as that it was God; they tooke a round way,   [Joh. 1.1]
and often practised, to condemne all that they did not understand,
and therefore refuse the whole *Gospell*. Indeed his *whole Gospell* is
comprehended in the beginning thereof. In this *first Chapter* is contracted all that which is extensively spred, and dilated through the
whole Booke. For here is first, the *Foundation* of all, the *Divinitie*
of Christ, to the 15. verse. Secondly, the *Execution* of all, the *Offices*
of Christ, to the 35. verse. And then the *Effect*, the *Working*, the
Application of all, that is, who were to *Preach* all this, to the ends of
the world, the *calling of his Apostles*, to the end of the Chapter. For
the first, *Christs Divinity*, there is enough expressed in the very first
verse alone: for, there is his *Eternitie*, intimated in that word, *In*
principio, in the beginning. The first booke of the Bible, *Genesis*, and
the last booke, (that is, that which was *last written*) this *Gospell*,
begin both with this word, *In the beginning*. But the *last* beginning
was the *first*, if *Moses* beginning doe onely denote the *Creation*, which

was not 6000. yeares since, and Saint *Johns,* the *Eternity of Christ,* which no Millions, multiplied by Millions, can calculate. And then, as his *Eternitie,* so his *distinction of Persons,* is also specified in this 1. verse, when the *Word,* (that is, *Christ*) is said to have been *apud Deum, with God.* For, therefore, (saith Saint *Basil*) did the *Holy Ghost* rather choose to say *apud Deum,* then *in Deo, with God,* then *in God, ne auferendæ Hypostaseos occasionem daret,* lest he should give any occasion of denying the same *Nature,* in divers *Persons;* for it doth more clearly notifie a distinction of Persons, to say, he was *with him,* then to say, he was *in him;* for the severall Attributes of God, (*Mercy* and *Justice,* and the rest) are *in God,* and yet they are not distinct Persons. Lastly, there is also expressed in this 1. verse Christs *Equality* with God, in that it is said, *& Verbum erat Deus,* and *this Word was God.* As it was *in the beginning,* and therefore *Eternall,* and as it was *with God,* and therefore a *distinct* Person, so it was *God,* and therefore *equall* to the Father; which phrase doth so vexe and anguish the *Arians,* that being disfurnished of all other escapes, they corrupted the place, onely with a false interpunction, and broke of the words, where they admitted no such pause; for, they read it thus, *Verbum erat apud Deum;* (so far, well) *Et Deus erat.* There they made their point; and then followed in another sentence: *Verbum hoc erat in principio,* &c.

The first part then of this Chapter, (and indeed of the whole Gospell) is in that 1. verse the *manifestation* of his *Divine Nature,* in his *Eternitie,* in the *distinction* of Persons, in the *equalitie* with the Father. The second part of the Chapter layeth downe the *Office of Christ,* his *Propheticall,* his *Priestly,* his *Royall Office.* For the first, the Office of a *Prophet* consisting in three severall *exercises,* to *manifest* things *past,* to *foretell* things *to come,* and to *expound* things *present,* Christ declared himself to be a Prophet in all these three: for, for the first, he was not onely a *Verball,* but an *Actuall* manifester of former *Prophecies,* for all the former Prophecies were accomplished in his *Person,* and in his *deeds,* and *words,* in his *actions* and *Passion.* For the second, his foretelling of *future* things, he foretold the state *of the Church,* to the end of the world. And for the third (declaring of *present things*) He told the *Samaritan woman,* so exquisitely, all her own History, that she gave presently that attestation, *Sir, I see*

John 4.19

that thou art a Prophet: so his *Propheticall* Office, is plainly laid
down. For his *second* Office, his *Priesthood,* that is expressed in the
36. verse, *Behold the Lambe of God;* f.. ⁻, in this, he was our *Priest,*
that he was our *Sacrifice;* he was our *Priest,* in that he offered himselfe for our sinnes. Lastly, his *Royall Office* was the *most naturall* to
him of all the rest. The Office of a *Prophet* was *Naturall* to none;
none was *born* a Prophet. Those who are called the *children of the
Prophets,* and the *sonnes of the Prophets,* are but the *Prophets Disciples.* Though the Office of *Priesthood,* by being annexed to *one
Tribe,* may (in some sense) be called *Naturall,* yet in Christ it could
not be so, for he was not of that Tribe of *Levi:* so that he had no
interest in the *legall Priesthood,* but *was a Priest according to the
Order of Melchisedec.* But his Title to be *King,* was *naturall,* by
descent, he was of the *bloud Royall,* and the nearest in succession; so
that he, and onely he, had, *De Jure,* all the *three unctions* upon him.
David had *two;* he was both a *Prophet,* and a *King;* he had those two
capacities; *Melchisedec* had *two* too; he was both a *King* and a *Priest;*
he had two: Onely Christ had all *three,* both a *Prophet,* and *Priest,*
and *King.*

    In the third part of the Chapter, which is *the calling of foure of his
Apostles,* we may observe that the first that was called, was not *Peter,*
but *Andrew;* that there might be laid at first some interruption, some
stop to their zealous fury, who will still force, and heap up every
action which any way concerns Saint *Peter,* to the building up of his
imaginary *primacy,* which primacy, they cared not though *Peter*
wanted, if they could convey that primacy to his *Successor,* by any
other Title; for which Successours sake it is, and not for Saint *Peters*
own, that they are so over diligent in advancing his *prerogative.* But,
it was not *Peter,* that was called, but *Andrew.* In *Andrews* present
and earnest application of himself to *Christ,* we may note, (and onely
so) divers particulars, fit for use and imitation. In his first question,
Master, where dwellest thou? there is not onely, (as *Cyrill* observes) a
reverent ascribing to him *a power of instructing* in that compellation,
Master, but a desire to have more time afforded to hearken to his
instructions, *Where dwellest thou,* that I may dwell with thee? And
as soon as ever he had taken in some good portion of knowledge
himselfe, he conceives presently a desire to communicate his hap-

[Psa. 110.4;
Heb. 6.20]

pinesse with *others;* and he seeks his brother *Peter,* and tells him, *Invenimus Messiam, we have found the Messias;* which is, (as Saint *Chrysostome* notes) *vox quærentis:* In this, that he rejoyces in the finding of him, he testifies that he had sought him, and that he had continued in the expectation of a *Messias* before. *Invenit Messiam,* he had found the *Messias;* but, saith the Text, *Duxit ad Jesum,* he brought his brother the glorious newes of having found a *King,* the King of the Jewes, but he led him to *Jesus,* to a *Saviour;* that so, all kinds of happinesse, *temporall* and *spirituall,* might be intimated in this discovery of a *King,* and of a *Saviour;* What may not his servants hope for at his hands, who is both those, a *King* and a *Saviour,* and hath *worldly* preferments, and the Glory of *Heaven in his power?*

Now, though the words of this Text, (*He was not that light, but was sent to beare witnesse of that light*) are placed in the first part of the Chapter, that which concernes *Christs Divine nature,* yet they belong, and they have a respect to all three; To his *Divine nature,* to his *Offices,* and to his *Calling of his Apostles:* For, first, *light* denotes his *Divine nature;* secondly, the testimony that is given of him by *John Baptist,* (of whom the words of our Text are spoken) declares him to be the *Messias,* and *Messias,* (which signifies *anointed*) involves all his *Offices,* for his *three Offices,* are his *three vocations,* and thirdly, the Application of this testimony, given by *Iohn Baptist* here, by the *Apostles* and their *Successors* after, intimates or brings to our memory this their first *vocation,* in this Chapter. So that the Gospel of Saint *Iohn* containes all *Divinity,* this Chapter *all the Gospell,* and this Text all the *Chapter.* Therefore it is too large to goe through at this time; at this time we shall insist upon such branches as arise out of that consideration, *what, and who this light is,* (for, we shall finde it to be both a *personall light,* (it is *some body*) and, otherwise too, a *reall light,* (it is *some thing*) therefore we inquire, *what,* this light is, (*what thing*) and *who* this light is, (*what person*) which *John Baptist* is denied to be. Hereafter we shall consider, *the Testimony* which is given of this light; in which part in due time, we shall handle, the *person* of the witnesse *John Baptist,* in whom we shall finde many considerable, and extraordinary circumstances: and then, his *Citation,* and calling to this testimony; and thirdly, the *testimony* it selfe that he gave: and lastly, *why any testimony* was requisite to so evident a thing as *light*. But the first part, *who*, and *what* this light is, belongs most properly to *this day*, and will fill that portion of the day, which is afforded us for this exercise. Proceed we therefore to that, *John Baptist* was not that light, *who was, what was?*

Though most expositors, as well ancient, as modern agree with one generall, and unanime consent, that *light* in this *verse* is intended and meant of *Christ*, Christ is this light, yet in some precedent and subsequent passages in this Chapter, I see other senses have been admitted of this word, *light*, then perchance those places will beare; certainly other then those places need: particularly in the *fourth verse* (*In it was life, and that life was the light of men*) there they understand *life*, to be nothing but this *naturall life* which we breath, and *light* to be onely that *naturall light, naturall reason*, which distinguishes us *men*, from other creatures. Now, it is true that they may have a pretence for some ground of this interpretation in antiquity it selfe, for, so says Saint *Cyrill, Filius Dei Creativè illuminat*, Christ doth enlighten us, in creating us. And so some others of the *Fathers*, and some of the *Schooles*, understand by that light *naturall Reason*, and that life, conservation in life. but this interpretation seemes to me subject to both these dangers, that it goes so farre, and yet reaches not home. So far, in wresting in *divers* senses into a word, which needs but *one*, and is of it selfe cleare enough, that is *light*, and yet reaches not home, for it reaches not to the *essentiall light*, which is *Christ Jesus*, nor to the *supernaturall light*, which is *Faith* and *Grace*, which seemes to have been the Evangelists principall scope, to declare the comming of *Christ*, (who is the *essentiall light*) and his purpose in comming, to raise and establish a Church, by *Faith* and *Grace*, which is the *supernaturall light:* For, as the holy Ghost himselfe interprets *life* to be meant of Christ, (*He that hath the Sonne hath life*) so we may justly doe of *light* too, *he that sees* the Sonne, the *Sonne of God hath light*. For, light is never, (to my remembrance) found in any place of the Scripture, where it must necessarily signifie the light of nature, *naturall reason;* but wheresoever it is transferred from the naturall to a figurative sense, it takes a higher signification then *that;* either it signifies *Essentiall* light, Christ Jesus, (which answers our first question, *Quis lux, who is this light*, it is *Christ, personally*) or it signifies the *supernaturall light* of *Faith* and *Grace*,

1 Part
Quis lux

1 Ioh. 5.12

(which answers our second question, *Quid lux, what is this light,* for it is the *working of Christ,* by his Spirit, in his *Church,* in the infusion of *Faith* and *Grace,* for *beliefe,* and *manners*) And therefore though it be ever lawfull, and often times very usefull, for the raising and exaltation of our devotion, and to present the plenty, and abundance of the *holy Ghost* in the *Scriptures,* who satisfies us as with marrow, and with fatnesse, to induce the *diverse senses* that the Scriptures doe admit, yet this may not be admitted, if there may be danger thereby, to neglect or weaken the *literall sense* it selfe. For there is no necessity of that *spirituall wantonnesse* of finding more then necessary senses; for, the more *lights* there are, the more *shadows* are also cast by those many lights. And, as it is true in religious duties, so is it in interpretation of matters of Religion, *Necessarium & Satis convertuntur;* when you have done that you ought to doe in your calling, you have done enough; there are no such *Evangelicall counsailes,* as should raise workes of *supererogation,* more then you are bound to doe, so when you have the *necessary sense,* that is the meaning of the holy Ghost in that place, you have senses enow, and not till then, though you have never so many, and never so delightfull.

Light therefore, is in all this Chapter fitliest understood of *Christ;* who is noted here, with that distinctive article, *Illa lux, that light.* For, *non sic dicitur lux, sicut lapis;* Christ is not so called *Light,* as he is called a *Rock,* or a *Cornerstone;* not by a metaphore, but truly, and properly. It is true that the Apostles are said to be *light,* and that with an article, *the light;* but yet with a limitation and restriction, *the light of the world,* that is, set up to convey light to the world. It is true that *John Baptist* himselfe was called *light,* and with large additions, *Lucerna ardens, a burning, and a shining lampe,* to denote both his owne *burning zeale,* and the *communicating* of this his light to others. It is true, that *all the faithfull* are said to be *light in the Lord;* but all this is but to signifie that they had been in darknesse before; they had been beclouded, but were now illustrated; they were light, but light by *reflexion,* by illustration of a greater light. And as in the first creation, *vesper & mane dies unus, The evening and the morning made the day, evening* before *morning, darknesse* before *light,* so in our *regeneration,* when wee are made *new Creatures,* the Spirit of God findes us in *naturall darknesse,* and by him we are made *light in*

Illa lux

Augustin.

Mat. 5.[14]

Ioh. 5.[35]

Ephe. 5.[8]

[Gen. 1.5]

the Lord. But Christ himselfe, and hee onely, is *Illa lux, vera lux; that light, the true light.* Not so opposed to those other lights, as though the *Apostles,* or *John Baptist,* or the *faithfull,* who are called *lights,* were *false* lights; but that they were *weake* lights. But Christ was *fons lucis,* the fountaine of all their light; light so, as no body else was so; so, as that hee was nothing but light. Now, neither the *Apostles,* nor *John Baptist,* nor the *Elect,* no nor the *virgin Mary* (though wee should allow all that the *Roman Church* aske in her behalfe) for the Roman Church is not yet come to that searednesse, that obduratenesse, that impudency, as to pronounce that the *virgin Mary* was *without originall sinne,* (though they have done many shrewd acts towards it, to the prejudice of the contrary opinion) yet none of these were so light, as they were nothing but light. *Moses* himselfe who received and delivered the law, was not so; and to intimate so much, there was an illustration, and irradiation upon *his face,* but not so of *all his body.* Nay, *Christ Jesus* himselfe, who fulfilled the law, *as man,* was not so; which he also intimated in the greatest degree of glorification which he accepted upon earth, which was his *transfiguration,* for, though it be said in that, *That the fashion of his Countenance was changed, and his garment was white, and glistered,* yet, *lineamenta Petro agnoscibilia servavit,* hee kept that former proportion of body, that *Peter* could know him by it. So that this was not a glorifying of the body, and making it *thorough light;* but hee suffered his *Divine nature* to appeare and shine thorough his *flesh,* and not to swallow, or annihilate that flesh. All other men, by occasion of this flesh, have darke *clouds,* yea *nights,* yea long and frozen winter nights of *sinne,* and of the *works of darknesse.* Christ was incapable of any such nights, or any such clouds, any approaches towards *sinne;* but yet Christ admitted some *shadowes,* some such degrees of *humane infirmity,* as by *them,* he was willing to show, that the nature of man, in the best perfection thereof, is not *vera lux, tota lux,* true light, all light, which he declared in that *Si possibile,* and that *Transeat calix, If it bee possible, let this cup passe;* words, to which himselfe was pleased to allow so much of a retractation, and a correction, *Veruntamen, yet Father,* whatsoever the sadnesse of my soule have made mee say, *yet, not my will but thine be done; not mine, but thine;* so that they were not altogether, *all one;* humane

Luke 9.29

Tertull.

Mat. 26.39

infirmity made some difference. So that no one man, not Christ, (considered but so as man) was *tota lux,* all light, no cloud. No not *mankinde,* consider it *collectively,* can bee light so, as that there shall bee no darknesse. It was not so, when all mankind was in one *person,* in *Adam.* It is said sometimes in School, that *no man* can keep the commandements, yet *man, collectively,* may keep them. They intend no more herein, but that some one man may abstaine from doing any act against worshipping of *Images,* another from *stealing,* another from *adultery,* and others from others. But if it were possible to compose a man of such elements, as that the principallest vertues, and eminencies of all other men, should enter into his composition, and if there could bee found a man, as perfect in all particular vertues, as *Moses* was in meeknesse, (who was a *meeke man, above all the men that were upon the earth*) yet this man would not bee *vera lux, tota lux,* true light, all light. *Moses* was not so *meeke,* but that hee *slew the Egyptian,* nor so meek, but that hee disputed and expostulated with *God* many times, passionately. Every man is so far from beeing *tota lux,* all light, as that he hath still *within him,* a darke vapor of *originall sinne,* and the cloud of *humane flesh without him.*

Numb. 12.
[3]

Nay not onely no man, (for so we may consider him in the whole course of his life) but *no one act,* of the most perfect, and religious man in the world, though that act employ but halfe a minute in the doing thereof, can bee *vera lux,* true light, all light, so perfect light, as that it may serve another, or thy selfe, for a lanthorne to his, or thy feet, or a light to his, or thy steps, so that hee or thou may thinke it enough to doe so still. For, another man may doe so good works, as it may justly work to thy shame, and confusion, and to the aggravating of thy condemnation, that thou livest not as well as *hee,* yet, it would not perchance serve thy turne, to live *but* so well; for, *to whom God gives more, of him he requires more.* No man hath *veram lucem,* true light, thorough light; no man hath *meridiem, Augem,* that high point that casts no shadow, because, besides *originall sinne,* that ever smoakes up, and creates a soote in the soule, and besides *naturall infirmities,* which become sinnes, when wee consider *Grace,* no man does carry his good actions to that heighth as, by that grace, which God affords him, hee might doe. Slacker men have a declination even in their *mornings;* a *West* even in their *East;* coolings, and

[Luke
12.48]

faintnesses and after-noones, as soon as they have any dawnings, any breake of day, any inchoation of any spirituall action or purpose. Others have some farther growth, and increasing, and are more diligent in the observation of spirituall duties; but yet they have not their *meridiem,* their *Augem,* their noon, their *south point,* no such heighth, as that they might not have a higher, by that *grace* which they have received. In the best degree of our best actions, particularly in this service, which wee doe to God at this houre, if we brought with us hither a religious purpose to sanctifie this festivall, if wee answer to the callings of his most blessed Spirit, whilest wee are here, if wee carry away a detestation of our sinnes, and a holy purpose of amendment of life, this is a good degree of proficiency, and God bee blessed, if any of us all arrive to that degree; but yet, this is not *vera lux,* true light, all light; for, who amongst us can avoid the testimony of his conscience, that since he begun this present service to God, his thoughts have not strayed upon *pleasures* and *vanities* or *profit,* and leapt the walls of this Church, yea, perchance within the walls of this flesh, which should bee the *Temple of the holy Ghost?* Besides, to become *vera lux, tota lux,* true light, thorough light, requires *perseverance* to the end. So that till our naturall light goe out, wee cannot say that wee have this light; for, as the darknesse of hell fire is, so this light of this heavenly fire, must bee everlasting. If ever it go cleane out, it was never throughly kindled, but kindled to our farther damnation; it was never *vera lux,* true light, for, as one office of the *law* is, but to show sinne, so all the *light of grace* may end in this, to show me my desperate estate, from the abuse of grace. In all Philosophy there is not so darke a thing as *light;* As the sunne, which is *fons lucis naturalis,* the beginning of naturall light, is the most evident thing to bee seen, and yet the hardest to be looked upon, so is naturall light to our reason and understanding. Nothing clearer, for it is *clearnesse* it selfe, nothing darker, it is enwrapped in so many scruples. Nothing nearer, for it is round about us, nothing more remote, for wee know neither entrance, nor limits of it. Nothing more *easie,* for a child discerns it, nothing more *hard,* for no man understands it. It is apprehensible by *sense,* and not comprehensible by *reason.* If wee winke, wee cannot chuse but see it, if we stare, wee know it never the better. No man is *yet* got so neare to the knowledge of the qualities of light, as to know whether *light* it selfe be a *quality,* or a *substance*. If then this *naturall light* be so darke to our naturall reason, if wee shall offer to pierce so far, into the light of this text, the *Essentiall light Christ Jesus,* (in his nature, or but in his *offices*) or the *supernaturall light* of *faith* and *grace,* (how far *faith* may be had, and yet lost, and how far the *freewill* of man may concur and cooperate with *grace,* and yet *still* remaine nothing in it selfe) if wee search farther into these points, then the Scripture hath opened us a way, how shall wee hope to unentangle, or extricate our selves? They had a precious composition for *lamps,* amongst the *ancients,* reserved especially for *Tombes,* which kept light for many hundreds of yeares; we have had *in our age* experience, in some casuall openings of ancient vaults, of finding such lights, as were kindled, (as appeared by their inscriptions) *fifteen* or *sixteen hundred* yeares before; but, as soon as that light comes to our light, it vanishes. So this *eternall,* and this *supernaturall light, Christ* and *faith,* enlightens, warmes, purges, and does all the profitable offices of *fire,* and *light,* if we keep it in the right spheare, in the proper place, (that is, if wee consist in *points necessary* to salvation, and *revealed* in the Scripture) but when wee bring this light to the common light of *reason,* to our inferences, and consequencies, it may be in danger to vanish it selfe, and perchance extinguish our reason too; we may search so far, and reason so long of *faith* and *grace,* as that we may lose not onely *them,* but even our reason too, and sooner become *mad* then *good.* Not that we are bound to believe any thing *against reason,* that is, to believe, we know not why. It is but a slacke opinion, it is not *Beliefe,* that is not grounded upon reason. He that should come to a *Heathen man,* a meere naturall man, uncatechized, uninstructed in the rudiments of the Christian Religion, and should at first, without any preparation, present him first with this necessitie; Thou shalt burn in fire and brimstone eternally, except thou believe *a Trinitie of Persons, in an unitie of one God,* Except thou believe the *Incarnation* of the second Person of the Trinitie, the Sonne of God, Except thou believe that *a Virgine had a Sonne,* and the same Sonne that God had, and that God was Man too, and being the immortall God, yet died, he should be so farre from working any spirituall cure upon this poore soule, as that he should rather bring Christian Mysteries into scorne, then *him* to a beliefe. For, that man, if you proceed so, Believe all, or you burne in Hell, would finde an easie, an obvious way to escape all; that is, first not to believe *Hell* it selfe, and then nothing could binde him to believe the rest.

The *reason* therefore of Man, must first be satisfied; but the way of such satisfaction must be *this,* to make him see, That this World, a frame of so much harmony, so much concinnitie and conveniencie, and such a correspondence, and subordination in the parts thereof, must necessarily have had a workeman, for nothing can make it selfe: That no such workeman would deliver over a frame, and worke, of so much Majestie, to be governed by *Fortune,* casually, but would still retain the Administration thereof in his owne hands: That if he doe so, if he made the World, and *sustaine* it still by his watchfull Providence, there belongeth a worship and service to him, for doing so: That therefore he hath certainly revealed to man, what kinde of worship, and service, shall be acceptable to him: That this manifestation of his Will, must be permanent, it must be *written,* there must be a *Scripture,* which is his *Word* and his *Will:* And that therefore, from that Scripture, from that Word of God, all Articles of our Beliefe are to bee drawne.

If then his *Reason* confessing all this, aske farther proofe, how he shall know that *these Scriptures* accepted by the Christian Church, are the true Scriptures, let him bring any other Booke which pretendeth to be the Word of God, into comparison with these; It is true, we have not a *Demonstration;* not such an Evidence as that one and two, are three, to prove these to be Scriptures of God; God hath not proceeded in that manner, to drive our Reason into a pound, and to force it by a peremptory necessitie to accept these for Scriptures, for then, here had been no exercise of our *Will,* and our assent, if we could not have resisted. But yet these Scriptures have so orderly, so sweet, and so powerfull a working upon the reason, and the understanding, as if any third man, who were utterly discharged of all preconceptions and anticipations in matter of Religion, one who were altogether *neutrall,* disinterested, unconcerned in either party, nothing towards a *Turke,* and as little toward a *Christian,* should heare a *Christian* pleade for his Bible, and a *Turke* for his Alcoran, and should weigh the evidence of both; the Majesty of the *Style,* the

punctuall accomplishment of the *Prophecies,* the harmony and concurrence of the *foure Evangelists,* the consent and unanimity of the
Christian Church ever since, and many other such reasons, he would
be drawne to such an Historicall, such a Grammaticall, such a Logicall
beliefe of our Bible, as to preferre it before any other, that could be
pretended to be the Word of God. He would believe it, and he would
know *why* he did so. For let no man thinke that *God* hath given him
so much ease here, as to save him by believing he knoweth not what,
or why. *Knowledge* cannot save us, but we cannot be saved without
Knowledge; Faith is not on this side Knowledge, but beyond it; we
must necessarily come to *Knowledge* first, though we must not stay
at it, when we are come thither. For, a regenerate Christian, being
now a *new Creature,* hath also *a new facultie of Reason:* and so
believeth the Mysteries of Religion, out of another Reason, then as a
meere naturall Man, he believed naturall and morall things. He believeth them for their own sake, by *Faith,* though he take *Knowledge*
of them before, by that common Reason, and by those humane Arguments, which worke upon other men, in naturall or morall things.
Divers men may walke by the Sea side, and the same beames of the
Sunne giving light to them all, one gathereth by the benefit of that
light pebles, or speckled shells, for curious vanitie, and another
gathers precious Pearle, or medicinall Ambar, by the same light. So
the common light of reason illumins us all; but one imployes this
light upon the searching of impertinent vanities, another by a better
use of the same light, finds out the Mysteries of Religion; and when
he hath found them, loves them, not for the lights sake, but for the
naturall and true worth of the thing it self. Some men by the benefit
of this light of Reason, have found out things profitable and usefull
to the whole world; As in particular, *Printing,* by which the learning
of the whole world is communicable to one another, and our minds
and our inventions, our wits and compositions may trade and have
commerce together, and we may participate of one anothers under-
standings, as well as of our Clothes, and Wines, and Oyles, and other
Merchandize: So by the benefit of this light of reason, they have
found out *Artillery,* by which warres come to quicker ends then heretofore, and the great expence of bloud is avoyded: for the numbers of
men slain now, since the invention of Artillery, are much lesse then

before, when the sword was the executioner. Others, by the benefit
of this light have searched and found the secret corners of gaine, and
profit, wheresoever they lie. They have found wherein the weakenesse of another man consisteth, and made their profit of that, by
circumventing him in a bargain: They have found his riotous, and
wastefull inclination, and they have fed and fomented that disorder,
and kept open that leake, to their advantage, and the others ruine.
They have found where was the easiest, and most accessible way, to
sollicite the Chastitie of a woman, whether *Discourse, Musicke,* or
Presents, and according to that discovery, they have pursued *hers,* and
their own eternall destruction. By the benefit of this light, men see
through the darkest, and most impervious places, that are, that is,
Courts of Princes, and the greatest *Officers* in Courts; and can submit
themselves to second, and to advance the humours of men in great
place, and so make their profit of the weaknesses which they have
discovered in these great men. All the wayes, both of *Wisdome,* and
of *Craft* lie open to this light, this light of naturall reason: But when
they have gone all these wayes by the benefit of this light, they have
got no further, then to have walked by a tempestuous Sea, and to have
gathered pebles, and speckled cockle shells. Their light seems to be
great out of the same reason, that a Torch in a misty night, seemeth
greater then in a clear, because it hath kindled and inflamed much
thicke and grosse Ayre round about it. So the light and wisedome of
worldly men, seemeth great, because he hath kindled an admiration,
or an applause in Aiery flatterers, not because it is so in deed.

But, if thou canst take this light of reason that is in thee, this poore
snuffe, that is almost out in thee, thy faint and dimme knowledge of
God, that riseth out of this light of nature, if thou canst in those
embers, those cold ashes, finde out one small coale, and wilt take the
paines to kneell downe, and blow that coale with thy devout *Prayers,*
and light thee a *little candle,* (a *desire* to reade that Booke, which
they call the Scriptures, and the Gospell, and the Word of God;) If
with that little candle thou canst creep humbly into low and poore
places, if thou canst finde thy Saviour in a *Manger,* and in his
swathing clouts, in his humiliation, and blesse God for that beginning, if thou canst finde him flying into Egypt, and finde in thy
selfe a disposition to accompany him in a persecution, in a banish-

ment, if not a bodily banishment, a locall banishment, yet a *reall, a spirituall banishment,* a banishment from those sinnes, and that sinnefull conversation, which thou hast loved more then thy *Parents,* or *Countrey,* or thine owne body, which perchance thou hast consumed, and destroyed with that sinne; if thou canst finde him contenting and containing himselfe at home in his fathers house, and not breaking out, no not about the worke of our salvation, till the due time was come, when it was to be done. And if according to that example, thou canst contain thy selfe in that station and vocation in which God hath planted thee, and not, through a hasty and precipitate *zeale,* breake out to an imaginary, and intempestive, and unseasonable *Reformation,* either in *Civill* or *Ecclesiasticall* businesse, which belong not to thee; if with this little poore light, these *first degrees* of *Knowledge* and *Faith,* thou canst follow him into the *Garden,* and gather up some of the droppes of his precious Bloud and sweat, which he shed for thy soule, if thou canst follow him to *Jerusalem,* and pick up some of those *teares,* which he shed upon that City, and upon thy soule; if thou canst follow him to the place of his scourging, and to his crucifying, and provide thee some of that balme, which must cure thy soule; if after all this, thou canst turne this little light inward, and canst thereby discerne where thy diseases, and thy wounds, and thy corruptions are, and canst apply those teares, and blood and balme to them, (all this is, That if thou attend the light of naturall reason, and cherish that, and exalt that, so that that bring thee to a *love of the Scriptures,* and that *love to a beleefe* of the truth thereof, and that *historicall faith* to a *faith of application, of appropriation,* that as all those things were certainly done, so they were certainly done *for thee*) thou shalt never envy the lustre and glory of the great lights of worldly men, which are great by the infirmity of others, or by their own opinion, great because others think them great, or because they think themselves so, but thou shalt finde, that howsoever they magnifie their lights, their wit, their learning, their industry, their fortune, their favour, and *sacrifice to their owne nets,* yet thou shalt see, that thou by thy small light hast gathered *Pearle* and *Amber,* and they by their great lights nothing but shels and pebles; they have determined the light of nature, upon the booke of nature, this world, and thou hast carried the light of nature higher, thy naturall reason, and even *humane arguments,* have brought thee to reade the Scriptures, and to that *love,* God hath set to the seale of *faith.* Their light shall set at noone; even in their heighth, some heavy crosse shall cast a damp upon their soule, and cut off all their succours, and devest them of all comforts, and thy light shall grow up, from a *faire hope,* to a modest assurance and *infallibility,* that that light shall never go out, nor the *works of darknesse,* nor the *Prince of darknesse* ever prevaile upon thee, but as thy light of *reason* is exalted by *faith* here, so thy light of *faith* shall be exalted into the light of *glory,* and fruition in the Kingdome of heaven. Before the sunne was made, there was *a light* which did that office of distinguishing night and day; but when the sunne was created, that did all the offices of the former light, and more. *Reason* is that first, and primogeniall light, and goes no farther in a naturall man; but in a man regenerate by faith, that light does all that reason did, *and more;* and all his *Morall,* and *Civill,* and *Domestique,* and indifferent actions, (though they be never done *without Reason*) yet their principall scope, and marke is the glory of God, and though they seeme but *Morall,* or *Civill,* or *domestique,* yet they have a deeper tincture, a heavenly nature, a relation *to God,* in them.

The light in our Text then, is *essentially* and *personally Christ* himself, from *him* flowes the *supernaturall light* of *faith* and *grace,* here also intended; and because this light of *faith,* and *grace* flowing from that fountaine of light Christ Jesus, works upon the light of *nature,* and *reason,* it may conduce to the raising of your devotions, if we do (without any long insisting upon the severall parts thereof) present to you some of those many and divers lights, which are in this world, and admit an application to this light in our Text, the *essentiall* light, *Christ Jesus;* and the *supernaturall* light, *faith* and *grace.*

Of these lights we shall consider some few couples; and the first payre, *Lux Essentiæ,* and *Lux Gloriæ,* the light of the *Essence of God,* and the light of the *glory of his Saints.* And though the first of these, be that essentiall light, by which we shall *see God face to face, as he is,* and the effluence and emanation of beams, from the face of God, which make that place *Heaven,* of which light it is said, *That God who onely hath Immortality, dwels in luce inaccessibili,* in the light that none can attaine to, yet by the light of faith, and grace in

Lux
Essentiæ

[1 Cor.
13.12;
1 John 3.2]
1 Tim. 6.16

sanctification, we may come to such a *participation* of that light of Essence, or such a *reflection* of it in this world, that it shall be true of us, which was said of those Ephesians, *You were once darknesse, but now are light in the Lord;* he does not say *enlightned,* nor *lightsome,* but *light* it self, light *essentially,* for *our conversation is in heaven;* And as God sayes of *Jerusalem,* and his blessings here in this world, *Calceavi te Ianthino, I have shod thee, with Badgers skinne,* (some *translate* it) (which the Antients take for some *precious* stuffe) that is, I have enabled thee to tread upon all the most estimable things of this world, (for as the Church it self is presented, so every true member of the Church is endowed, *Luna sub pedibus,* the Moone, and all under the Moone is under our feet, we tread upon this world, even when we are trodden upon in it) so the *precious promises of Christ, make us partakers of the Divine Nature,* and the light of faith, makes us the same *Spirit with the Lord;* And this is our participation of the light of essence, in this life. The next is the light of glory.

This is that *Glorification* which we shall have at the last day, of which glory, we consider a great part to be in that *Denudation,* that manifestation of all to all; as, in this world, a great part of our inglorious servitude is in those disguises, and palliations, those colours, and pretences of *publique good,* with which men of power and authority apparell their oppressions of the poore; In this are we the more miserable, that we cannot see *their ends,* that there is none of this denudation, this laying open of our selves to one another, which shall accompany that state of glory, where we shall see one anothers *bodies,* and *soules, actions* and *thoughts.* And therefore, as if this place were now that Tribunall of Christ Jesus, and this that day of Judgement, and denudation, we must be here, as we shall be there, content to stand *naked* before him; content that there be a discovery, a revealing, a manifestation of all our sinnes, wrought upon us, at least to our owne *consciences,* though not to the congregation; If we will have glory, we must have this *denudation.* We must not be glad, when our sins scape the *Preacher.* We must not say, (as though there were a comfort in that) though he have hit such a mans *Adultery,* and anothers *Ambition,* and anothers *extortion,* yet, for all his diligence, he hath missed *my sinne;* for, if thou wouldest faine have it mist, thou wouldest faine hold it still. And then, why camest thou

Marginal notes:
5.8
Phil. 3.20
Ezek. 16.10
Apo. 12.1
2 Pet. 1.4
1 Cor. 6.17
Lux Gloriæ

hither? What camest thou for to *Church,* or to the *Sacrament?* Why doest thou delude God, with this *complementall visit,* to come to his house, if thou bring not with thee, a disposition to his honour, and his service? Camest thou onely to try whether God *knew* thy sinne, and could tell thee of it, by the Preacher? Alas, he knowes it infal- libly; And, if he take no knowledge of his knowing it, to thy *con- science,* by the words of the Preacher, thy state is the more desperate. God sends us to preach *forgivenesse of sinnes;* where wee finde no sinne, we have no Commission to execute; How shall we finde your sinnes? In the old sacrifices of the law, the Priest did not fetch the sacrifice from the herd, but he received it from him that brought it, and so sacrificed it for him. Doe thou therefore prevent the Preacher; Accuse thyselfe before he accuse thee; offer up thy sinne thy selfe; Bring it to the top of thy memory, and thy conscience, that he finding it there, may sacrifice it for thee; Tune the instrument, and it is the fitter for his hand. Remember thou thine own sins, first, and then every word that fals from the preachers lips shall be a drop of the *dew of heaven,* a dram of the *balme of Gilead,* a portion of the bloud of thy Saviour, to wash away that sinne, so presented by thee to be so sacrified by him; for, if thou onely of all the congregation finde that the preacher hath not touched *thee,* nor hit *thy sinnes,* know then, that thou wast not in his Commission for the *Remission* of sinnes, and be afraid, that thy conscience is either *gangrend,* and unsensible of all incisions, and *cauterizations,* that can be made by denouncing the *Judgements* of God, (which is as far as the preacher can goe) or that thy whole constitution, thy complexion, thy com- position is sinne; the preacher cannot hit thy particular sinne, be- cause thy whole life, and the whole body of thy actions is one con- tinuall sin. As long as a man is alive, if there appeare any offence in his breath, the physician will assigne it to some *one* corrupt *place,* his *lungs,* or *teeth,* or *stomach,* and thereupon apply convenient remedy thereunto. But if he be dead, and putrefied, no man askes *from whence that ill aire and offence comes,* because it proceeds from thy whole carcasse. So, as long as there is in you a *sense* of your sinnes, as long as we can touch the offended and wounded part, and be felt by you, you are not desperate, though you be froward, and impatient of our increpations. But when you *feele nothing,* whatsoever wee

[Gen. 27.28; Jer. 8.22]

say, your soule is in an *Hectique fever,* where the distemper is not in any one humor, but in the whole substance; nay, your soule it selfe is become a carcasse. This then is our first couple of these lights, by our *Conversation in heaven* here, (that is, a watchfulnesse, that we fall not into sinne) we have *lucem essentiæ,* possession and fruition of heaven, and of the light of Gods presence; and then, if we doe, by infirmity, fall into sinne, yet, by this *denudation* of our soules, this manifestation of our sinnes to God by *confession,* and to that purpose, a gladnesse when we heare our sinnes spoken of by the preacher, we have *lumen gloriæ,* an inchoation of our glorified estate; and then, an other couple of these lights, which we propose to be considered, is *lumen fidei,* and *lumen naturæ,* the light of *faith,* and the light of *nature.*

Lux fidei   Of these two lights, *Faith* and *Grace,* first, and then *Nature* and *Reason,* we said something before, but never too much, because contentious spirits have cast such clouds upon both these lights, that some have said, *Nature* doth *all* alone, and others, that Nature hath *nothing* to do at all, but all is *Grace:* we decline wranglings, that tend not to edification, we say onely to our present purpose, (which is the operation of these severall couples of lights) that by this light of *Faith,* to him which hath it, all that is involved in *Prophecies,* is clear, and evident, as in a History already done; and all that is wrapped up in *promises,* is his own already in *performance.* That man needs not goe so high, for his assurance of a *Messias* and *Redeemer,* as to the first

Gen. 3.15   promise made to him in *Adam,* nor for the limitation of the stock and race from whence this *Messias* should come: so far as to the renewing

12.3   of this promise in *Abraham:* nor for the description of this *Messias*
Esay 7.14   who he should be, and of whom he should be born, as to *Esaias;* nor
Mich. 5.2   to *Micheas,* for the *place;* nor for the *time* when he should accom-
Dan. 9.24   plish all this, so far as to *Daniel;* no, nor so far, as to the *Evangelists* themselves, for the History and the evidence, that all this that was to be done in his behalf by the *Messias,* was done 1600. yeares since. But he hath a whole *Bible,* and an abundant Library in his own heart, and there by this light of *Faith,* (which is not onely a knowing, but an applying, an *appropriating* of all to thy benefit) he hath a better knowledge then all this, then either *Propheticall,* or *Evangelicall;* for though both these be irrefragable, and infallible proofs of a Mes-

sias, (the Propheticall, that he *should*, the Evangelicall, that he *is*
come) yet both these might but concern others: this light of Faith
brings him home *to thee*. How sure so ever I be, that the *world* shall
never perish by *water*, yet *I may* be drowned; and how sure so ever
that the *Lamb of God hath taken away the sinnes of the world*, I may
perish, without I have this *applicatory Faith*. And as he needs not
looke back to *Esay*, nor *Abraham*, nor *Adam*, for the Messias, so
neither needs he to looke forward. He needs not stay in expectation
of the *Angels Trumpets*, to awaken the dead; he is not put to his
usquequo Domine, How long, Lord, wilt thou defer our restitution?
but he hath already *died the death of the righteous;* which is, to die
to sinne; He hath already had his *buriall*, by being *buried with Christ
in Baptisme*, he hath had his *Resurrection* from sinne, his *Ascension*
to holy purposes of amendment of life, and his *Judgement*, that is,
peace of Conscience, sealed unto him, and so by this light of applying
Faith, he hath already apprehended an eternall possession of Gods
eternall Kingdome. And the other light in this second couple is *Lux
naturæ*, the light of Nature.

    This, though a fainter light, directs us to the other, *Nature to Faith:*
and as by the quantitie in the light of the *Moone*, we know the position and distance of the *Sunne*, how far, or how neare the Sunne is
to her, so by the working of the light of *Nature* in us, we may discern, (by the measure and virtue and heat of that) how near to the
other greater light, the light of *Faith*, we stand. If we finde our *naturall faculties rectified*, so as that that *free will* which we have in
Morall and *Civill* actions, be bent upon the *externall duties of Religion*, (as every naturall man may, out of the use of that *free will,
come to Church, heare the Word preached, and believe it to be true*)
we may be sure, the other greater light is about us. If we be *cold* in
them, in actuating, in exalting, in using our *naturall faculties* so farre,
we shall be deprived of all light; we shall not see the *Invisible* God,
in *visible things*, which Saint *Paul* makes so *inexcusable*, so unpar-
donable a thing, we shall not see the hand of God in all our *worldly
crosses*, nor the seal of God in all our *worldly blessings*; we shall not
see the face of God in his House, his presence here in the *Church*, nor
the mind of God in his *Gospell*, that his gracious purposes upon mankinde, extend so particularly, or reach so far, as to include us. I shall

[Joh. 1.29]

[Rev. 6.10]
[Num.
23.10]
[Col. 2.12]

Lux Naturæ

Rom. 1.20

heare in the Scripture his *Venite omnes, come all,* and yet I shall
thinke that his eye was not upon me, that his eye did not becken me
and I shall heare the *Deus vult omnes salvos, that God would save
all,* and yet I shall finde some perverse reason in my selfe, why it is
not likely that God will save *me.* I am commanded *scrutari Scripturas, to search the scriptures;* now, that is not to be able to *repeat* any
history of the Bible without booke, it is not to *ruffle* a Bible, and
upon any word to turne to the Chapter, and to the verse; but this is
exquisita scrutatio, the true searching of the Scriptures, to finde all
the *histories* to be *examples* to me, all the *prophecies* to induce a
Saviour for *me,* all the *Gospell* to apply Christ Jesus to *me.* Turne
over all the folds, and plaits of thine owne heart, and finde there the
infirmities, and waverings of thine *owne faith,* and an ability to say,
Lord, I beleeve, help mine unbeleefe, and then, though thou have no
Bible in thy hand, or though thou stand in a dark corner, nay though
thou canst not read a letter, thou hast searched that Scripture, thou
hast turned to *Marke 9. ver. 24.* Turne thine eare to God, and heare
him turning to thee, and saying to thy soule, *I will marry thee to my
selfe for ever;* and thou hast searched that Scripture, and turned to
Hos. 2. ver. 19. Turne to thine owne *history,* thine *owne life,* and if
thou canst reade there, that thou hast endeavoured to turne thine
ignorance into *knowledge,* and thy knowledge into *Practice,* if thou
finde thy selfe to be an example of that rule of Christs, *If you know
these things, blessed are you, if you do them,* then thou hast searched
that Scripture, and turned to *Jo. 13. ver. 17.* This is *Scrutari Scripturas,
to search the Scriptures,* not as though thou wouldest make a *con-
cordance,* but an *application;* as thou wouldest search a *wardrobe,*
not to make an *Inventory* of it, but to finde in it something fit for
thy wearing. *John Baptist was not the light,* he was not Christ, *but
he bore witnesse of him.* The light of *faith,* in the highest exaltation
that can be had, in the *Elect,* here, is not that very *beatificall vision,*
which we shall have in heaven, but it beares witnesse of that light.
The light of *nature,* in the highest exaltation is not *faith,* but it *beares
witnesse* of it. The lights of *faith,* and of *nature,* are subordinate *John
Baptists: faith* beares me witnesse, that I have *Christ,* and the light of
nature, that is, the *exalting of my naturall faculties* towards *religious
uses,* beares me witnesse that I have *faith.* Onely that man, whose

conscience testifies to himself, and whose *actions* testifie to the world, that he *does* what he *can,* can beleeve himself, or be beleeved by others, that he hath the true light of faith.

And therefore, as the Apostle saith, *Quench not the Spirit,* I say too, *Quench not the light of Nature,* suffer not *that* light to goe out; study your *naturall faculties;* husband and improve them, and love the *outward acts of Religion,* though an *Hypocrite,* and though a naturall man may doe them. Certainly he that loves not the *Militant Church,* hath but a faint faith in his interest in the *Triumphant.* He that cares not though the *materiall Church* fall, I am afraid is falling from the *spirituall.* For, can a man be sure to have his *money,* or his *plate,* if his *house* be burnt? or to preserve his *faith,* if the *outward exercises* of Religion faile? He that undervalues *outward things,* in the religious service of God, though he begin at *ceremoniall* and *rituall* things, will come quickly to call *Sacraments* but outward things, and *Sermons,* and *publique prayers,* but outward things, in contempt. As some *Platonique* Philosophers, did so over-refine Religion, and devotion, as to say, that nothing but the *first thoughts* and *ebullitions* of a devout heart, were fit to serve God in. If it came to any *outward action* of the body, *kneeling,* or lifting up of *hands,* if it came to be but invested in our *words,* and so made a *Prayer,* nay if it passed but a revolving, a turning in our inward thoughts, and thereby were mingled with our *affections,* though *pious affections,* yet, say they, it is not pure enough for a service to God; nothing but the *first motions* of the heart is for him. Beloved, outward things apparell God; and since God was content to take *a body,* let not us leave him naked, nor ragged; but, as you will bestow not onely some *cost,* but some *thoughts,* some *study,* how you will clothe your *children,* and how you will clothe your *servants,* so bestow both cost and thoughts, thinke seriously, execute cheerfully in outward declarations, that which becomes the dignity of him, who evacuated himselfe for you. The *zeale of his house* needs not *eat you up,* no nor eat you out of house and home; God asks not *that* at your hands. But, if you eat *one dish the lesse* at your feasts for his house sake, if you spare somewhat for his reliefe, and his glory, you will not be the leaner, nor the weaker, for that abstinence. *John Baptist* bore witnesse of the light, *outward things* beare witnesse of your faith, the exalting of our *nat-*

1 Thes. 5.19

[Psa. 69.9;
Joh. 2.17]

urall faculties beare witnesse of the supernaturall. We do not compare the master and the servant, and yet we thank that servant that brings us to his master. We make a great difference between the *treasure* in the chest, and the *key* that opens it, yet we are glad to have that key in our hands. The *bell* that cals me to *Church,* does not catechise me, nor preach to me, yet I observe the sound of that bell, because it brings me to *him* that does those offices to me. The light of *nature* is far from being enough; but, as a *candle* may kindle a *torch,* so into the faculties of nature, well imployed, God infuses *faith.* And this is our second couple of lights, the subordination of the light of *nature,* and the light of *faith.* And a third payre of lights of *attestation,* that beare witnesse to the light of our Text, is *Lux æternorum Corporum,* that light which the *Sunne* and *Moone,* and those glorious bodies give from heaven, and *lux incensionum,* that light, which those things, that are naturally combustible, and apt to take fire, doe give upon earth; both these beare witnesse of this light, that is, admit an application to it. *For,* in the first of these, the glorious lights of heaven, we must take nothing for *stars,* that are *not stars;* nor make Astrological and fixed conclusions out of *meteors,* that are but transitory; they may be *Comets,* and *blazing starres,* and so portend much mischiefe, but they are none of those *æterna corpora,* they are not fixed stars, not stars of heaven. So is it also in the *Christian Church,* (which is the proper spheare in which the light of our text, *That light* the *essentiall light* Christ Jesus moves by that supernaturall light of *faith* and *grace,* which is truly the *Intelligence* of that spheare, the Christian Church) As in the heavens the stars were created at once, with one *Fiat,* and then being so made, stars doe not beget new stars, so the *Christian doctrine necessary* to salvation, was delivered at once, that is, intirely in one spheare, in the body of the Scriptures. And then, as stars doe not beget stars, Articles of faith doe not beget Articles of faith; so, as that the *Councell of Trent* should be brought to bed of *a new Creed,* not conceived before by the *holy Ghost* in the Scriptures, and, (which is a monstrous birth) the child greater then the Father, as soon as it is borne, the new Creed of the *Councell of Trent* to containe more Articles, then the old Creed of the Apostles did. Saint *Jude* writing of the *common salvation,* (as he calls it) (for, Saint *Jude,* it seems, knew no such *particular salvation,* as that it was

impossible for *any man* to have, salvation is *common salvation*) ex-
horts them to *contend earnestly for that faith, which was once delivered unto the Saints. Semel, once;* that is, *at once, semel, simul,
once altogether.* For this is also *Tertullians* note; that the rule of faith   Tertull.
is, that it be *una, immobilis, irreformabilis;* it must not be *deformed,*
it cannot be *Reformed;* it must not be mard, it cannot be mended;
whatsoever needs mending, and *reformation,* cannot be the rule of
faith, says *Tertullian. Other foundation can no man lay then Christ;*   1 Cor. 3.11
not onely no *better,* but no *other;* what other things soever are added
by men, enter not into the nature and condition of a foundation. The
additions, and traditions, and superedifications of the Roman Church,
they are not *lux æternorum corporum,* they are not fixed bodies, they
are not stars to direct us; they may be *meteors,* and so exercise our discourse, and Argumentation, they may raise controversies; And they
may be *Comets,* and so exercise our feares, and our jealousies, they
may raise *rebellions* and *Treasons,* but they are not fixed and glorious
bodies of heaven, they are not *stars.* Their *non-communions,* (for,
communions where there are no communicants, are no communions)
when they admit no bread at all, no wine at all, all is *transubstan-
tiated,* are no communions; their *semi-communions,* when they admit
the *bread* to be given, but *not the wine;* their *sesqui-communions,*
Bread and Wine to the taste, and to all other trialls of bread and
wine, and yet that bread and wine, the very body, and the very bloud
of Christ; their *quotidian miracles,* which destroy and contradict even
the nature of the miracle, to make miracles ordinary, and fixed, constant and certain; (for, as that is not a miracle which nature does, so
that's not a miracle which man can doe certainly, constantly, infallibly every day, and every day, every Priest can miraculously change
bread into the body of Christ, and besides they have certaine fixed
shops, and *Marts of miracles,* in one place a shop of miracles for
barrennesse, in another, a shop for the *tooth-ache*) To contract this,
their *occasionall Divinity,* doctrines to serve present occasions, that in
eighty eight, an Hereticall Prince must necessarily be excommunicated, and an Hereticall Prince excommunicated must necessarily
be deposed, but at another time it may be otherwise, and *conveniencies,* and *dispensations* may be admitted, these, and such as these,
traditionall, occasionall, Almanack Divinity, they may bee *Comets,*

they may be *Meteors,* they may raine bloud, and raine fire, and raine
hailestones, *hailstones as big as Talents,* (as it is in the Revelation)
milstones, to grinde the world by their oppressions, but they are not
lux æternorum corporum, the light of the stars and other heavenly
bodies, for, they were made *at once,* and diminish not, encrease not.
Fundamentall articles of faith, are always the same. And that's our
application of this *lux æternorum corporum,* the light of those heavenly bodies, to the light of our Text, Christ working in the Church.

Now, for the consideration of the other light in this third couple,
which is *lux incensionum,* the light of things, which take, and give
light here upon earth, if we reduce it to application and practise, and
contract it to one Instance, it will appeare that the *devotion* and *zeale*
of him, that is best affected, is, for the most part, in the disposition of
a *torch,* or a *knife,* ordained to take *fire,* and to give *light.* If it have
never been *lightned,* it does not easily take light, but it must be
bruised, and *beaten* first; if it have been lighted and put out, though
it cannot take fire *of it self,* yet it does easily conceive fire, if it be
presented within any convenient distance. Such also is the soule of
man towards the fires of the *zeale* of Gods glory, and *compassion* of
others misery. If there be any that *never* tooke this fire, that was never
affected with either of these, the glory of God, the miseries of other
men, can I hope to kindle him? It must be Gods worke to *bruise* and
beat him, with his rod of affliction, before he will take fire. *Paulus
revelatione compulsus ad fidem,* St. *Paul* was compelled to believe;
not the light which he saw, but the power which he felt wrought
upon him; not because that light shined from heaven, but because it
strooke him to the earth. *Agnoscimus Christum in Paulo prius co-
gentem, deinde docentem;* Christ begun not upon St. *Paul,* with
a catechisme, but with *a rod.* If therefore here be any in *Pauls* case,
that were never kindled before, Almighty God proceed the same way
with *them,* and come so neare to a friendship towards them, as to be
at enmity with them; to be so mercifull to them, as to seeme unmerci-
full; to be so well pleased, as to seeme angry; that so by inflicting
his *medicinall afflictions,* he may give them comfort by discomfort,
and life by death, and make them seeke his face, by turning his face
from them; and not to suffer them to continue in a stupid *inconsideration,* and lamentable *senslesnesse* of their miserable condition, but

[Rev. 16.21]

*Lux incen-
sionum*

Hierom.

August.

bruise and *breake* them with his rod, that they may take fire. But for you, who have taken this fire before, that have been enlightned in both *Sacraments*, and in the *preaching* of the word; in the *meanes*, and in some measure of *practise* of *holinesse* heretofore, if in not supplying *oyle* to your Lamps, which God by his ordinance had kindled in you, you have let this light go out by negligence or inconsideration, or that storms of *worldly calamities* have blowne it out, do but now at this instant call to minde, *what* sin of *yesterday*, or t'other day, or long ago, begun, and practised, and prevailed upon you, or *what future sinne*, what purpose of doing a sinne to night, or to morrow, possesses you; do but thinke seriously *what sinne*, or *what crosse* hath blown out that light, that grace, which was formerly in you, before that sinne, or that crosse invaded you, and turne your soul, which hath been enlightned before, towards this fire which Gods Spirit blowes this minute, and you will conceive new fire, new zeale, new compassion. As this *Lux incensionum*, kindles easily, when it hath been kindled before, so the soule accustomed to the presence of God in *holy meditations*, though it fall asleep in some darke corner, in some *sinne of infirmity*, a while, yet, upon every holy occasion, it takes fire againe, and the meanest *Preacher* in the Church, shall worke more upon him, then the *foure Doctors* of the Church should be able to do, upon a person who had never been enlightned before, that is, never accustomed to the presence of God in his *private meditations*, or in his *outward acts* of Religion. And this is our third couple of lights, that *beares witnesse*, that is, admit an application to the light of our Text; and then the fourth and last couple, which we consider, is *Lux Depuratarum Mixtionum*, the light and lustre of *precious stones*, and then *Lux Repercussionum*, the light of *Repercussion*, and *Reflexion*, when one body, though it have no light in it self, casts light upon other bodies.

In the application of the first of these lights, *Depuratarum Mixtionum, precious stones*, we shall onely apply their *making* and their *value*. Precious stones are first *drops of the dew* of heaven, and then refined by the sunne of heaven. When by long lying they have exhal'd, and evaporated, and breathed out all their grosse matter, and received another concoction from the sunne, then they become precious in the eye, and estimation of men: so those *actions* of ours, that shall be precious or acceptable in the eye of God, must at first have been conceived from *heaven,* from the *word* of God, and then receive *another concoction,* by a holy *deliberation,* before we bring those actions to *execution,* lest we may have mistaken the roote thereof. Actions precious, or acceptable in Gods eye, must be *holy purposes* in their beginning, and then *done in season;* the *Dove* must lay the *egge,* and hatch the *bird;* the *holy Ghost* must infuse the purpose, and *sit* upon it, and *overshadow* it, and mature and ripen it, if it shall be precious in Gods eye. The *reformation of abuses* in *State* or *Church,* is a holy purpose, there is that drop of the dew of heaven in it; but if it be *unseasonably attempted,* and have not a farther concoction, then the *first motions of our owne zeale,* it becomes ineffectuall. Stones precious in the estimation of men, begin with the *dew of Heaven,* and proceed with the *sunne of Heaven;* Actions precious in the acceptation of God, are purposes conceived by his Spirit, and executed in his time *to his Glory,* not conceived out of *Ambition,* nor executed out of *sedition.* And this is the application of this *Lux depuratarum mixtionum,* of precious stones, out of their *making;* we proposed another out of their *valuation,* which is this, That whereas a Pearle or Diamond of such a bignesse, of so many *Carats,* is so much worth, one that is twice as big, is ten times as much worth. So, though God vouchsafe to value every good work thou dost, yet as they grow greater he shall multiply his estimation of them infinitely; When he hath prized at a high rate, the *chastitie* and *continency* of thy *youth,* if thou adde to this, a *moderation* in thy *middle age,* from *Ambition,* and in thy latter age from *covetousnesse* and *indevotion,* there shall be no price in Gods treasure (not the last drop of the blood of his Sonne) too deare for thee, no roome, no state in his Kingdome (not a *Jointenancie* with his onely Sonne) too glorious for thee. This is one light in this Couple; The lustre of precious stones: the other the last is *Lux Repercussionum,* The light of Repercussion, of Reflexion.

Lux Repercussionum

This is, when Gods light cast upon us, reflecteth upon *other men too,* from us; when God doth not onely accept our works for *our selves,* but imployes those works of ours upon *other* men. And here is a true, and a Divine *Supererogation;* which the *Devill,* (as he doth all *Gods Actions,* which fall into his compasse) did mischievously

counterfeit in the *Romane Church*, when he induced their Doctrine
of *Supererogation*, that a man might do so much more then he was
bound to do *for God*, as that *that superplusage* might *save* whom he
would; and that if he did not direct them in his intention, upon any
particular person, the *Bishop of Rome*, was generall *Administrator*
to all men, and might bestow them where he would. But here is a
true supererogation; not from *Man*, or *his Merit*, but *from God;*
when our good works shall not onely profit *us*, that *do* them, but
others that *see them* done; and when we by this light of *Repercus-*
sion, of *Reflexion*, shall be made *specula divinæ gloriæ, quæ accipiunt*   Tertull.
& reddunt, such looking glasses as *receive* Gods face upon our selves,
and *cast it upon others by a holy life*, and *exemplary conversation.*

    To end all, we have no *warmth* in *our selves;* it is true, but Christ   Conclusi
came even in the *winter:* we have *no light* in our selves; it is true,
but he came even in the *night*. And now, I appeall to your own *Con-*
sciences, and I aske you all, (not as a *Judge*, but as an *Assistant* to
your Consciences, and *Amicus Curiæ*,) whether any man have made
as good use of this light, as he might have done. Is there any man that
in the compassing of his *sinne*, hath not met this light by the way,
Thou shouldest not do this? Any man, that hath not onely as *Balaam*   Numb.
did, met this light as an *Angell*, (that is, met *Heavenly inspirations*   22.22
to avert him,) but that hath not *heard* as *Balaam* did, *his own Asse;*
that is, those reasons that use to carry him, or those very *worldly*
respects that use to carry him, dispute against that sinne, and tell him,
not onely that there is more *soule* and more *heaven*, and more *salva-*
tion, but more *body*, and more *health*, more *honour*, and more *repu-*
tation, more *cost*, and more *money*, more *labour*, and more *danger*
spent upon such a sinne, then would have carried him the right way?

    They that sleep, sleep in the night, and they that are drunke, are   *Recapitu-*
drunke in the night. But to you the *Day starre*, the *Sunne of Right-*   *latio*
eousnesse, the Sonne of God is risen this day. The day is but a little   1 Thes. 5.7
longer now, then at *shortest;* but a *little* it is. Be a little better now,
then when you came, and mend a little at every coming, and in lesse
then seaven *yeares apprentissage*, which your occupations cost you,
you shall learn, not the Mysteries of your *twelve Companies*, but the
Mysteries of the *twelve Tribes*, of the *twelve Apostles*, of their *twelve*
Articles, whatsoever belongeth to the *promise*, to the performance,

to the *Imitation* of Christ Jesus. He, who is *Lux una,* light and *light alone,* and *Lux tota,* light and *all light,* shall also, by that light, which he sheddeth from himselfe upon all his, the light *of Grace,* give you all these Attestations, all these witnesses of that his light; he shall

Essentiæ

give you *Lucem essentiæ,* (really, and essentially to be incorporated into him, to be made partakers of the Divine Nature, and the same Spirit with the Lord, by a Conversation in Heaven, here) and *lucem*

Gloriæ

gloriæ, (a gladnesse to give him glory in a *denudation* of your souls, and your sinnes, by humble *confession* to him, and a gladnesse to receive a denudation and manifestation of your selves to your selves, by his messenger, in his *medicinall* and *musicall increpations,* and a gladnesse to receive an inchoation of future glory, in the remission

Fidei

of those sinnes.) He shall give you *lucem fidei,* (faithfull and unremovable possession of future things, in the present, and make your

Naturæ

hereafter, now, in the fruition of God.) And *Lucem naturæ* (a love of the *outward beauty* of his house, and *outward testimonies* of this love, in inclining your *naturall faculties* to religious duties.) He shall

Æternorum Corporum

give you *Lucem æternorum Corporum,* (a love to walk in the light of the stars of heaven, that never change, a love so perfect in the *fundamentall articles* of Religion, without impertinent additions.)

Incensionum Depuratarum Mixtionum

And *Lucem incensionum,* (an aptnesse to take holy fire, by what *hand,* or *tongue,* or *pen* soever it be presented unto you, according to Gods Ordinance, though that light have formerly been suffered to go out in you.) He shall give you *Lucem depuratarum Mixtionum,* (the lustre of precious stones, made of the dew of heaven, and by the heat of heaven, that is, *actions* intended at first, and produced at last, *for his glory;* and every day multiply their value, in the sight of God, because thou shalt every day grow up from grace to grace.) And

Repercussionum

Lucem Repercussionum, (he shall make you able to reflect and cast this light upon others, to his glory, and their establishment.)

Lighten our darknesse, we beseech thee, O Lord, with all these lights; that in thy light we may see light; that in this Essentiall *light, which is Christ, and in this* Supernaturall *light, which is* grace, *we may see all these, and all other beames of light, which may bring us to thee, and* him, *and that blessed Spirit which proceeds from both. Amen.*

Number 7.

*Preached at White-hall, the first
Friday in Lent.* [*1622/3*]

JOHN 11.35. *IESUS WEPT.*

I AM NOW but upon the Compassion of Christ. There is much difference betweene his Compassion and his Passion, as much as between the men that are to handle them here. But *Lacryma passionis Christi est vicaria:* A great personage may speake of his Passion, of his blood; My vicarage is to speake of his Compassion and his teares. Let me chafe the wax, and melt your soules in a bath of his Teares now, Let him set to the great Seale of his effectuall passion, in his blood, then. It is a Common place I know to speake of teares: I would you knew as well, it were a common practise, to shed them. Though it be not so, yet bring S. *Bernards* patience, *Libenter audiam, qui non sibi plausum, sed mihi planctum moveat;* be willing to heare him, that seeks not your acclamation to himselfe, but your humiliation to his and your God; not to make you praise with them that praise, but to make you weepe with them that weepe, *And Iesus wept.*

The Masorites (the Masorites are the Critiques upon the Hebrew Bible, the Old Testament) cannot tell us, who divided the Chapters of the Old Testament into verses; Neither can any other tell us, who did it in the New Testament. Whoever did it seemes to have stopped in an amazement in this Text, and by making an intire verse of these two words, *Iesus wept,* and no more, to intimate that there needs no more for the exalting of our devotion to a competent heighth, then to consider, how, and where, and when, and why *Iesus wept.* There

August.

1 Thes.
5.16

is not a shorter verse in the Bible, nor a larger Text. There is another as short; *Semper gaudete, Rejoyce evermore,* and of that holy Joy, I may have leave to speake here hereafter, more seasonably, in a more Festivall time, by my ordinary service. This is the season of generall Compunction, of generall Mortification, and no man priviledged, for *Iesus wept.*

Divisio

In that Letter which *Lentulus* is said to have written to the Senate of Rome, in which he gives some Characters of Christ, he saies, That Christ was never seene to laugh, but to weepe often. Now in what number he limits his *often*, or upon what testimony he grounds his number, we know not. We take knowledge that he wept thrice. Hee wept here, when he mourned with them that mourned for *Lazarus;* He wept againe, when he drew neare to Jerusalem, and looked upon that City; And he wept a third time in his Passion. There is but one Euangelist, but this, S. *Iohn,* that tells us of these first teares, the rest say nothing of them; There is but one Euangelist, S. *Luke,* that tells us of his second teares, the rest speake not of those; There is no Euangelist, but there is an Apostle that tells us of his third teares, S. *Paul* saies, *That in the daies of his flesh, he offered up prayers with strong cries, and teares;* And those teares, Expositors of all sides referre to his Passion, though some to his Agony in the Garden, some to his Passion on the Crosse; and these in my opinion most fitly; because those words of S. *Paul* belong to the declaration of the Priesthood, and of the Sacrifice of Christ; and for that function of his, the Crosse was the Altar; and therefore to the Crosse we fixe those third teares. The first were Humane teares, the second were Propheticall, the third were Pontificall, appertaining to the Sacrifice. The first were shed in a Condolency of a humane and naturall calamity fallen upon one family; *Lazarus* was dead: The second were shed in Contemplation of future calamities upon a Nation; Jerusalem was to be destroyed: The third, in Contemplation of sin, and the everlasting punishments due to sin, and to such sinners, as would make no benefit of that Sacrifice, which he offered in offering himselfe. His friend was dead, and then Jesus wept; He justified naturall affections and such offices of piety: Jerusalem was to be destroyed, and then Jesus wept; He commiserated publique and nationall calamities, though a private person: His very giving of himselfe for sin, was to

Luke 19.41

Heb. 5.7

become to a great many ineffectuall; and then Jesus wept; He declared how indelible the naturall staine of sin is, that not such sweat as his, such teares, such blood as his could absolutely wash it out of mans nature. The teares of the text are as a Spring, a Well, belonging to one houshold, the Sisters of *Lazarus:* The teares over Jerusalem, are as a River belonging to a whole Country: The teares upon the Crosse, are as the Sea belonging to all the world; and though literally there fall no more into our text, then the Spring, yet because the Spring flowes into the River, and the River into the Sea, and that wheresoever we find that Jesus wept, we find our Text, (for our Text is but that, *Iesus wept*) therefore by the leave and light of his blessed Spirit, we shall looke upon those lovely, those heavenly eyes, through this glasse of his owne teares, in all these three lines, as he wept here over *Lazarus,* as he wept there over Jerusalem, as he wept upon the Crosse over all us. For so often Jesus wept.

First then, Jesus wept *Humanitus,* he tooke a necessary occasion to shew that he was true Man. He was now in hand with the greatest Miracle that ever he did, the raising of *Lazarus,* so long dead. Could we but do so in our spirituall raising, what a blessed harvest were that? What a comfort to finde one man here to day, raised from his spirituall death, this day twelve-month? Christ did it every yeare, and every yeare he improved his Miracle. In the first yeare, he raised the Governours Daughter: she was newly dead, and as yet in the house. In the beginning of sin, and whilst in the house, in the house of God, in the Church, in a glad obedience to Gods Ordinances and Institutions there, for the reparation and resuscitation of dead soules, the worke is not so hard. In his second yeare, Christ raised the Widows Son; and him he found without, ready to be buried. In a man growne cold and stiffe in sin, impenetrable, inflexible by denouncing the Judgements of God, almost buried in a stupidity, and insensiblenesse of his being dead, there is more difficultie. But in his third yeare, Christ raised this *Lazarus;* he had been long dead, and buried, and in probability, putrified after foure daies.

This Miracle Christ meant to make a pregnant proofe of the Resurrection, which was his principall intention therein. For, the greatest arguments against the Resurrection, being for the most part of this kinde, when a Fish eates a man, and another man eates that fish, or

1 Part
Humanitus

Mat. 9.25

Luke 7.15

when one man eates another, how shall both these men rise again?
When a body is resolv'd in the grave to the first principles, or is passed
into other substances, the case is somewhat neere the same; and therefore Christ would worke upon a body neare that state, a body putrified. And truly, in our spirituall raising of the dead, to raise a sinner
putrified in his owne earth, resolv'd in his owne dung, especially that
hath passed many transformations, from shape to shape, from sin to
sin, (he hath beene a Salamander and lived in the fire, in the fire successively, in the fire of lust in his youth, and in his age in the fire of
Ambition; and then he hath beene a Serpent, a Fish, and lived in the
waters, in the water successively, in the troubled water of sedition in
his youth, and in his age in the cold waters of indevotion) how shall
we raise this Salamander and this Serpent, when this Serpent and this
Salamander is all one person, and must have contrary musique to
charme him, contrary physick to cure him? To raise a man resolv'd
into diverse substances, scattered into diverse formes of severall sinnes,
is the greatest worke. And therefore this Miracle (which implied
that) S. *Basil* calls *Miraculum in Miraculo,* a pregnant, a double
Miracle. For here is *Mortuus redivivus,* A dead man lives; that had
been done before; but *Alligatus ambulat,* saies *Basil;* he that is fet-
tered, and manacled, and tyed with many difficulties, he walks.

And therfore as this Miracle raised him most estimation, so (for
they ever accompany one another) it raised him most envy: Envy
that extended beyond him, to *Lazarus* himselfe, who had done nothing; and yet, *The chiefe Priests consulted how they might put Lazarus
to death, because by reason of him, many beleeved in Iesus.* A disease,
a distemper, a danger which no time shall ever be free from, that
wheresoever there is a coldnesse, a dis-affection to Gods Cause, those
who are any way occasionally instruments of Gods glory, shall finde
cold affections. If they killed *Lazarus,* had not Christ done enough
to let them see that he could raise him againe? for *Cæca sævitia, si aliud
videtur mortuus, aliud occisus;* It was a blinde malice, if they thought,
that Christ could raise a man naturally dead, and could not if he were
violently killed. This then being his greatest Miracle, preparing the
hardest Article of the Creed, the Resurrection of the body, as the
Miracle it selfe declared sufficiently his Divinity, that nature, so in this
declaration that he was God, he would declare that he was man too,
and therefore *Iesus wept.*

John 12.10

August.

He wept as man doth weepe, and he wept as a man may weepe; for these teares were *Testes naturæ, non Indices diffidentiæ,* They declared him to be true man, but no distrustfull, no inordinate man. In *Iob* there is a question ask'd of God, *Hast thou eyes of flesh, and doest thou see, as man sees?* Let this question be directed to God manifested in Christ, and Christ will weepe out an answer to that question, I have eyes of flesh, and I do weep as man weepes. Not as sinfull man, not as a man, that had let fall his bridle, by which he should turne his horse: Not as a man that were cast from the rudder, by which he should steere his Ship: Not as a man that had lost his interest and power in his affections, and passions; Christ wept not so. Christ might goe farther that way, then any other man: Christ might ungirt himselfe, and give more scope and liberty to his passions, then any other man: both because he had no Originall sin within, to drive him, no inordinate love without to draw him, when his affections were moved; which all other men have.

God sayes to the Jews, *That they had wept in his eares;* God had heard them weep: but for what, and how? *they wept for flesh.* There was a tincture, there was a deep dye of murmuring in their tears. Christ goes as far in the passion, in his agony, and he comes to a passionate deprecation, in his *Tristis anima,* and in the *Si possibile,* and in the *Transeat calix.* But as all these passions were sanctified in the roote, from which no bitter leafe, no crooked twig could spring, so they were instantly washed with his *Veruntamen,* a present and a full submitting of all to Gods pleasure, *Yet not my will O Father, but thine be done.* It will not be safe for any man to come so neare an excesse of passions, as he may finde some good men in the Scriptures to have done: That because he heares *Moses* say to God, *Dele me, Blot my name out of the book of life,* Therefore he may say, God damne me, or I renounce God. It is not safe for a man to expose himself to a tentation, because he hath seen another passe through it. Every man may know his own Byas, and to what sin that diverts him: The beauty of the person, the opportunity of the place, the importunity of the party, being his Mistresse, could not shake *Iosephs* constancy. There is one such example, of one that resisted a strong tentation: But then there are in one place, two men together, that sinned upon their own bodies, *Her* and *Onan,* then when no tenta-

Non inordinatè Bernard Iob 10.4

Numb. 11.18

[Mat. 26.38, 39]

[Exod. 32.32]

[Gen. 39.7-12]

tion was offered, nay when a remedy against tentation was ministred to them.

Some man may be chaster in the Stews, then another in the Church; and some man will sin more in his dreams, then another in his discourse. Every man must know how much water his own vessell draws, and not to think to saile over, wheresoever he hath seen another (he knows not with how much labour) shove over: No nor to adventure so far, as he may have reason to be confident in his own strength: For though he may be safe in himself, yet he may sin in another, if by his indiscreete, and improvident example, another be scandalized. Christ was alwayes safe; *He was led of the Spirit:* of what spirit? his own Spirit: *Led* willingly *into the wildernesse, to be tempted of the devill.* No other man might do that; but he who was able to say to the Sun, *Siste sol,* was able to say to Satan, *Siste Lucifer.* Christ in another place gave such scope to his affections, and to others interpretations of his actions, that his friends and kinsfolks thought him mad, besides himself: But all this while, Christ had his own actions, and passions, and their interpretations in his own power: he could do what he would. Here in our Text, Jesus was troubled, and he groaned; and vehemently, and often, his affections were stirred: but as in a clean glasse, if water be stirred and troubled, though it may conceive a little light froth, yet it contracts no foulenesse in that clean glasse, the affections of Christ were moved, but so: in that holy vessell they would contract no foulenesse, no declination towards inordinatenesse. But then every Christian is not a Christ; and therefore as he that would fast forty dayes, as Christ did, might starve; and he that would whip Merchants out of the Temple, as Christ did, might be knockt downe in the Temple; So he [that] knowing his owne inclinations, or but the generall ill inclination of all mankind, as he is infected with Originall sin, should converse so much with publicans and sinners, might participate of their sins. The rule is, we must avoid inordinatenesse of affections; but when we come to examples of that rule, our selves well understood by our selves, must be our owne examples; for it is not alwaies good to go too far, as some good men have gone before.

Now though Christ were farre from both, yet he came nearer to an excesse of passion, then to an Indolencie, to a senselesnesse, to a priva-

tion of naturall affections. Inordinatenesse of affections may sometimes make some men like some beasts; but indolencie, absence,
emptinesse, privation of affections, makes any man at all times, like
stones, like dirt. *In novissimis,* saith S. *Peter,* In the last, that is, in the [2 Pet. 3.3]
worst dayes, in the dregs, and lees, and tartar of sin, then shall come
men, lovers of themselves; and that is ill enough in man; for that is
an affection peculiar to God, to love himselfe. *Non speciale vitium,
sed radix omnium vitiorum,* saies the Schoole in the mouth of
Aquinas: selfe-love cannot be called a distinct sin, but the roote of all
sins. It is true that *Iustin Martyr* saies, *Philosophandi finis est Deo
assimilari,* The end of Christian Philosophy is to be wise like God;
but not in this, to love our selves; for the greatest sin that ever was,
and that upon which even the blood of Christ Jesus hath not wrought,
the sin of Angels was that, *Similis ero Altissimo,* to be like God. To [Isa. 14.14]
love our selves, to be satisfied in our selves, to finde an omni-sufficiency
in our selves, is an intrusion, an usurpation upon God: And even
God himselfe who had that omni-sufficiency in himselfe, conceived
a conveniency for his glory, to draw a Circumference about that
Center, Creatures about himselfe, and to shed forth lines of love upon
all them, and not to love himselfe alone. Selfe-love in man sinks deep:
but yet you see, the Apostle in his order, casts the other sin lower, that
is, into a worse place, *To be without naturall affections.* [2 Tim. 3.3]

S. *Augustine* extends these naturall affections, to Religious affections, because they are naturall to a supernaturall man, to a regenerate
man, who naturally loves those, that are of the houshold of the faithfull, that professe the same truth of Religion: and not to be affected
with their distresses, when Religion it selfe is distressed in them, is
impietie. He extends these affections to Morall affections; the love
of Eminent and Heroicall vertues in any man: we ought to be affected
with the fall of such men. And he extends them to civill affections,
the love of friends; not to be moved in their behalfe, is argument
enough that we doe not much love them.

For our case in the Text, These men whom Jesus found weeping,
and wept with them, were none of his kindred: They were Neighbours, and Christ had had a conversation, and contracted a friendship
in that Family; *He loved Martha, and her sister, and Lazarus,* saies the V. 5
Storie: and he would let the world see that he loved them: for so the

V. 36

Jewes argued that saw him weepe, *Behold how he loved them;* without outward declarations, who can conclude an inward love? to assure that, *Iesus wept.*

Lacrymæ

To an inordinatenesse of affections it never came; to a naturall tendernesse it did; and so far as to teares; and then who needs be

[Isa. 22.4]

ashamed of weeping? *Look away far from me, for I will weep bitterly,* sayes Hierusalem in *Esay.* But *look upon me,* sayes Christ in

[Lam. 1.12]

the Lamentations, *Behold and see if ever there were any sorrow, any teares like mine:* Not like his in value, but in the roote as they proceeded from naturall affection, they were teares of imitation, and we may, we must weepe teares like his teares. They scourged him, they crowned him, they nailed him, they pierced him, and then blood came; but he shed teares voluntarily, and without violence: The blood came from their ill, but the teares from his owne good nature: The blood was drawne, the teares were given. We call it a childish thing to weepe, and a womanish; and perchance we meane worse in that then in the childish; for therein we may meane falshood to be mingled with weaknesse. Christ made it an argument of his being man, to weepe, for though the lineaments of mans bodie, eyes and eares, hands and feet, be ascribed to God in the Scriptures, though the affections of mans mind be ascribed to him, (even sorrow, nay Repentance it selfe, is attributed to God) I doe not remember that ever God is said to have wept: It is for man. And when God shall come

[Rev. 7.17]

to that last Act in the glorifying of Man, when he promises, *to wipe all teares from his eyes,* what shall God have to doe with that eye that never wept?

He wept out of a naturall tendernesse in generall; and he wept now out of a particular occasion. What was that? *Quia mortuus,* because *Lazarus* was dead. We stride over many steps at once; waive many such considerable circumstances as these; *Lazarus* his friend was dead, therefore he wept, *Lazarus,* the staffe and sustentation of that family was dead, he upon whom his Sisters relied, was dead, therefore he wept. But I stop onely upon this one step, *Quia mortuus,* that he was dead. Now a good man is not the worse for dying, that is true and capable of a good sense, because he is established in a better world: but yet when he is gone out of this world he is none of us, he is no longer a man. The stronger opinion in the Schoole, is, That Christ himselfe, when he lay dead in the grave, was no man. Though the Godhead never departed from the Carcasse, (there was no divorce of that Hypostaticall union) yet because the Humane soule was departed from it, he was no man. *Hugo de S. Victor,* who thinks otherwise, that Christ was a man then, thinkes so upon a weak ground: He thinkes, that because the soule is the form of man, the soul is man; and that therefore the soul remaining, the man remaines. But it is not the soule, but the union of the soul, that makes the man. The Master of the Sentences, *Peter Lombard,* that thinks so too, that Christ was then a man, thinkes so upon as weak a ground: He thinkes that it is enough to constitute a man, that there be a soul and body, though that soul and body be not united; but still it is the union that makes the man: And therefore when he is disunited, dead, he is none of us, he is no man; and therefore we weep how well soever he be. *Abraham* was loath to let go his wife, though the King had her: A man hath a naturall lothnesse to let go his friend, though God take him to him.

[Gen. 12.14–20]

S. *Augustine* sayes, that he knew well enough, that his mother was in heaven; and S. *Ambrose,* that he knew wel enough that his master *Theodosius* the Emperor was in heaven, but because they saw not in what state they were, they thought that something might be asked at Gods hands in their behalf; and so out of a humane and pious offi-ciousnesse, in a devotion perchance indigested, uncocted, and retaining yet some crudities, some irresolutions, they strayed into prayers for them after they were dead. *Lazarus* his sisters made no doubt of their brothers salvation; they beleeved his soul to be in a good estate: And for his body, they told Christ, Lord we know that he shall rise at the last day: And yet they wept.

Here, in this world, we who stay, lack those who are gone out of it: we know they shall never come to us; and when we shall go to them, whether we shall know them or no, we dispute. They who think that it conduces to the perfection of happinesse in heaven, that we should know one another, think piously if they think we shall. For, as for the maintenance of publique peace, States, and Churches, may think diversly in points of Religion, that are not fundamentall, and yet both be true and Orthodoxall Churches; so for the exaltation of private devotion in points that are not fundamentall, divers men may think diversly, and both be equally good Christians. Whether we shall

know them there, or no, is problematicall and equall; that we shall
not till then, is dogmaticall and certain: Therefore we weep. I know
there are Philosophers that will not let us weep, nor lament the death
of any: And I know that in the Scriptures there are rules, and that
there are instructions convayed in that example, that *David* left
mourning as soon as the childe was dead; And I know that there are
Authors of a middle nature, above the Philosophers, and below the
Scriptures, the Apocryphall books, and I know it is said there, Comfort thy selfe, for thou shalt do him no good that is dead, *Et teipsum
pessimabis* (as the vulgat reads it) thou shalt make thy self worse and
worse, in the worst degree. But yet all this is but of inordinate
lamentation; for in the same place, the same Wise man sayes, My
Son, let thy tears fall down over the dead; weep bitterly and make
great moane, as he is worthy. When our Saviour Christ had uttered
his *consummatum est,* all was finished, and their rage could do him
no more harm, when he had uttered his *In manus tuas,* he had delivered and God had received his soul, yet how did the whole frame
of nature mourn in Eclipses, and tremble in earth-quakes, and dis-
solve and shed in pieces in the opening of the Temple, *Quia mortuus,*
because he was dead.

Truly, to see the hand of a great and mighty Monarch, that hand
that hath governed the civill sword, the sword of Justice at home, and
drawn and sheathed the forraigne sword, the sword of war abroad,
to see that hand lie dead, and not be able to nip or fillip away one of
his own wormes (and then *Quis homo,* what man, though he be one
of those men, of whom God hath said, *Ye are gods,* yet *Quis homo,
what man is there that lives, and shall not see death?*) To see the brain
of a great and religious Counsellor (and God blesse all from making,
all from calling any great that is not religious) to see that brain that
produced means to becalme gusts at Councell tables, stormes in
Parliaments, tempests in popular commotions, to see that brain
produce nothing but swarmes of wormes and no Proclamation to
disperse them; To see a reverend Prelate that hath resisted Heretiques
and Schismatiques all his life, fall like one of them by death, and
perchance be called one of them when he is dead; To re-collect all, to
see great men made no men, to be sure that they shall never come to
us, not to be sure, that we shall know them when we come to them, to

[2 Sam.
12.19–20]

Ecclus.
38.21, 23

[Joh. 19.30]
[Lu. 23.46]

[Psa. 82.6]
[Psa. 89.48]

see the Lieutenants and Images of God, Kings, the sinews of the State, religious Counsellors, the spirit of the Church, zealous Prelates, And then to see vulgar, ignorant, wicked, and facinorous men thrown all by one hand of death, into one Cart, into one common Tide-boate, one Hospitall, one Almeshouse, one Prison, the grave, in whose dust no man can say, This is the King, this is the Slave, this is the Bishop, this is the Heretique, this is the Counsellor, this is the Foole, even this miserable equality of so unequall persons, by so foule a hand, is the subject of this lamentation, even *Quia mortuus,* because *Lazarus* was dead, *Iesus wept.*

He wept even in that respect, *Quia mortuus,* and he wept in this respect too, *Quia non adhibita media,* because those means which in appearance might have saved his life, by his default were not used, for when he came to the house, one sister, *Martha* sayes to him, *Lord if thou hadst been here, my brother had not dyed;* and then the other sister, *Mary* sayes so too, *Lord if thou hadst been here, my brother had not dyed:* They all cry out, that he who only, only by comming, might have saved his life, would not come. Our Saviour knew in himself that he abstained to better purpose, and to the farther glory of God: for when he heard of his death, he said to his Disciples, *I am glad for your sakes that I was not there.* Christ had certain reserved purposes which conduced to a better establishing of their faith, and to a better advancing of Gods Kingdome, the working of that miracle. But yet because others were able to say to him, it was in you to have saved him, and he did not, even this *Quia non adhibita media,* affected him; and *Iesus wept.*

Quia non adhibita media

He wept, *Etsi quatriduanus,* though they said unto him, *He hath been foure dayes dead, and stinkes.* Christ doth not say, there is no such matter, he doth not stink; but though he do, my friend shall not lack my help. Good friends, usefull friends, though they may commit some errors, and though for some misbehaviours they may stink in our nostrils, must not be derelicted, abandoned to themselves. Many a son, many a good heire, findes an ill ayre from his Father; his Fathers life stinkes in the nostrils of all the world, and he heares every where exclamations upon his Fathers usury, and extortion, and oppression: yet it becomes him by a better life, and by all other means to rectifie and redeem his Fathers fame. *Quatriduanus est,* is no plea

Etsi quat-riduanus

for my negligence in my family; to say, My son, or my servant hath proceeded so far in ill courses, that now it is to no purpose to go about to reform him, because *Quatriduanus est. Quatriduanus est,* is no plea in my pastorall charge, to say that seducers, and practisers, and perswaders, and sollicitors for superstition, enter so boldly into every family, that now it is to no purpose to preach religious warinesse, religious discretion, religious constancy. *Quatriduanus est,* is no plea for my Usury, for my Simony; to say, I do but as all the world doth, and hath used to do a long time. To preach there where reprehension of growing sin is acceptable, is to preach in season; where it is not acceptable, it is out of season; but yet we must preach in season, and out of season too. And when men are so refractary, as that they forbeare to heare, or heare and resist our preaching, we must pray; and where they dispise or forbid our praying, we must lament them, we must weep: *Quatriduanus erat, Lazarus* was far spent, yet *Iesus wept.*

Etsi sus-citandus

He wept, *Etsi suscitandus;* Though he knew that *Lazarus* were to be restored, and raised to life again: for as he meant to declare a great good will to him at last, so he would utter some by the way; he would do a great miracle for him, as he was a mighty God; but he would weep for him too, as he was a good natured man. Truly it is no very charitable disposition, if I give all at my death to others, if I keep all all my life to my self. For how many families have we seen shaked, ruined by this distemper, that though the Father mean to alien nothing of the inheritance from the Son at his death, yet because he affords him not a competent maintenance in his life, he submits his Son to an encumbring of his fame with ignominious shiftings, and an encumbring of the estate with irrecoverable debts. I may mean to feast a man plentifully at Christmas, and that man may starve before in Lent: Great persons may think it in their power to give life to persons and actions by their benefits, when they will, and before that will be up and ready, both may become incapable of their benefits. Jesus would not give this family, whom hee pretended to love, occasion of jealousie, of suspition, that he neglected them; and therefore though he came not presently to that great worke, which hee intended at last, yet hee left them not comfortlesse by the way, *Iesus wept.*

And so (that we may reserve some minutes for the rest) we end this part, applying to every man that blessed exclamation of S. *Ambrose, Ad monumentum hoc digneris accedere Domine Iesu,* Lord Jesus be pleased to come to this grave, to weep over this dead *Lazarus,* this soule in this body: And though I come not to a present rising, a present deliverance from the power of all sin, yet if I can feele the dew of thy teares upon me, if I can discern the eye of thy compassion bent towards me, I have comfort all the way, and that comfort will flow into an infallibility in the end.

And be this the end of this part, to which we are come by these steps. *Iesus wept,* That as he shewed himself to be God, he might appeare to be man too: he wept not inordinately; but he came nearer excesse then indolency: He wept because he was dead; and because all means for life had not been used; he wept, though he were far spent; and he wept, though he meant to raise him again.

We passe now from his humane to his propheticall teares, from Jesus weeping in contemplation of a naturall calamity fallen upon one family, *Lazarus* was dead, to his weeping in contemplation of a Nationall calamity foreseen upon a whole people; Jerusalem was to be destroyed. His former teares had some of the spirit of prophecy in them; for therefore sayes *Epiphanius,* Christ wept there, because he foresaw how little use the Jews would make of that miracle, his humane teares were propheticall, and his propheticall teares are humane too, they rise from good affections to that people. And therefore the same Author sayes, That because they thought it an uncomely thing for Christ to weep for any temporall thing, some men have expunged and removed that verse out of S. *Lukes* Gospell, That Jesus when he saw that City, wept: But he is willing to be proposed, and to stand for ever for an example of weeping in contemplation of publique calamities; Therefore *Iesus wept.*

He wept first, *Inter acclamationes,* in the midst of the congratulations and acclamations of the people, then when the whole multitude of his Disciples cried out, *Vivat Rex, Blessed be the King, that comes in the name of the Lord,* Jesus wept. When *Herod* tooke to himselfe the name of the Lord, when he admitted that grosse flattery, *It is a God and not a man that speakes,* It was no wonder that present occasion of lamentation fell upon him. But in the best times, and under the best Princes, (first, such is the naturall mutability of all worldly

2 Part

[Lu. 19.41]

Inter acclamationes
Luke 19.38

[Acts 12.22]

things; and then (and that especially) such is the infinitenesse, and enormousnesse of our rebellious sin) then is ever just occasion of feare of worse, and so of teares. Every man is but a spunge, and but a spunge filled with teares: and whether you lay your right hand or your left upon a full spunge, it will weep. Whether God lay his left hand, temporall calamities, or his right hand, temporall prosperity; even that temporall prosperity comes alwaies accompanied with so much anxiety in our selves, so much uncertainty in it selfe, and so much envy in others, as that that man who abounds most, that spunge shall weep.

Jesus wept, *Inter acclamationes,* when all went well enough with him; to shew the slipperinesse of worldly happinesse, and then he wept *Inter judicia;* then when himselfe was in the act of denouncing judgements upon them, Jesus wept, To shew with how ill a will he inflicted those judgements, and that themselves, and not he, had

drawne those judgements upon them. How often doe the Prophets repeat that phrase, *Onus visionis,* O the burden of the judgements that I have seene upon this, and this people! It was a burden that pressed teares from the Prophet *Esay, I will water thee with my teares, O Heshbon:* when he must pronounce judgements upon her, he could not but weep over her. No Prophet so tender as Christ, nor so compassionate; and therefore he never takes rod into his hand, but with teares in his eyes. Alas, did God lack a footstoole, that he should make man only to tread and trample upon? Did God lack glory, and could have it no other way, but by creating man therefore, to afflict him temporally here, and eternally hereafter? whatsoever Christ weeps for in the way of his mercy, it is likely he was displeased with it in the way of his Justice: If he weep for it, he had rather it were not so. If then those judgements upon Jerusalem were only from his owne primary, and positive, and absolute Decree, without any respect to their sins, could he be displeased with his owne act, or weep and lament that which onely himselfe had done? would

God ask that question of Israel, *Quare moriemini domus Israel?* why will you dye O house of Israel? if God lay open to that answer, We die therefore, because you have killed us? Jerusalem would not judge her selfe, therefore Christ judged her; Jerusalem would not weep for her self, and therefore Jesus wept; but in those teares of his, he shewed, that he had rather her own teares had averted, and washed away those judgements.

He wept, *cum appropinquavit*, sayes the Text there, *when Iesus came near the City and saw it, then he wept;* not till then. If we will not come neare the miseries of our brethren, if we will not see them, we will never weep over them, never be affected towards them. It was *cum ille*, not *cum illi*, when Christ himselfe, not when his Disciples, his followers, who could doe Jerusalem no good, tooke knowledge of it. It was not *cum illi*, nor it was not *cum illa*, not when those judgements drew neare; It is not said so; neither is there any time limited in the Text, when those judgements were to fall upon Jerusalem; it is onely said generally, indefinitely, these dayes shall come upon her. And yet Christ did not ease himselfe upon that, that those calamities were remote and farre off, but though they were so, and not to fall till after his death, yet he lamented future calamities then, then Jesus wept. Many such little Brookes as these fall into this River, the consideration of Christs Propheticall teares; but let it be enough to have sprinkled these drops out of the River; That Jesus, though a private person, wept in contemplation of publique calamities; That he wept in the best times, fore-seeing worse; That he wept in their miseries, because he was no Author of them: That he wept not till he tooke their miseries into his consideration: And he did weep a good time, before those miseries fell upon them. There remaine yet his third teares, his pontificall teares, which accompany his sacrifice; Those teares we called the Sea, but a Sea which must now be bounded with a very little sand.

To saile apace through this Sea; these teares, the teares of his Crosse, were expressed by that inestimable waight, the sinnes of all the world. If all the body were eye, argues the Apostle in another place; why, here all the body was eye; every pore of his body made an eye by teares of blood, and every inch of his body made an eye by their bloody scourges. And if Christs looking upon *Peter,* made *Peter* weep, shall not his looking upon us here, with teares in his eyes, such teares in such eyes, springs of teares, rivers of teares, seas of teares make us weep too? *Peter* who wept under the waight of his particular sin, wept bitterly: how bitterly wept Christ under the waight of all the sins of all the world? In the first teares, Christs humane teares

Cum appro-
pinquavit

Non cum
illi

3 Part

[1 Cor.
12.17]

[Lu. 22.61,
62]

(those we called a spring) we fetched water at one house, we con-
doled a private calamity in another; *Lazarus* was dead. In his second
teares, his Propheticall teares, wee went to the condoling of a whole
Nation; and those we called a River. In these third teares, his
pontificall teares, teares for sin, for all sins (those we call a Sea)
here is *Mare liberum,* a Sea free and open to all; Every man may saile
home, home to himselfe, and lament his own sins there.

I am farre from concluding all to be impenitent, that doe not
actually weep and shed teares; I know there are constitutions, com-
plexions, that doe not afford them. And yet the worst Epithet, which
the best Poet could fixe upon *Pluto* himselfe, was to call him
Illachrymabilis, a person that could not weep. But to weep for other
things, and not to weep for sin, or if not to teares, yet not to come to
that tendernesse, to that melting, to that thawing, that resolving of the
bowels which good soules feele; this is a spunge (I said before, every
man is a spunge) this is a spunge dried up into a Pumice stone;
the lightnesse, the hollownesse of a spunge is there still, but (as the
Pumice is) dried in the Ætnaes of lust, of ambition, of other flames
in this world.

I have but three words to say of these teares of this weeping. What
it is, what it is for, what it does; the nature, the use, the benefit of
these teares, is all. And in the first, I forbeare to insist upon S. *Basils*
Metaphor, *Lachrymæ sudor animi male sani;* Sin is my sicknesse,
the blood of Christ Jesus is my Bezar, teares is the sweat that that
produceth. I forbeare *Gregory Nyssens* Metaphor too, *Lachryma
sanguis cordis defœcatus;* Teares are our best blood, so agitated, so
ventilated, so purified, so rarified into spirits, as that thereby I become
Idem spiritus, one spirit with my God. That is large enough, and
imbraces all, which S. *Gregory* sayes, That man weeps truly, that
soul sheds true teares, that considers seriously, first, *ubi fuit in inno-
centia,* the blessed state which man was in, in his integrity at first, *ubi
fuit;* and then considers, *ubi est in tentationibus,* the weak estate that
man is in now, in the midst of tentations, where, if he had no more,
himself were tentation too much, *ubi est;* and yet considers farther,
ubi erit, in gehenna, the insupportable, and for all that, the inevitable,
the irreparable, and for all that, undeterminable torments of hell, *ubi
erit;* and lastly, *ubi non erit, in cœlis,* the unexpressible joy and glory

which he loses in heaven, *ubi non erit,* where he shall never be. These foure to consider seriously, where man was, where he is, where he shall be, where he shall never be, are foure such Rivers, as constitute a Paradise. And as a ground may be a weeping ground, though it have no running River, no constant spring, no gathering of waters in it; so a soule that can poure out it self into these religious considerations, may be a weeping soule, though it have a dry eye: This weeping then is but a true sorrow, (that was our first) and then, what this true sorrow is given us for, and that is our next Consideration.

As water is in nature a thing indifferent, it may give life, (so the first living things that were, were in the water) and it may destroy life, (so all things living upon the earth, were destroyed in the water) but yet though water may, though it have done good and bad, yet water does now one good office, which no ill quality that is in it can equall, it washes our soules in Baptisme; so though there be good teares and bad teares, teares that wash away sin, and teares that are sin, yet all teares have this degree of good in them, that they are all some kinde of argument of good nature, of a tender heart; and the Holy Ghost loves to work in Waxe, and not in Marble. I hope that is but meerly Poeticall which the Poet saies, *Discunt lachrymare decenter;* that some study to weep with a good grace; *Quoque volunt plorant tempore, quoque modo,* they make use and advantage of their teares, and weep when they will. But of those who weep not when they would, but when they would not, do half imploy their teares upon that for which God hath given them that sacrifice, upon sin? God made the Firmament, which he called Heaven, after it had divided the waters: After we have distinguished our teares, naturall from spirituall, worldly from heavenly, then there is a Firmament established in us, then there is a heaven opened to us: and truly, to cast Pearles before Swine, will scarce be better resembled, then to shed teares which resemble pearles for worldly losses.

Ad quid

Are there examples of men passionately enamored upon age? or if upon age, upon deformity? If there be examples of that, are they not examples of scorn too? doe not all others laugh at their teares? and yet such is our passionate doting upon this world. *Mundi facies,* sayes S. *Augustine,* (and even S. *Augustine* himselfe hath scarce said any thing more pathetically) *tanta rerum labe contrita, ut etiam*

speciem seductionis amiserit: The face of the whole world is so defaced, so wrinkled, so ruined, so deformed, as that man might be
trusted with this world, and there is no jealousie, no suspition that
this world should be able to minister any occasion of tentation to
man: *Speciem seductionis amisit.* And yet, *Qui in seipso aruit, in
nobis floret,* sayes S. *Gregory,* as wittily as S. *Augustine,* (as it is easie
to be witty, easie to extend an Epigram to a Satyre, and a Satyre to
an Invective, in declaiming against this world) that world which
findes it selfe truly in an Autumne, in it selfe, findes it selfe in a
spring, in our imaginations. *Labenti hæremus,* sayes that Father;
Et cum labentem sistere non possumus, cum ipso labimur; The world
passes away, and yet wee cleave to it; and when wee cannot stay it
from passing away, wee passe away with it.

To mourne passionately for the love of this world, which is de-
crepit, and upon the deathbed, or imoderately for the death of any
that is passed out of this world, is not the right use of teares. That
hath good use which *Chrysologus* notes, that when Christ was told
of *Lazarus* death, he said he was glad; when he came to raise him to
life, then hee wept: for though his Disciples gained by it, (they were
confirmed by a Miracle) though the family gained by it, (they had
their *Lazarus* againe) yet *Lazarus* himselfe lost by it, by being re-
imprisoned, re-committed, re-submitted to the manifold incommodi-
ties of this world. When our Saviour Christ forbad the women to
weepe for him, it was because there was nothing in him, for teares
to worke upon; no sin: *Ordinem flendi docuit,* saies S. *Bernard,*
Christ did not absolutely forbid teares, but regulate and order their
teares, that they might weepe in the right place; first for sin. *David*
wept for *Absolon;* He might imagine, that he died in sin, he wept
not for the Child by *Bathsheba,* he could not suspect so much danger
in that. *Exitus aquarum,* saies *David, Rivers of waters ran downe from
mine eyes,* why? *Quia illi, Because they,* who are they? not other men,
as it is ordinarily taken; but *Quia illi, Because mine owne eyes* (so
Hilary, and *Ambrose,* and *Augustine* take it) *have not kept thy Lawes:*
As the calamities of others, so the sins of others may, but our owne
sins must be the object of our sorrow. *Thou shalt offer to me,* saies
God, *the first of thy ripe fruits, and of thy liquors,* as our Translation
hath it: The word in the Originall is *Vedingnacha, lachrymarum,*

Psal.
119.136

Exod. 22.29

and of thy teares: Thy first teares must be to God for sin: The second
and third may be to nature and civility, and such secular offices. But
Liquore ad lippitudinem apto quisquamne ad pedes lavandos abute-
tur? It is S. *Chrysostomes* exclamation and admiration, will any wash
his feet in water for sore eyes? will any man embalme the Carcasse of
the world, which he treads under foote, with those teares which
should embalme his soule? Did *Ioseph* of Arimathea bestow any of
his perfumes (though he brought a superfluous quantity, a hundred
pound waight for one body) yet did he bestow any upon the body of
either of the Thieves? Teares are true sorrow, that you heard before;
True sorrow is for sin, that you have heard now; All that remaines is
how this sorrow works, what it does.

The Fathers have infinitely delighted themselves in this descant,
the blessed effect of holy teares. He amongst them that remembers us,
that in the old Law all Sacrifices were washed, he meanes, That our
best sacrifice, even prayer it selfe, receives an improvement, a dignity,
by being washed in teares. He that remembers us, that if any roome
of our house be on fire, we run for water, meanes that in all tentations, we should have recourse to teares. He that tels us, that money
being put into a bason, is seene at a farther distance, if there be water
in the bason, then if it be emptie, meanes also, that our most pretious
devotions receive an addition, a multiplication by holy teares. S. *Ber-*
nard meanes all that they all meane in that, *Cor lachrymas nesciens*
durum, impurum, A hard heart is a foule heart. Would you shut up
the devill in his owne channell, his channell of brimstone, and make
that worse? S. *Hierom* tels the way, *Plus tua lachryma, &c.* Thy
teares torment him more then the fires of hell; will you needs have
holy water? truly, true teares are the holiest water. And for Purgatory,
it is liberally confessed by a Jesuit, *Non minùs efficax, &c.* One teare
will doe thee as much good, as all the flames of Purgatory. We have
said more then once, that man is a spunge; And *in Codice scripta,*
all our sins are written in Gods Booke, saies S. *Chrysostome:* If there
I can fill my spunge with teares, and so wipe out all my sins out of
that Book, it is a blessed use of the Spunge.

I might stand upon this, the manifold benefits of godly teares, long:
so long, as till you wept, and wept for sin; and that might be very
long. I contract all to this one, which is all: To how many blessed-

Quid ope-
rantur

Mendoza
in 1 Sam.

Iob 10.20

Psal. 42.3

Mendoza

Cant. 2.12

2 Sam. 22.50

nesses must these teares, this godly sorrow reach by the way, when as it reaches to the very extreme, to that which is opposed to it, to Joy? for godlie sorrow is Joy. The words in *Iob* are in the Vulgat, *Dimitte me ut plangam dolorem meum: Lord spare me a while that I may lament my lamentable estate:* and so ordinarily the Expositors that follow that Translation, make their use of them. But yet it is in the Originall, *Lord spare me a while, that I may take comfort:* That which one cals *lamenting,* the other calls *rejoycing:* To conceive true sorrow and true joy, are things not onely contiguous, but continuall; they doe not onely touch and follow one another in a certaine succession, Joy assuredly after sorrow, but they consist together, they are all one, Joy and Sorrow. *My teares have beene my meat day and night,* saies *David:* not that he had no other meate, but that none relisht so well. It is a Grammaticall note of a Jesuit, (I doe not tell you it is true; I have almost told you that it is not true, by telling you whose it is, but that it is but a Grammaticall note) That when it is said *Tempus cantus, The time of singing is come,* it might as well be rendred out of the Hebrew, *Tempus plorationis, The time of weeping is come;* And when it is said, *Nomini tuo cantabo, Lord I will sing unto thy Name,* it might be as well rendred out of the Hebrew, *Plorabo, I will weepe, I will sacrifice my teares unto thy Name.* So equall, so indifferent a thing is it, when we come to godly sorrow, whether we call it sorrow or joy, weeping or singing.

To end all, to weep for sin is not a damp of melancholy, to sigh for sin, is not a vapour of the spleene, but as *Monicaes* Confessor said still unto her, in the behalfe of her Son S. *Augustine, filius istarum lachrymarum,* the son of these teares cannot perish; so wash thy selfe in these three examplar bathes of Christs teares, in his humane teares, and be tenderly affected with humane accidents, in his Propheticall teares, and avert as much as in thee lieth, the calamities imminent upon others, but especially in his pontificall teares, teares for sin, and I am thy Confessor, *non ego, sed Dominus;* not I, but the spirit of God himself is thy Confessor, and he absolves thee, *filius istarum lachrymarum,* the soule bathed in these teares cannot perish: for this is *trina immersio,* that threefold dipping which was used in the Primitive Church in baptisme. And in this baptisme, thou takest a new Christian name, thou who wast but a Christian, art now a re-

generate Christian; and as *Naaman* the Leper came cleaner out of
Jordan, then he was before his leprosie, (for his flesh came as the
flesh of a child) so there shall be better evidence in this baptisme of
thy repentance, then in thy first baptisme; better in thy self, for then
thou hadst no sense of thy own estate, in this thou hast: And thou
shalt have better evidence from others too; for howsoever some others
will dispute, whether all children which dye after Baptisme, be certainly saved or no, it never fell into doubt or disputation, whether all
that die truely repentant, be saved or no. Weep these teares truly, and
God shall performe to thee, first that promise which he makes in
Esay, The Lord shall wipe all teares from thy face, all that are fallen
by any occasion of calamity here, in the militant Church; and he shall
performe that promise which he makes in the Revelation, *The Lord
shall wipe all teares from thine eyes,* that is, dry up the fountaine of
teares; remove all occasion of teares hereafter, in the triumphant
Church.

[2 Kings
5.14]

Esay 25.[8]

Revel. 7.17

Number 8.

Preached at Pauls, upon Christmas Day,
in the Evening. 1624.

Esiah 7.14. [and Matthew 1.23] PART OF THE
FIRST LESSON, THAT EVENING. *THEREFORE*
THE LORD SHALL GIVE YOU A SIGNE;
BEHOLD, A VIRGIN SHALL CONCEIVE, AND
BEARE A SON, AND SHALL CALL HIS
NAME IMMANUEL.

SAINT *Bernard* spent his consideration upon three remarkable
conjunctions, this Day. First, a Conjunction of God, and Man
in one person, Christ Jesus; Then a conjunction of the incompatible Titles, Maid and Mother, in one blessed woman, the blessed
Virgin *Mary:* And thirdly a conjunction of Faith, and the Reason of
man, that so beleeves, and comprehends those two conjunctions. Let
us accompany these three with another strange conjunction, in the
first word of this Text, *Propterea, Therefore;* for that joynes the anger
of God, and his mercy together. God chides and rebukes the King
Achaz by the Prophet, he is angry with him, and *Therefore,* sayes the
Text, because he is angry he will give him a signe, a seale of mercy,
Therefore the Lord shall give you a signe, Behold, a Virgin, &c. This
Therefore, shall therefore be a first part of this Exercise, That God
takes any occasion to shew mercy; And a second shall be, The particular way of his mercy, declared here, *The Lord shall give you a*
signe; And then a third and last, what this signe was, *Behold, a*
Virgin, &c.

In these three parts, we shall walk by these steps; Having made our
entrance into the first, with that generall consideration, that Gods
mercy is alwaies in season, upon that station, upon that height we shall

look into the particular occasions of Gods mercy here, what this King *Achaz* had done to alien God, and to avert his mercy, and in those two branches we shall determine that part. In the second, we shall also first make this generall entrance, That God persists in his own waies, goes forward with his own purposes, And then what his way, and his purpose here was, he would give them a signe: and farther we shall not extend that second part. In the third we have more steps to make; First, what this sign is in generall, it is, that there is a Redeemer given. And then how, thus; First, *Virgo concipiet, a Virgin shall conceive,* she shall be a Virgin then; And *Virgo pariet, a Virgin shall bring forth,* she shall be a Virgin then; And *Pariet filium, she shall beare a Son,* and therefore he is of her substance, not only man, but man of her; And this Virgin shall call this Son *Immanuel, God with us,* that is, God and Man in one person. Though the Angel at the Conception tell *Ioseph,* That he shall call his name Jesus, and tell *Mary* her selfe, that she shall call his name Jesus, yet the blessed Virgin her selfe shall have a further reach, a clearer illustration, *She shall call his name Immanuel, God with us:* Others were called *Iesus, Iosuah* was so, divers others were so; but, in the Scriptures there was never any but Christ called *Immanuel.* Though *Iesus* signifie a Saviour, *Ioseph* was able to call this childe *Iesus,* upon a more peculiar reason, and way of salvation then others who had that name, because they had saved the people from present calamities, and imminent dangers; for, the Angel told *Ioseph,* that he should therefore be called *Iesus, because he should save the people from their sins;* and so, no *Iosuah,* no other *Iesus* was a *Iesus.* But the blessed Virgin saw more then this; not only that he should be such a *Iesus* as should save them from their sins, but she saw the manner how, that he should be *Immanuel, God with us,* God and man in one person; That so, being Man, he might suffer, and being God, that should give an infinite value to his sufferings, according to the contract passed between the Father and him; and so he should be *Iesus,* a Saviour, a Saviour from sin, and this by this way and meanes. And then that all this should be established, and declared by an infallible signe, with this *Ecce, Behold;* That whosoever can call upon God by that name *Immanuel,* that is, confesse Christ to bee come in the flesh, that Man shall have an *Ecce,* a light, a sign, a token, an assurance that this *Immanuel,* this Jesus, this Saviour belongs unto

Mat. 1.21
Luc. 1.31

him, and he shall be able to say, *Ecce, Behold, mine eyes have seen thy salvation.*

We begin with that which is elder then our beginning, and shall over-live our end, The mercy of God. *I will sing of thy mercy and judgement,* sayes *David;* when we fixe our selves upon the meditation and modulation of the mercy of God, even his judgements cannot put us out of tune, but we shall sing, and be chearefull, even in them. As God made grasse for beasts, before he made beasts, and beasts for man, before he made man: As in that first generation, the Creation, so in the regeneration, our re-creating, he begins with that which was necessary for that which followes, Mercy before Judgement. Nay, to say that mercy was first, is but to post-date mercy; to preferre mercy but so, is to diminish mercy; The names of first or last derogate from it, for first and last are but ragges of time, and his mercy hath no relation to time, no limitation in time, it is not first, nor last, but eternall, everlasting; Let the Devill make me so far desperate as to conceive a time when there was no mercy, and he hath made me so far an Atheist, as to conceive a time when there was no God; if I despoile him of his mercy, any one minute, and say, now God hath no mercy, for that minute I discontinue his very Godhead, and his beeing. Later Grammarians have wrung the name of mercy out of misery; *Misericordia præsumit miseriam,* say these, there could be no subsequent mercy, if there were no precedent misery; But the true roote of the word mercy, through all the Prophets, is *Racham,* and *Racham* is *diligere,* to love;

as long as there hath been love (and *God is love*) there hath been mercy: And mercy considered externally, and in the practise and in the effect, began not at the helping of man, when man was fallen and become miserable, but at the making of man, when man was nothing. So then, here we consider not mercy as it is radically in God, and an essentiall attribute of his, but productively in us, as it is an action, a working upon us, and that more especially, as God takes all occasions to exercise that action, and to shed that mercy upon us: for particular mercies are feathers of his wings, and that prayer, *Lord let thy mercy lighten upon us, as our trust is in thee,* is our birdlime; particular mercies are that cloud of Quailes which hovered over the host of Israel, and that prayer, *Lord let thy mercy lighten upon us,* is our net to catch, our Gomer to fill of those Quailes. The aire is not so full of

Moats, of Atomes, as the Church is of Mercies; and as we can suck in
no part of aire, but we take in those Moats, those Atomes; so here in
the Congregation we cannot suck in a word from the preacher, we
cannot speak, we cannot sigh a prayer to God, but that that whole
breath and aire is made of mercy. But we call not upon you from this
Text, to consider Gods ordinary mercy, that which he exhibites to all
in the ministery of his Church; nor his miraculous mercy, his extraordinary deliverances of States and Churches; but we call upon particular Consciences, by occasion of this Text, to call to minde Gods
occasionall mercies to them; such mercies as a regenerate man will
call mercies, though a naturall man would call them accidents, or
occurrences, or contingencies; A man wakes at midnight full of unclean thoughts, and he heares a passing Bell; this is an occasionall
mercy, if he call that his own knell, and consider how unfit he was to
be called out of the world then, how unready to receive that voice,
Foole, this night they shall fetch away thy soule. The adulterer, whose   [Luke
eye waites for the twy-light, goes forth, and casts his eyes upon for-   12.20]
bidden houses, and would enter, and sees a *Lord have mercy upon us*
upon the doore; this is an occasionall mercy, if this bring him to know
that they who lie sick of the plague within, passe through a furnace,
but by Gods grace, to heaven; and hee without, carries his own furnace
to hell, his lustfull loines to everlasting perdition. What an occasionall
mercy had *Balaam,* when his Asse Catechized him? What an occa-   [Luke
sionall mercy had one Theefe, when the other catechized him so, *Art*   23.40]
thou not afraid being under the same condemnation? What an occasionall mercy had all they that saw that, when the Devil himself fought
for the name of Jesus, and wounded the sons of *Sceva* for exorcising
in the name of Jesus, with that indignation, with that increpation,
Iesus we know, and Paul we know, but who are ye? If I should declare   Act. 19.15
what God hath done (done occasionally) for my soule, where he
instructed me for feare of falling, where he raised me when I was
fallen, perchance you would rather fixe your thoughts upon my illnesse, and wonder at that, then at Gods goodnesse, and glorifie him
in that; rather wonder at my sins, then at his mercies, rather consider
how ill a man I was, then how good a God he is. If I should inquire
upon what occasion God elected me, and writ my name in the book
of Life, I should sooner be afraid that it were not so, then finde a reason

why it should be so. God made Sun and Moon to distinguish seasons, and day, and night, and we cannot have the fruits of the earth but in their seasons: But God hath made no decree to distinguish the seasons of his mercies; In paradise, the fruits were ripe, the first minute, and in heaven it is alwaies Autumne, his mercies are ever in their maturity. We ask *panem quotidianum,* our daily bread, and God never sayes you should have come yesterday, he never sayes you must againe to morrow, but *to day if you will heare his voice,* to day he will heare you. If some King of the earth have so large an extent of Dominion, in North, and South, as that he hath Winter and Summer together in his Dominions, so large an extent East and West, as that he hath day and night together in his Dominions, much more hath God mercy and judgement together: He brought light out of darknesse, not out of a lesser light; he can bring thy Summer out of Winter, though thou have no Spring; though in the wayes of fortune, or understanding, or conscience, thou have been benighted till now, wintred and frozen, clouded and eclypsed, damped and benummed, smothered and stupified till now, now God comes to thee, not as in the dawning of the day, not as in the bud of the spring, but as the Sun at noon to illustrate all shadowes, as the sheaves in harvest, to fill all penuries, all occasions invite his mercies, and all times are his seasons.

[Psa. 95.7]

Achaz case

If it were not thus in generall, it would never have been so in this particular, in our case, in the Text, in King *Achaz;* If God did not seeke occasion to doe good to all, he would never have found occasion to doe good to King *Achaz.* Subjects are to look upon the faults of Princes, with the spectacles of obedience, and reverence, to their place, and persons; little and dark spectacles, and so their faults, and errors are to appeare little, and excusable to them; Gods perspective glasse, his spectacle is the whole world; he looks not upon the Sun, in his spheare onely, but as he works upon the whole earth: And he looks upon Kings, not onely what harme they doe at home, but what harme they occasion abroad; and through that spectacle, the faults of Princes, in Gods eye, are multiplyed, farre above those of private men. *Achaz* had such faults, and yet God sought occasion of Mercy. *Iotham,* his Father, is called *a good King,* and yet all Idolatry was not removed in his time, and he was a good King, for all that. *Achaz* is called *ill,* both because himselfe sacrificed Idolatrously, (And the King was a commanding person) And because he made the Priest *Vriah* to doe so, (And the Priest was an exemplar person) And because he made his Son commit the abominations of the heathen; (And the actions of the Kings Son pierce far in leading others.) *Achaz* had these faults, and yet God sought occasion of mercy. *If the evening skie be red, you promise your selves a faire day,* sayes Christ; you would not doe so if the evening were black and cloudy: when you *see the fields white with corne, you say harvest is ready;* you would not doe so if they were white with frost. *If ye consent, and obey, you shall eat the good things of the Land,* sayes God in the Prophet; shall ye doe so if you refuse, and rebell? *Achaz* did, and yet God sought occasion of mercy. There arise diseases for which there is no *probatum est,* in all the bookes of Physitians; There is scarce any sin of which we have not had experiments of Gods mercies; He concludes with no sin, excludes no occasion, precludes no person: And so we have done with our first part, Gods generall disposition, for the Rule, declared in *Achaz* case for the example.

Our second part consists of a Rule, and an Example too: The Rule, That God goes forward in his own wayes, proceeds, as he begun, in mercy; The Example, what his proceeding, what his subsequent mercy to *Achaz* was. One of the most convenient Hieroglyphicks of God, is a Circle; and a Circle is endlesse; whom God loves, hee loves to the end: and not onely to their own end, to their death, but to his end, and his end is, that he might love them still. His hailestones, and his thunder-bolts, and his showres of bloud (emblemes and instruments of his Judgements) fall downe in a direct line, and affect and strike some one person, or place: His Sun, and Moone, and Starres, (Emblemes and Instruments of his Blessings) move circularly, and communicate themselves to all. His Church is his chariot; in that, he moves more gloriously, then in the Sun; as much more, as his begotten Son exceeds his created Sun, and his Son of glory, and of his right hand, the Sun of the firmament; and this Church, his chariot, moves in that communicable motion, circularly; It began in the East, it came to us, and is passing now, shining out now, in the farthest West. As the Sun does not set to any Nation, but withdraw it selfe, and returne againe; God, in the exercise of his mercy, does not set to thy soule, though he benight it with an affliction. Remember that our Saviour

Mat. 16.2

Joh. 4.35

Esay 1.19

2 Part

Christ himselfe, in many actions and passions of our humane nature, and infirmities, smothered that Divinity, and suffered it not to worke, but yet it was alwayes in him, and wrought most powerfully in the deepest danger; when he was absolutely dead, it raised him again: If Christ slumbred the God-head in himselfe, The mercy of God may be slumbred, it may be hidden from his servants, but it cannot be taken away, and in the greatest necessities, it shall break out. The Blessed Virgin was overshadowed, but it was with the Holy Ghost that over-shadowed her: Thine understanding, thy conscience may be so too, and yet it may be the work of the Holy Ghost, who moves in thy dark-nesse, and will bring light even out of that, knowledge out of thine ignorance, clearnesse out of thy scruples, and consolation out of thy Dejection of Spirit. *God is thy portion,* sayes *David; David* does not speak so narrowly, so penuriously, as to say, God hath given thee thy portion, and thou must look for no more; but, *God is thy portion,* and as long as he is God, he hath more to give, and as long as thou art his, thou hast more to receive. Thou canst not have so good a Title, to a subsequent blessing, as a former blessing; where thou art an ancient tenant, thou wilt look to be preferred before a stranger; and that is thy title to Gods future mercies, if thou have been formerly accustomed to them. The Sun is not weary with sixe thousand yeares shining; God cannot be weary of doing good; And therefore never say, God hath given me these and these temporall things, and I have scattered them wastfully, surely he will give me no more; These and these spirituall graces, and I have neglected them, abused them, surely he will give me no more; For, for things created, we have instruments to measure them; we know the compasse of a Meridian, and the depth of a Di-ameter of the Earth, and we know this, even of the uppermost spheare in the heavens: But when we come to the Throne of God himselfe, the Orbe of the Saints, and Angels that see his face, and the vertues, and powers that flow from thence, we have no balance to weigh them, no instruments to measure them, no hearts to conceive them: So, for temporall things, we know the most that man can have; for we know all the world; but for Gods mercy, and his spirituall graces, as that language in which God spake, the Hebrew, hath no superlative, so, that which he promises, in all that he hath spoken, his mercy hath no superlative; he shewes no mercy, which you can call his Greatest

Mercy, his Mercy is never at the highest; whatsoever he hath done for thy soule, or for any other, in applying himselfe to it, he can exceed that. Onely he can raise a Tower, whose top shall reach to heaven: The Basis of the highest building is but the Earth; But though thou be but a Tabernacle of Earth, God shall raise thee peece by peece, into a spirituall building; And after one Story of Creation, and another of Vocation, and another of Sanctification, he shall bring thee up, to meet thy selfe, in the bosome of thy God, where thou wast at first, in an eternall election: God is a circle himselfe, and he will make thee one; Goe not thou about to square eyther circle, to bring that which is equall in it selfe, to Angles, and Corners, into dark and sad suspicions of God, or of thy selfe, that God can give, or that thou canst receive no more Mercy, then thou hast had already.

This then is the course of Gods mercy, He proceeds as he begun, which was the first branch of this second part; It is alwayes in motion, and always moving towards *All,* alwaies perpendicular, right over every one of us, and always circular, alwayes communicable to all; And then the particular beame of this Mercy, shed upon *Achaz* here in our Text, is, *Dabit signum, The Lord shall give you a signe.* It is a great Degree of Mercy, that he affords us signes. A naturall man is not made of Reason alone, but of Reason, and Sense: A Regenerate man is not made of Faith alone, but of Faith and Reason; and Signes, externall things, assist us all.

Signum

In the Creation, it was part of the office of the Sunne and Moone, to be significative; he created them for signes, as well as for seasons: hee directed the Jews to Christ, by signes, by sacrifices, and Sacraments, and ceremonies; and he entertaines us with Christ, by the same meanes to; we know where to finde Christ; In his House, in his Church; And we know at what signe he dwels; where the Word is rightly Preached, and the Sacraments duly administred. It is truly, and wisely said, *Sic habenda fides verbo Dei, ut subsidia minimè contemnamus;* We must so farre satisfie our selves, with the word of God, as that we despise not those other subsidiary helps, which God in his Church hath afforded us: which is true (as of Sacraments especially) so of other Sacramentall, and Rituall, and Ceremoniall things, which assist the working of the Sacraments, though they infuse no power into the Sacraments. For, therefore does the Prophet say, when

Calvin

V. 13

Achaz refused a signe, *Is it a small thing to weary* (or disobey) *men, but that you will weary* (disobey) *God himselfe?* He disobeyes God, in the way of contumacy, who refuses his signes, his outward assistances, his ceremonies which are induced by his authority, derived from him, upon men, in his Church, and so made a part, or a help, of his ordinary service, as Sacraments and Sacramentall things are.

There are signes of another sort, not fixed by Gods Ordinance, but signes which particular men, have sometimes desired at Gods hand, for a farther manifestation of Gods will, in which, it is not, otherwise, already fully manifested, and revealed. For, to seeke such signes, in things which are sufficiently declared by God, or to seeke them, with a resolution, That I will leave a duty undone, except I receive a signe, this is to tempt God, and to seeke a way to excuse my selfe, for not doing that, which I was bound to doe, by the strength of an old commandement, and ought not to look for a new signe. But the greatest fault in this kinde, is, that if God, of his abundant goodnesse, doe give me a signe, for my clearer directions, and I resist that signe, I dispute against that signe, I turne it another way, upon nature, upon fortune, upon mistaking, that so I may goe mine owne way, and not be bound, by beleeving that signe to be from God, to goe that way, to which God by that signe calls me. And this was *Achaz* case; God

V. 11

spoke unto him, and said, *Aske a signe* (that he would deliver him, from the enemy, that besieged Jerusalem) and he said, *I will not aske a signe, nor tempt God;* For, though St. *Augustine,* and some with him, ascribe this refusall of *Achaz,* to a religious modesty, yet St. *Hierome,* and with him, the greatest party, justly impute this, for a fault to *Achaz:* both because the signe was offered him from God, and not sought by himselfe, (which is the case that is most subject to errour) And because the Prophet, who understood Gods minde, and the Kings minde to, takes knowledge of it, as of a great fault, *In this, thou hast contemned, and wearyed, not Man but God.* For, though there be but a few cases, in which we may put God to give a signe,

Mat. 12.39
Exod. 4

Gen. 15.8

(for Christ calls the Pharisees *an evill, and an adulterous generation,* therefore, because they *sought a signe*) yet God gave *Moses* a signe, of a Rod changed into a Serpent, and a signe of good flesh changed into leprous, and leprous into good, unasked: And after, *Abraham* askes a signe, whereby shall I know, that I shall inherit the land?

and God gave him a signe. So *Gideon,* in a modest timorousnesse
askes a signe, and presses God to a second signe: First, he would
have all the dew upon the fleece, and then, none of the dew upon the
fleece. God does give signes, and when he does so, he gives also irradi-
ations, illustrations of the understanding, that they may be discerned
to be his signes; and when they are so, it is but a pretended modesty,
to say, we will not tempt God to ask a sign, we will not trouble God
to tell us whether this be a sign or no, but against all significations
from God, goe on, as though all were but naturall accidents.

God gives signes *rectè petentibus,* to them that aske them upon due
grounds, (so to *Abraham,* so to *Gideon*) And it is too long for this
time, to put cases, when a man may or may not put God to a signe;
He gives signes also *Non petentibus,* without being asked, to illustrate
the case, and to confirme the person, and so he did to *Moses.* Both
these are high expressions of his mercy; for what binds God, to begin
with man, and give him a signe before he aske; or to waite upon man,
and give it him, when he askes? But the highest of all, is, to persever
in his mercy so far, as to give a signe, though upon the offer thereof,
it be refused; And that is *Achaz* case: *Aske ye,* says God, And, *I will
not,* says *Achaz,* and then, It is not *Quamvis,* for all that, though thou
refuse, but it is *Propterea, Therefore,* because thou refusest, *The Lord
himselfe shall give thee a signe.* His fault is carried thus high: Because he had treasure to pay an army, because he had contracted with
the Assyrians to assist him with men, therefore he refuses the assistance offerd by the Prophet from God, and would faine goe his owne
wayes, and yet would have a religious pretext, *He will not tempt God.*
Nay his fault is carried thus much higher, That which we read, *Non
tentabo, I will not tempt,* is in the Originall, *Nasas;* and *Nasas* is *non
Extollam, non glorificabo,* I will not glorifie God so much, that is, I
will not be beholden to God for this victory, I will not take him into
the league for this action, I will do it of my selfe: And yet, (and then,
who shall doubt of the largenesse of Gods mercy?) God proceeds in
his purpose: *Aske a signe,* will ye not? *Therefore the Lord shall give
you a signe:* Because you will doe nothing for your selfe, the Lord shall
doe all; which is so transcendent a mercy, as that, howsoever God
afforded it to *Achaz* here, we can promise it to no man hereafter.

We are come to our third part, which is more peculiar to this Day:

It is, first, what the signe is in generall, And then, some more particular circumstances, *Behold a Virgin shall conceive, &c.* In generall
then, the signe that God gives *Achaz* and his company, is, That there
shall bee a Messias, a Redeemer given. Now, how is this future thing,
(There shall be a Messias) a signe of their present deliverance from
that siege? First, In the notion of the Prophet, it was not a future
thing; for, as in Gods owne sight, so in their sight, to whom he opens

Esay 9.6

himselfe, future things are present. So this Prophet says, *Puer datus,
filius natus, unto us a child is borne, unto us a Son is given:* He was
not given, he was not borne in six hundred yeares after that; but such
is the clearenesse of a Prophets sight, such is the infallibility of Gods
declared purpose. So then, if the Prophet could have made the King
beleeve, with such an assurednesse, as if he had seene it done, that
God would give a deliverance, to all mankinde, by a Messias, that
had beene signe enough, evidence enough to have argued thereupon,
That God who had done so much a greater worke, would also give
him a deliverance from that enemy, that pressed him then: If I can
fixe my selfe, with the strength of faith, upon that which God hath
done for man, I cannot doubt of his mercy, in any distresse: If I lacke
a signe, I seeke no other but this, That God was made man for me;
which the Church and Church-writers, have well expressed by the
word Incarnation, for that acknowledges, and denotes, that God was
made my flesh: It were not so strange, that he who is spirit, should
be made my spirit, my soule, but he was made my flesh: Therefore
have the Fathers delighted themselves, in the variation of that word;
so far, as that *Hilarie* cals it *Corporationem,* That God assumed my
Body; And *Damascen* cals it *Inhumanationem,* That God became
this man, soule and body; And *Irenæus* cals it *Adunationem,* and
Nysen Contemperationem, A mingling, says one, an uniting, saies
the other, of two, of God and man, in one person. Shall I aske, what
needs all this? what needed God to have put himselfe to this? I may
say with S. *Augustine, Alio modo poterat Deus nos liberare, sed si
aliter faceret, similiter vestræ stultitiæ displiceret:* What other way
soever God had taken for our salvation, our curiosity would no more
have beene satisfied in that way, than in this: But God having chosen
the way of Redemption, which was the way of Justice, God could do
no otherwise: *Si homo non vicisset inimicum hominis, non justè victus*

esset inimicus, saies *Irenæus;* As, if a man should get a battaile by the power of the Devill, without fighting, this were not a just victory; so, if God, in mans behalfe, had conquered the devill, without man, without dying, it had not beene a just conquest. I must not aske why God tooke this way, to Incarnate his Son; And shall I aske how this was done? I doe not aske how *Rheubarb,* or how *Aloes* came by this, or this vertue, to purge this, or this humour in my body: *In talibus*   August. *rebus, tota ratio facti, est potentia facientis:* Even in naturall things, all the reason of all that is done, is the power, and the will of him, who infused that vertue into that creature. And therefore much more, when we come to these supernaturall points, such as this birth of Christ, we embrace S. *Basils* modesty, and abstinence, *Nativitas ista silentio honoretur,* This mysterie is not so well celebrated, with our words, and discourse, as with a holy silence, and meditation: *Immo potius ne cogitationibus permittatur,* Nay, (saies that Father) there may be danger in giving our selves leave, to thinke or study too much of it. *Ne dixeris quando,* saies he, *præteri hanc interrogationem:* Aske not thy selfe overcuriously, when this mystery was accomplished; be not over-vehement, over-peremptory, (so far, as to the perplexing of thine owne reason and understanding, or so far, as to the despising of the reasons of other men) in calculating the time, the day or houre of this nativity: *Præteri hanc interrogationem,* pass over this question, in good time, and with convenient satisfaction, *Quando,* when Christ was borne; But *noli inquirere Quomodo,* (saies S. *Basil* still) never come to that question, how it was done, *cum ad hoc nihil sit quod responderi possit,* for God hath given us no faculties to comprehend it, no way to answer it. That's enough, which we have in S. *Iohn,* *Every spirit, that confesses, that Iesus is come in the flesh, is of God:*   I Ioh. 4.2 for, since it was a comming of Iesus, Iesus was before; so he was God; and since he came in the flesh, hee is now made man; And, that God and Man, are so met, is a signe to mee, that God, and I, shall never bee parted.

This is the signe in generall; That God hath had such a care of all   *Virgo* men, is a signe to me, That he hath a care of me: But then there are signes of this signe; Divers; All these; *A Virgin shall conceive,* A Virgin shall *bring forth,* Bring forth *a Son, And* (whatsoever have been prophesied before) *she shall call his name Immanuel.*

First, a Virgin shall be a mother, which is a very particular signe, and was seene but once. That which *Gellius,* and *Plinie* say, that a Virgin had a child, almost 200. yeares before Christ, that which *Genebrard* saies, that the like fell out in France, in his time, are not within our faith, and they are without our reason; our faith stoopes not downe to them, and our Reason reaches not up to them; of this Virgin in our text, If that be true, which *Aquinas* cites out of the Roman story, that in the times of *Constantine* and *Irene,* upon a dead body found in a sepulchre, there was found this inscription, in a plate of gold, *Christus nascetur ex Virgine, & ego credo in eum,* Christ shall be borne of a Virgin, and I beleeve in that Christ, with this addition, in that inscription, *O Sol, sub Irenæ, & Constantini temporibus, iterum me videbis,* Though I be now buried from the sight of the sun, yet in *Constantines* time, the sun shall see me againe; If this be true, yet our ground is not upon such testimonie; If God had not said it, I would never have beleeved it. And therefore I must have leave to doubt of that which some of the Roman Casuists have delivered, That a Virgin may continue a virgin upon earth, and receive the particular dignity of a Virgin in Heaven, and yet have a child, by the insinuation and practise of the Devill; so that there shall be a father, and a mother, and yet both they Virgins. That this Mother, in our text, was a Virgin, is a peculiar, a singular signe, given, as such, by God; never done but then; and it is a singular testimony, how acceptable to God, that state of virginity is; Hee does not dishonour physick, that magnifies health; nor does hee dishonour marriage, that praises Virginity; let them embrace that state, that can; and certainly, many more might doe it, then do, if they would try whether they could, or no; and if they would follow S. *Cyprians* way, *Virgo non tantum esse, sed & intelligi esse debet, & credi:* It is not enough for a virgin to bee a virgin in her owne knowledge, but she must governe her selfe so, as that others may see, that she is one, and see, that shee hath a desire, and a disposition, to continue so still; *Ita, ut nemo, cum virginem viderit, dubitet an sit virgo,* saies that Father, She must appeare in such garments, in such language, and in such motions, (for, as a wife may weare other clothes, so she may speake other words, then a virgin may do) as they that see her, may not question, nor dispute, whether she be a maid or no. The word in the Text, is derived *à latendo,* from retiring, from privatenesse: And *Tertullian,* who makes the note, notes withall, that *Ipsa concupiscentia non latendi, non est pudica,* The very concupiscence of conversation, and visits, is not chaste: *Studium placendi, publicatione sui, periclitatur,* saies the same Author: Curious dressings are for publique eyes; and the Virgin that desires to publish her selfe, is weary of that state: It is usefully added by him, *Dum percutitur oculis alienis, frons duratur, & pudor teritur,* the eyes of others, that strike upon her, (if she be willing to stand out that battery) dry up that blood, that should blush, and weare out that chastity, which should be preserved. So precious is virginity in Gods eye, as that hee lookes upon that, with a more jealous eye, than upon other states.

This blessed Mother of God, in our text, was a Virgin: when? *Virgo concipiet,* saies our Text, *A Virgin shall conceive,* when she conceived, she was a Virgin. There are three Heresies, all noted by S. *Augustine,* that impeach the virginity of this most blessed Woman: The Cerinthians said she conceived by ordinary generation; *Iovinian* said, she was delivered by ordinary meanes; And *Helvidius* said, she had children after: All against all the world besides themselves, and against one another. For the first, that is enough which S. *Basil* sayes, that if the word Virgin in our text signified no more but *adolescentulam,* a yong woman (as they pretend) it had been an impertinent, an absurd thing for the Prophet to have made that a sign, and a wonder, that a yong woman should have a childe. This is enough, but that is abundantly enough, that S. *Matthew,* who spoke with the same spirit that *Esay* did, sayes in a word, which can admit no mis-interpretation, That that was fulfilled which *Esay* had said, *A Virgin shall conceive;* S. *Matthews* word without question, is a Virgin, and not a yong woman, and S. *Matthew* took *Esaies* word to be so too; and S. *Matthew* (at least he that spake in S. *Matthew*) did not, could not mistake, and mistake himself, for it was one and the same Holy Ghost that spake both. Christ sayes therefore of himself, *vermis sum,* I am a worm, but sayes S. *Ambrose, vermis de Manna,* a worm out of a pure substance, a holy Man, from a blessed Virgin; *Virgo concepit,* she was a Virgin then, then when she had conceived.

She was so to, *In partu,* then when she was delivered; *Iovinian* denied that: A better then he (*Tertullian*) denied it: *Virgo quantum à viro, non quantum à partu,* says he, she was such a Virgin as knew

Concepit

Mat. 1.23

Ps. 22.[6]
[22 : 21 F
as in Vulg.]

In partu

no man, not such a Virgin as needed no midwife: *Virgo concepit,* sayes he, *in partu nupsit,* a Virgin in her conception, but a wife in the deliverance of her Son. Let that be wrapped up amongst *Tertullians* errors, he had many; The text cleares it, *A virgin shall conceive, a virgin shall beare a Son:* The Apostles Creed cleares it, sayes S. *Augustine,* when it sayes, *Born of the Virgin Mary;* and S. *Ambrose* cleares it, when hee says, with such indignation, *De via iniquitatis produntur dicere, virgo concepit, sed non virgo generavit,* It is said, that there are some men so impious, as to deny that she remained a Virgin at the birth of her Son: S. *Ambrose* wondred there should be, scarce beleeved it to be any other then a rumour, or a slander, that there could be any so impious, as to deny that: And yet there have beene some so impious, as to charge *Calvin,* with that impiety, with denying her to be a Virgin then; It is true, he makes it not a matter of faith, to defend her perpetuall virginity; but that's not this case, of her Virginity in her Deliverance: And even of that, (of her perpetuall virginity) he saies thus, *Nemo unquam quæstionem movebit, nisi curiosus, nemo pertinaciter insistet, nisi contentiosus rixator;* He is over-curious, that will make any doubt of it; but no man will persist in the denyall of it, but a contentious wrangler; And in that very point, S. *Basil* saies fully as much, as *Calvin.* But, at his birth, and after his birth, there is evidence enough in this text, *A Virgin shall conceive, A Virgin shall bring forth, A Virgin shall call him Immanuel,* In all those future, and subsequent Acts, still it is the same person, and in the same condition.

Pariet, & pariet filium, She shall bring forth a Son; If a Son, then of the substance of his Mother; that the Anabaptists deny; But had it not beene so, Christ had not beene true Man, and then, man were yet unredeemed. He is her Son, but not her ward; his Father cannot dye: Her Son, but yet he asked her no leave, to stay at Jerusalem, nor to dispute with the Doctors, nor to goe about his Fathers worke: His setling of Religion, his governing the Church, his dispensing of his graces, is not by warrant from her: They that call upon the Bishop of Rome, in that voyce, *Impera Regibus,* command Kings and Emperors, admit of that voyce, *Impera filio,* to her, that she should command her Sonne. The naturall obedience of children to Parents, holds not in such civill things, as are publique; A woman may be a Queen-

Cramerus

Filium

Dowager, and yet a subject; The blessed Virgin *Mary* may be in a high
ranke, and yet no Soveraigne; *Blessed art thou amongst women,* saies Luke 1.28
the Angell to her; Amongst women, above women; but not above
any person of the Trinity, that she should command her Son. *Luther*
was awake, and risen, but he was not readie; Hee had seene light,
and looked toward it, but yet saw not so clearely by it, then, when
he said, That the blessed Virgin was of a middle condition, betweene
Christ, and man; that man hath his conception, and his quickning
(by the infusion of the soule) in originall sin; that Christ had it in
neither, no sin in his conception, none in his inanimation, in the
infusion of his soule; But, saies *Luther,* howsoever it were at the conception, certainly at the inanimation, at the quickning, she was preserved from originall sin. Now, what needs this? may I not say, that
I had rather be redeemed by Christ Jesus then bee innocent? rather
be beholden to Christs death, for my salvation, then to *Adams* standing in his innocencie? *Epiphanius* said enough, *Par detrimentum
afferunt religioni,* they hurt Religion as much, that ascribe too little, to
the blessed Virgin, as they who ascribe too much; much is due to her,
and this amongst the rest, That she had so cleare notions, above all
others, what kind of person, her Son was, that as *Adam* gave names,
according to natures, so the Prophet here leaves it to her, to name her
Son, according to his office, *She shall call his name Immanuel.*

Wee told you at first, that both *Ioseph* and *Mary,* were told by the *Immanuel*
Angel, that his name was to be Jesus, and we told you also, that others,
besides him, had beene called by that name of Jesus: but, as, though
others were called Jesus, (for *Iosuah* is called so, *Heb.* 4.8. *If Iesus had
given them rest;* that is, If *Iosuah* had &c. And the son of *Iosedech*
is called so, throughout the Prophet *Aggai*) yet there is observed a difference in the pointing, and sounding of those names, from this our
Jesus: so though other women were called *Mary,* as well as the blessed
Virgin, yet the Euangelists, evermore make a difference, betweene
her name, and the other *Maries;* for Her they call *Mariam,* and the
rest *Maria.* Now this Jesus, in this person, is a reall, an actuall Saviour,
he that hath already really, and actually accomplished our salvation;
But the blessed Virgin had a clearer illustration, then all that; for she
onely knew, or she knew best, the capacity, in which he could be a
Saviour, that is, as he is *Immanuel, God with us;* for she, and she

onely knew, that he was the Sonne of God, and not of naturall generation by man. How much is enwrapped in this name *Immanuel,* and how little time to unfold it? I am afraid none at all; A minute will serve to repeate that which S. *Bernard* saies, and a day, a life will not serve to comprehend it; (for to comprehend is not to know a thing, as far as I can know it, but to know it as far, as that thing can be knowne; and so onely God, can comprehend God.) *Immanuel est verbum infans,* saies the Father; He is the ancient of daies, and yet in minority; he is the Word it selfe, and yet speechlesse; he that is All, that all the Prophets spoke of, cannot speake: He addes more, He is *Puer sapiens,* but a child, and yet wiser then the elders, wiser in the Cradle, then they in the Chaire: Hee is more, *Deus lactens,* God, at whose breasts all creatures suck, sucking at his Mothers breast, and such a Mother, as is a maid. *Immanuel* is God with us; it is not we with God: God seeks us, comes to us, before wee to him: And it is God with us, in that notion, in that termination, *El,* which is *Deus fortis, The powerfull God;* not onely in infirmity, as when hee died in our nature, but as he is *Deus fortis,* able and ready to assist, and deliver us, in all encumbrances; so he is with us; And with us, *usque ad consummationem,* till the end of the world, in his Word, and in

Cornelius the Sacraments: for, though I may not say, as some have said, That by the word of Consecration, in the administration of the Sacrament, Christ is so infallibly produced, as that, if Christ had never been incarnate before, yet, at the pronouncing of those words of consecration, he must necessarily be incarnate then, yet I may say, that God is as effectually present, with every worthy receiver, as that hee is not more effectually present with the Saints in Heaven.

Ecce And this is that, which is intimated in that word, which we seposed at first, for the last of all, *Ecce, Behold; Behold, a Virgin shall conceive, &c.* God does not furnish a roome, and leave it darke; he sets up lights in it; his first care was, that his benefits should be seene; he made light first, and then creatures, to be seene by that light: He sheds himselfe from my mouth, upon the whole auditory here; he

[Rom. powres himselfe from my hand, to all the Communicants at the table;
16.20] I can say to you all here, *The grace of our Lord Iesus Christ be with you, and remaine with you all;* I can say to them all there, *The Body of our Lord Iesus Christ which was given for you, preserve you to*

everlasting life: I can bring it so neare; but onely the worthy hearer, and the worthy receiver, can call this Lord, this Jesus, this Christ, *Immanuel, God with us;* onely that Virgin soule, devirginated in the blood of *Adam,* but restored in the blood of the Lambe, hath this *Ecce,* this testimony, this assurance, that God is with him; they that have this *Ecce,* this testimony, in a rectified conscience, are Godfathers to this child Jesus, and may call him *Immanuel, God with us;* for, as no man can deceive God, so God can deceive no man; God cannot live in the darke himselfe, neither can he leave those, who are his, in the darke: If he be with thee, he will make thee see, that he is with thee; and never goe out of thy sight, till he have brought thee, where thou canst never goe out of his.

Number 9.

A Sermon Preached to the Houshold at
White-hall, April 30. 1626.

MATTH. 9.13. *I AM NOT COME TO CALL THE*
RIGHTEOUS, BUT SINNERS TO REPENTANCE.

SOME THINGS the several Evangelists record severally, one, and no more. S. *Matthew,* and none but S. *Matthew,* records *Josephs* jealousie and suspicion, that his wife *Mary* had been in a fault, before her marriage; And then his temper withall, not frequent in that distemper of jealousie, not to exhibit her to open infamy for that fault; And yet his holy discretion too, Not to live with a woman faulty that way, but to take some other occasion, and to put her away privily: In which, we have three elements of a wise husband; first, not to be utterly without all jealousie and providence, and so expose his wife to all tryals, and tentations, And yet not to be too apprehensive and credulous, and so expose her to dishonour and infamy; but yet not to be so indulgent to her faults, when they were true faults, as by his connivence, and living with her, to make her faults, his: And all this we have out of that which S. *Matthew* records, and none but

he. S. *Mark,* and none but S. *Mark,* records that story, of Christs recovering a dumb man, and almost deaf, of both infirmities: In which, when we see, that our Saviour Christ, though he could have recover'd that man with a word, with a touch, with a thought, yet was pleas'd to enlarge himself in all those ceremonial circumstances, of imposition of hands, of piercing his ears with his fingers, of wetting his tongue with spittle, and some others, we might thereby be instructed, not to under-value such ceremonies as have been instituted in the Church,

for the awakening of mens consideration, and the exalting of their
devotion; though those ceremonies, primarily, naturally, originally,
fundamentally, and meerly in themselves, be not absolutely and
essentially necessary: And this we have from that which is recorded
by S. *Mark,* and none but him. S. *Luke,* and none but S. *Luke,* records   2.42
the history of *Mary* and *Joseph*'s losing of Christ: in which we see,
how good and holy persons may lose Christ; and how long? They
had lost him, and were a whole day without missing him: A man
may be without Christ, and his Spirit, and lie long in an ignorance
and senslesness of that loss: And then, where did they lose him?
Even in *Jerusalem,* in the holy City: even in this holy place, and now
in this holy exercise, you lose Christ, if either any other respect then
his glory, brought you hither; or your mindes stray out of these walls,
now you are here. But when *they sought him,* and *sought him sor-
rowing,* and *sought him in the Temple,* then *they found him:* If in a
holy sadness and penitence, you seek him here, in his House, in his
Ordinance, here he is always at home, here you may always finde
him. And this we have out of that which S. *Luke* reports, and none
but he. S. *John,* and none but S. *John,* records the story of Christs   2.11
miraculous changing of water into wine, at the marriage in *Cana:*
In which, we see, both that Christ honour'd the state of Marriage,
with his personal presence, and also that he afforded his servants so
plentiful a use of his creatures, as that he was pleased to come to a
miraculous supply of wine, rather then they should want it. Some
things are severally recorded by the several Evangelists, as all these;
and then some things are recorded by all four; as *John Baptist*'s
humility, and lowe valuation of himself, in respect of Christ; which
he expresses in that phrase, *That he was not worthy to carry his shooes.*
The Holy Ghost had a care, that this should be repeated to us by all
four, That the best endeavours of Gods best servants, are unprofitable,
unavailable in themselves, otherwise then as Gods gracious acceptation inanimates them, and as he puts his hand to that plough which
they drive or draw. Now our Text hath neither this singularity, nor
this universality; it is neither in one onely, nor in all the Evangelists:
but it hath (as they speak in the Law) an interpretative universality,
a presumptive universality: for that which hath a plurality of voices,
is said to have all; and this Text hath so; for three of the four Evan-

gelists have recorded this Text: onely S. *John,* who doth especially extend himself about the divine nature of Christ, pretermits it; but [in] all the rest, who insist more upon his assuming our nature, and working our salvation in that, the Holy Ghost hath recorded, and repeated this protestation of our Saviour's, *I came to call not the righteous, but sinners to repentance.*

Which words, being spoken by Christ, upon occasion of the Pharisees murmuring at his admitting of Publicans and sinners to the Table with him, at that feast which S. *Matthew* made him, at his house, soon after his calling to the Apostleship, direct our consideration upon the whole story, and do, not afford but require, not admit but invite this Distribution; That, first, we consider the occasion of the words, and then the words themselves: for of these twins is this Text pregnant, and quick, and easily deliver'd. In the first, we shall see the pertinencie of Christs answer; and in the second, the doctrine thereof: In the first, how fit it was for them; in the other, how necessary for us: First, the Historical part, which was occasional; and then the Catechistical part, which is doctrinal. And in the first of these, the Historical and Occasional part, we shall see, first, That Christ by his personal presence justified Feasting, somewhat more then was meerly necessary, for society, and chearful conversation: He justified feasting, and feasting in an Apostles house: though a Church-man, and an Exemplar-man, he was not depriv'd of a plentiful use of Gods creatures, nor of the chearfulness of conversation. And then he justified feasting in the company of Publicans and sinners; intimating therein, that we must not be in things of ordinary conversation, over-curious, over-inquisitive of other mens manners: for whatsoever their manners be, a good man need not take harm by them, and he may do good amongst them. And then lastly, we shall see the calumny that the Pharisees cast upon Christ for this, and the iniquity of that calumny, both in the manner, and in the matter thereof. And in these Branches we shall determine that first, The Historical, the Occasional part: And in the second, The Catechistical and Doctrinal, (*I came to call not the righteous, but sinners to repentance*) we shall pass by these steps: first, we shall see the Actions; *venit,* he came; that is, first, *venit actu:* whereas he came by promise, even in Paradise; and by frequent ratification, in all the Prophets; now he is really, actually come; *venit,* he is come, we look for no other after him; we joyn no other, Angels nor Saints, with him: *venit,* he is actually come; and then, *venit sponte,* he is come freely, and of his good-will; we assigne, we imagine no cause in us, that should invite him to come, but humbly acknowledge all to have proceeded from his own goodness: and that's the Action, *He came.* And then the Errand, and purpose for which he came, is *vocare,* he came *to call:* It is not, *Occurrere,* That he came to meet them, who were upon the way before; for no man had either disposition in himself, or faculty in himself, neither will nor power to rise and meet him, no nor so much as to wish that Christ would call him, till he did call him: He came not *occurrere,* to meet us; but yet he came not *cogere,* to compel us, to force us, but onely *vocare,* to call us, by his Word, and Sacraments, and Ordinances, and lead us so; and that's his errand, and purpose in coming. And from that, we shall come to the persons upon whom his coming works: where we have first a Negative, a fearful thing in Christs lips; and then an Affirmative, a blessed seal in his mouth: first, an Exclusive, a fearful banishment out of his Ark; and then an Inclusive, a blessed naturalization in his Kingdom: *Non justos, I came to call, not the righteous, but sinners.* And then lastly, we have, not as before, his general intention and purpose, To call; but the particular effect and operation of this calling upon the godly, it brings them *to repentance.* Christ does not call us to a satisfaction of Gods justice, by our selves; that's impossible to us: it is not *ad satisfactionem;* but then it is not *ad gloriam,* he does not call us to an immediate possession of glory, without doing any thing before; but it is *ad Resipiscentiam; I came to call, not the righteous, but sinners, to Repentance.* And so have you the whole frame mark'd out, which we shall set up; and the whole compass design'd, which we shall walk in: In which, though the pieces may seem many, yet they do so naturally flow out of one another, that they may easily enter into your understanding; and so naturally depend upon one another, that they may easily lay hold upon your memory.

First then, our first Branch in the first Part, is, That Christ justified Feasting, festival and chearful conversation. For, as S. *Ambrose* says, *Frustra fecisset;* God, who made the world primarily for his own glory, had made Light in vain, if he had made no creatures to see, and to be seen by that light, wherein he might receive glory: so, *frustra*

Part I

Ambrose

fecisset, God, who intended secondarily mans good in the Creation, had made creatures to no purpose, if he had not allow'd Man a use, and an enjoying of those creatures. Our Mythologists, who think they have conveyed a great deal of Moral doctrine in their Poetical Fables, (and so, indeed they have) had mistaken the matter much, when they made it one of the torments of hell, to stand in a fresh River, and not be permitted to drink; and amongst pleasant fruits, and not to be suffered to eat; if God requir'd such a forbearing, such an abstemiousness in Man, as that being set to rule and govern the creatures, he might not use and enjoy them: Priviledges are lost, by abusing; but so they are, by not using too. Of those three Opinions, which have all pass'd through good Authors, Whether, before the Floud had impaired and corrupted the herbs and fruits of the earth, men did eat flesh or no; of which, the first is absolutely Negative, both in matter of law, and in matter of fact, No man might, no man did; and the second is directly contrary to this, Affirmative in both, All men might, all men did; and the third goes a Middle way, It was always lawful, and all men might, but sober and temperate men did forbear, and not do it: of these three, though the later have prevail'd with those Authors, and be the common opinion; yet the later part of that later opinion, would very hardly fall into proof, That all their sober and temperate men did forbear this eating of flesh, or any lawful use of Gods creatures. God himself took his portion in this world so, in meat and drink, in his manifold sacrifices; and God himself gave himself in this world so, in bread and wine, in the blessed Sacrament of his body and his bloud: And the very joys of heaven after the Resurrection, are convey'd to us also, in the Marriage-supper of the Lamb. That *mensa laqueus,* which is in the Psalm, is a curse: *Let their table be made a snare,* let their plenty and prosperity be an occasion of sin to them, that's a malediction: but for that *mensa propositionum,* The table of Shew-bread, where those blessings which God had given to man, were brought again, and presented in his sight, upon that table; the loaves were great in quantity, and many in number, and often renew'd: God gives plentifully, richly, and will be serv'd so himself. In all those festivals, amongst the Jews, which were of Gods immediate institution, as the Passover, and Pentecost, and the Trumpets, and Tabernacles, and the rest, you shall often meet in the Scriptures, these two phrases,

69.22

Num. 4.7

Humiliabitis animas; and then, *Lætaberis coram Domino:* first, upon that day, *you shall humble your souls,* (that you have, *Leviticus* 16.29. and very often) and then, upon that day, *You shall rejoyce before the Lord;* (and that you have, *Deuteronomy* 16.11. and very often besides.) Now some Interpreters have applied these two phrases to the two days; That upon the Eve we should humble our souls in Fasting, and upon the Day rejoyce before the Lord in a festival chearfulness: but both belong to the Day it self; that first we should humble our souls, as we do now, in these holy Convocations; and then return, and rejoyce before the Lord, in a chearful use of his creatures, our selves, and then send out a portion to them that want, as it is expresly enjoyn'd in that feast, *Nehemiah* 8.10. and in that, *Esther* 9.22. where their feasting is as literally commanded, as their giving to the poor. And besides those Stationary and Anniversary Feastings, which were of Gods immediate institution, And that Feast which was of the Churches institution after, in the time of the *Macchabees,* which was the *Encœnia,* The Dedication of the Temple; the Jews at this day, in their Dispersion, observe a yearly Feast, which they call *Festum Lætitiæ,* The feast of Rejoycing, in a festival thankfulness to God, that he hath brought the year about, and afforded them the use of the Law, another year. When Christ came to *Jairus* house, and commanded away the Musick, and all the Funeral-solemnities, it was not because he disallowed those solemnities, but because he knew there was no Funeral to be solemniz'd in that place, to which he came with an infallible purpose to raise that maid which was dead. Civil recreations, offices of society and mutual entertainment, and chearful conversation; and such a use of Gods creatures, as may testifie him to be a God, not of the valleys onely, but of the mountains too, not a God of necessity onely, but of plenty too; Christ justified by his personal presence at a Feast; which was our first: and then, at a Feast in an Apostles house; which is our second circumstance.

The Apostle then had a house, and means to keep a house, and to make occasional Feasts in his house, though he had bound himself to serve Christ in so near a place as an Apostle. The profession of Christs service, in the Ministery, does not take from any man, the use of Gods creatures, nor chearfulness of conversation. As some of the other Apostles are said to have followed Christ, *relictis retibus, They left*

In Domo Apost.

[Mat. 4.20]

their nets, and followed him; and yet upon occasion, they did at times
return to their nets and fishing after that; for Christ found them at
their nets, after his resurrection: so S. *Matthew* followed Christ, as

S. *Luke* expresses it; *Relictis omnibus, He left all, and followed Christ;*
but not so absolutely all, as S. *Basil* seems to take it, *Adeo ut non solum
lucra, sed & ipsa pericula contempserit,* that he did not onely neglect
the gain of his place, but the danger of displeasure by such a leaving
of his Place: for S. *Matthew* was a Publicane, and so a publike Officer,
and an Accountant to the State: But though he did so far leave all, as
that nothing retarded him from an immediate following of Christ;
yet, no doubt but he returned after, to the setling of his Office, and the
rectifying of his Accounts. When God sees it necessary or behoveful
for a man to leave all his worldly state, that he may follow him, God
tells him so; he gives him such a measure of light by his Spirit, as lets
him see, it is Gods will; and then, to that man, that is a full commandment, and bindes him to do it, and not onely an Evangelical
counsel, as they call it, which leaves him at liberty, to do it, or leave
it undone: Christ saw how much was necessary to that young man in

the Gospel, and therefore to him he said, *Vade & vende, Go and sell all
that thou hast, and then follow me:* And this was a commandment to
that man, though it be not a general commandment to all; upon
Matthew Christ laid no such commandment, but onely said to him,
Sequere me, Follow me; and he did so; but yet not so devest himself
of his worldly estate, as that he had not a house, and means to keep a

house, and that plentifully, after this. When *Eliah* us'd that holy
fascination upon *Elisha,* (we may not, I think, call it a fascination;
fascination, I think, hath never a good sense) but when *Eliah* used
that holy Charm and Incantation upon him, to spread his Mantle over
him, and to draw him with that, as with a net, after him; yet after
Elisha had thus receiv'd a character of Orders, after this imposition
of hands in the spreading of the Mantle, after he had this new filiation,
by which he was the son of the Prophet, yet *Elisha* went home, and
feasted his friends after this. So *Matthew* begun his Apostleship with

a feast; and though he, in modestie forbear saying so, S. *Luke,* who
reports the story, says that it was a *great feast.* He begun with a great,
but ended with a greater: for, (if we have S. *Matthews* history rightly
deliver'd to us) when he was at the greatest feast which this world

can present, when he was receiving and administring the blessed Sacrament, in that action, was he himself serv'd up as a dish to the table of the Lamb, and added to the number of the Martyrs then; and died for that Saviour of his, whose death for him, he did then celebrate.

This then was *festum Ablactationis; Abraham made a great feast, that day that Isaac was weaned:* Here was *Matthew* wean'd *ab uteribus mundi,* from the brests of this world; and he made a feast, a feast that was a Type of a Type, a prevision of a vision, of that vision which S. *Peter* had after, of a sheet, with all kinde of meats clean and unclean in it: for at this Table was the clean and unspotted Lamb, Christ Jesus himself; and at the same Table, those spotted and unclean Goats, the Publicans and sinners; which is our third, and next circumstance, He justified feasting, feasting in an Apostles house, feasting with Publicans and sinners.

Is there then any conversation with notorious sinners justifiable, excusable? We see when S. *Paul* came to be of that High Commission, to judge of notorious sinners, how he proceeded: he *deliver'd Alexander and Hymenæus to Satan;* and there, surely, he did not mean that any man should keep them company. What was their fault? It was but one Heretical point; a great one indeed; for they denied the Resurrection; and for this, the Apostle (as it is also said there) *sends them to Satan, that they might learn not to blaspheme:* And may there not be thus much intimated in that, That a man may learn more blasphemy with some men, then with Satan himself? That may be true: but the sending and delivering to Satan, is the excluding of that man from the Kingdom, that is, from the visible Church of Christ, by a just Excommunication: for, all without the Church, is Satans jurisdiction. Of which fearful state, *Gregory Nyssene* speaks pathetically; *Si haberet oculos anima,* If thy soul had eyes, to see souls, *Ostenderem tibi, tibi segregato,* I would shew thee, thee who hast wilfully incurr'd, and dost rebelliously continue under an Excommunication rightly grounded, duely proceeded in, and justly denounced; I would shew thee the picture of a man burning in Hell, for that's thy picture, says that Father, to that man; *Non Episcopalis arrogantiæ existimes,* says he, Think it not a passionate act of an insolent Bishop; *Cæpit in Lege, confirmatur in Gratia,* God began it in the Law, and confirm'd it in the Gospel; and where it is justly

Gen. 21.8

Act. 10.
[11 and 12]

Cum publicanis

1 Tim. 1.20

Nyssen.

grounded, and duely proceeded in, it is a fearful thing to be deliver'd over to Satan by excommunication; and S. *Paul* is so far from conversing with an Heretick in one point, as that he proceeds so far with him, as *to deliver him to Satan.*

Nay, for a fault much less then this, not opposed against God, as Heresie, but against Natural Honesty, the Apostle proceeds as far, in Incest; *Gather you,* says he, *with my spirit, and the power of the Lord Jesus, to deliver that incestuous man to Satan.* Nay, in less faults then that, he forbids Conversation; *If a fornicator, if a drunkard, if a covetous person, with him eat not.* Nay; for that which is less then these, he is as severe; *We command ye, Brethren, in the Name of the Lord Jesus Christ, that you withdraw your selves from every brother that walketh disorderly.* Where, *Calvin* thinks, (and, I think, aright, and many others must think so too; for a Jesuite thinks so, as well as *Calvin*) that the Apostle by the word *disorderly,* does not mean persons that live in any course of notorious sin; but by *disorderly,* he means *Ignavos, Inutiles,* idle and unprofitable persons; persons of no use to the Church, or to the State: that whereas this is *Ordo Divinus,* the order that God hath established in this world, that every man should embrace a Calling, and walk therein; they who do not so, pervert Gods order: and they are S. *Pauls disorderly persons.*

This then being so, that the Holy Ghost by S. *Paul,* separates not onely from all spiritual Communion, but from all civil Conversation, all notorious sinners, and disorderly persons, how descends Christ to this facility, and easiness of conversation with Publicans and Sinners? For, (to speak a word by the way, of the Office of a Publican) though Customes, and Tributes, and Impositions were due to the Kings of *Jewry,* due in natural right, and due in legal right, fixed and established by that Law in *Samuel;* and so the Farmers of those Customes, and Collectors of those Tributes, in that respect not to be blamed, or ill thought of; and though in the Roman State, (under whose Government, at this time the Jews were) the Office of a Publican were an honourable Office, (for so that great Statesman and Orator tells us, *Flos Equitum Romanorum, Ornamentum Civitatis, Firmamentum Reipublicæ*) Men of the best Families and Extraction in the State, Men of the best Credit and Reputation in the State, Men of the best Revenues and Possession in the State, were Publicans; yet when the

1 Cor. 5.5

v. 11

2 Thes.
3.6 and 14

Cornel.
Lapid.

1 Sam. 8.15

Cicero

Romans govern'd *Jewry* as a Province, and that these honourable Roman Publicans forbore to execute that Office in those remote parts, and making under-Farmers there, for the better advancing of that service, employed the Jews themselves, who best understood the ways and the persons: these Jews became more cruel and heavy to their Brethren, in these Exactions, then any strangers; and so, and justly, the most odious persons amongst them: and then why would Christ afford this conversation to these, and such as these, to Publicans and sinners? Christ was in himself a Dispensation upon any Law, because he was the Law-maker. But here he proceeded not in that capacity; he took no benefit of any Dispensation; he fulfilled the intention and purpose of the Law; for the Laws therefore forbad conversation with sinners, lest a man should take infection by such conversation: so the Jews were forbidden to eat with the Gentiles; but it was, lest in eating with the Gentiles, they might eat of things sacrificed to Idols: so they were forbidden conversation with leprous persons, lest by such conversation the disease should be propagated; but where the danger of infection ceas'd, all conversation might be open; and Christ was always far enough from taking any infection, by any conversation with any sinner. He might apply himself to them, because he could take no harm by them; but he did it especially, that he might do good upon them. Some forbear the company of sinners, out of a singularity, and pride in their own purity, and say, with those in *Esay, Stand by thyself, come not near me, for I am holyer then thou.* But, *Bonus non est, qui Malos tolerare non potest,* says S. *Augustine* upon those words, *Lilium inter spinas,* That Christ was a Lilie, though he grew amongst Thorns. A Lilie is not the less a Lilie, nor the worse, nor the darker a Lilie, because it grows amongst Thorns. That man is not so good as he should be, that cannot maintain his own integrity, and continue good; or that cannot maintain his charity, though others continue bad. It was S. *Paul's* way, *I am made all things to all men, that I might save some.* And in that place, which we mentioned before, where the Apostle names the persons, whom we are to forbear, amongst them, he names Idolators; and, as he does the rest, he calls even those Idolators, Brethren; *If any that is called a Brother, be an Idolator,* &c. In cases where we are safe from danger of infection, (and it lies much in our selves, to save our selves from infection) even some kind of

Exod. 34.[15]

Num. 5.[2]

65.5

Cant. 2.2

1 Cor. 9.22

1 Cor. 5.11

Idolators, are left by *S. Paul* under the name of Brethren; and some brotherly, and neighbourly, and pious Offices, belong to them, for all that. These faults must arm me to avoid all danger from them, but not extinguish all charity towards them. And therefore it was an unjust calumny in the Pharisees, to impute this for a fault to Christ, that he applyed himself to these men; which is the next and last Circumstance in this first part, *The Calumny of these Pharisees.*

Calumnia

Now in the manner of this Calumny, there was a great deal of iniquity, and a great deal in the matter: For, for the manner; That which they say of Christ, they say not to Christ himself, but they whisper it to his servants, to his Disciples. A Legal and Juridical Accusation, is justifiable, maintainable, because it is the proper way for remedy: a private reprehension done with discretion, and moderation, should be acceptable too; but a privy whispering is always Pharisaical. The Devil himself, though he be a Lyon, yet he is a roaring Lyon; a man may hear him: but for a privy Whisperer, we shall onely hear of him. And in their plot there was more mischief; for,

Matth. 12

when Christs Disciples plucked ears of Corn, upon the sabbath, the Pharisees said nothing to those Disciples, but they come to their Master, to Christ, and they tell him of it: Here, when Christ eats and drinks with these sinners, they never say any thing to Christ himself, but they go to his servants, and they tell him of it. By privy whisperings and calumnies, they would aliene Christ from his Disciples, and his Disciples from him; the King from his Subjects by some tales, and the Subject from the King by other: and they took this for the shortest way to disgrace both their preaching, to discredit both their lives; to defame Christ for a Wine-bibber, and a loose Companion, and to defame his Disciples for prophane men, and Sabbath-breakers:

Gregor.

for, *Cujus vita despicitur, restat ut ejus prædicatio contemnatur,* is an infallible inference and consequence made by S. *Gregory;* Discredit a mans life, and you disgrace his Preaching: Lay imputations upon the person, and that will evacuate and frustrate all his preaching; for whether it be in the corruption of our nature, or whether it be in the nature of the thing it self, so it is, if I believe the Preacher to be an ill man, I shall not be much the better for his good Sermons.

Thus they were injurious in the manner of their calumny; they were so too in the matter, to calumniate him therefore, because he

applyed himself to sinners. The Wise-man in *Ecclesiasticus* institutes
his meditation thus: *There is one that hath great need of help, full of* 11.12
poverty, yet the eye of the Lord looked upon him for good, and set
him up from his low estate, so that many that saw it, marvelled at it.
Many marvelled, but none reproached the Lord, chid the Lord,
calumniated the Lord, for doing so. And if the Lord will look upon
a sinner, and raise that bedrid man; if he will look with that eye, that
pierces deeper then the eye of heaven, the Sun, (and yet with a look
of that eye, the womb of the earth conceives) if he will look with that
eye, that conveys more warmth then the eye of the Ostrich, (and yet
with a look of that eye, that Bird is said to hatch her young ones,
without sitting) that eye that melted *Peter* into water, and made him
flow towards Christ; and rarified *Matthew* into air, and made him flee
towards Christ; if that eye vouchsafe to look upon a Publican, and
redeem a *Goshen* out of an *Egypt,* hatch a soul out of a carnal man,
produce a saint out of a sinner, shall we marvel at the matter? marvel
so, as to doubt Gods power? shall any thing be impossible to God? or
shall we marvel at the manner, at any way by which Christ shall be
pleased to convey his mercy? *Miraris eum peccatorum vinum bibere,* Chrysolog.
qui pro peccatoribus sanguinem fudit? shall we wonder that Christ
would live with sinners, who was content to die for sinners? Wonder
that he would eat the bread and Wine of sinners, that gave sinners his
own flesh to eat, and his own blood to drink? Or if we do wonder at
this, (as, indeed, nothing is more wonderful) yet let us not calumniate,
let us not mis-interpret any way, that he shall be pleased to take, to
derive his mercy to any man: but, (to use *Clement* of *Alexandria's* Clem. Alex.
comparison) as we tread upon many herbs negligently in the field,
but when we see them in an Apothecaries shop, we begin to think
that there is some vertue in them; so howsoever we have a perfect
hatred, and a religious despite against a sinner, as a sinner; yet if
Christ Jesus shall have been pleased to have come to his door, and to
have stood, and knock'd, and enter'd, and sup'd, and brought his dish,
and made himself that dish, and seal'd a reconciliation to that sinner,
in admitting him to that Table, to that Communion, let us forget the
Name of Publican, the Vices of any particular profession; and forget
the name of sinner, the history of any mans former life; and be glad
to meet that man now in the arms, and to grow up with that man now

in the bowels of Christ Jesus; since Christ doth not now begin to make that man his, but now declares to us, that he hath been his, from all eternity: For in the Book of Life, the name of *Mary Magdalen* was as soon recorded, for all her incontinency, as the name of the blessed Virgin, for all her integrity; and the name of St. *Paul* who drew his sword against Christ, as soon as St. *Peter,* who drew his in defence of him: for the Book of life was not written successively, word after word, line after line, but delivered as a Print, all together. There the greatest sinners were as soon recorded, as the most righteous; and here Christ comes *to call, not the righteous* at all, *but* onely *sinners to repentance.* And so we have done with those pieces which constitute our first part; Christ by his personal presence justified feasting, and feasting in an Apostles house, and feasting with Publicans and sinners, though the Pharisees calumniated him, malitiously in the manner, injuriously in the matter; and we pass to our other part; from the Historical and Occasional, to the Catechistical, the Doctrinal Part.

Part II

Respondet
Calumniæ

The other Part, the Occasion, the Connexion was of the Text; and we cannot say properly that this Part, the answer is in the Text; for, indeed, the Text is in it: the Text it self is but a piece of that Answer, which Christ gives to these Calumniators. First, Christ does afford an Answer even to Calumniators; for that is very often necessary: not onely because otherwise a Calumniator would triumph, but because otherwise a calumny would not appear to be a calumny. A calumny is fix'd upon the fame of a good man; he in a holy scorn, and religious negligence, pretermits it; and after, long after, the generation of those vipers come to say, In all this time, who ever denied it? A seasonable and a sober answer interrupts the prescription of a calumny, discontinues the continual claim of a calumny, disappoints and avoids that Fine which the calumny levied, to bar all posterity, if no man arise to make an answer. Truely, there are some passages in the Legend of Pope *Joan,* which I am not very apt to believe; yet, it is shrewd evidence, that in so many hundreds of years, six or seven, no man in that Church should say any thing against it: I would they had been pleas'd to have said something, somewhat sooner: for if there were slander mingled in the story, (and if there be, it must be their own Authors that have mingled it) yet slander it self should not be neglected. Christ does not neglect it; he justifies his conversation with these sinners:

and he gives answers proportionable to the men, with whom he dealt. First, because the Pharisees pretended a knowledge and zeal to the Scriptures, he answers out of the Scriptures, out of the Prophet, *Misericordiam volo, Mercy is better then sacrifice;* and an Evangelical desire to do good upon sinners, better then a Legal inhibition to come near them. And Christ seems to have been so full of this saying of *Ose,* as that he says it here, where the Pharisees calumniate him to his disciples; and when they calumniate the disciples about the sabbath, he says it there too. He answers out of Scriptures, because they pretend a zeal to them; and then because the Pharisees were learned, and rational men, he answers out of Reason too, *The whole have no need of the Physician:* I come in the quality of a Physician, and therefore apply my self to the sick. For, we read of many blinde and lame, and deaf and dumb, and dead persons, that came or were brought to Christ to be recovered; but we never read of any man, who being then in a good state of health, came to Christ to desire that he might be preserv'd in that state: The whole never think of a Physician; and therefore Christ, who came in that quality, applied himself to them that needed. And that he might give full satisfaction, even to Calumniators, every way, as he answer'd them out of Scriptures, and out of Reason; so because the Pharisees were States-men too, and led by Precedents and Records, he answers out of the tenour and letter of his Commission and Instructions, (which is that part of his answer that falls most directly into our Text) *Veni vocare, I came to call not the righteous, but sinners to repentance.*

First then, *venit,* he came, he is come: *venit actu;* he came in promise, often ratified before: now there is no more room for *John Baptist's* question, *Tune ille, Art thou he that should come, or must we look for another?* For another coming of the same Messias, we do look, but not for another Messias; we look for none after him, no post-Messias; we joyn none, Saints nor Angels, with him, no sub-Messias, no vice-Messias. The Jews may as well call the history of the Floud Prophetical, and ask when the world shall be drown'd according to that Prophecie; or the history of their deliverance from *Babylon* Prophetical, and ask when they shall return from thence to *Jerusalem,* according to that Prophecie, as seek for a Messias now amongst their Prophets, so long after all things being perform'd in Christ, which

Ose. 6.6.

Venit Actu

[Mat. 11.3]

were prophesied of the Messias; Christ hath so fully made Prophecie History.

Venit
sponte
[Joh. 3.16]

Venit actu, He is really, personally, actually come; and then *venit sponte,* he is come freely, and of his own meer goodness: How freely? Come, and not sent? Yes, he was sent: *God so loved the world, as that he gave his onely begotten Son for it;* There was enough done to magnifie the mercy of the Father, in sending him. How freely then?

[Luke 1.35]

Come and not brought? Yes, he was brought: *The holy Ghost over-shadowed the blessed virgin,* and so he was conceiv'd: there was enough done to magnifie the goodness of the holy Ghost in bringing him. He came to his prison, he abhorr'd not the Virgins womb; and not without a *Mittimus;* he was sent: He came to the Execution;

[Mat. 26.39]

and not without a desire of Reprieve, in his *Transeat Calix, If it be possible, let this cup pass from me;* and yet *venit sponte,* he came freely, voluntarily, of his own goodness. No more then he could have been left out at the Creation, and the world made without him, could he have been sent into this world, without his own hand to the War-rant, or have been left out at the decree of his sending. As when he was come, no man could have taken away his soul, if he had not laid it down; so, (if we might so speak) no God, no person in the Trinity, could have sent him, if he had not been willing to come. *Venit actu,* he is come; there's our comfort: *venit sponte,* he came freely; there's his goodness. And so you have the Action, *Venit,* He came.

Vocare

The next is his Errand, his Purpose, what he came to do, *Venit vocare, He came to call.* It is not *vocatus,* That Christ came, when we call'd upon him to come: Man had no power, no will, no not a faculty to wish that Christ would have come, till Christ did come, and call

Non
occurrere
August.

him. For, it is not *Veni occurrere,* That Christ came to meet them who were upon the way before: Man had no pre-disposition in Nature, to invite God to come to him. *Quid peto, ut venias in me, qui non essem si non esses in me?* How should I pray at first, that God would come into me, whenas I could not onely not have the spirit of prayer, but not the spirit of life, and being, except God were in me already? Where was I, when Christ call'd me out of my Raggs, nay out of my Ordure, and wash'd me in the Sacramental water of Baptism, and made me a Christian so? Where was I, when in the loyns of my sinful parents, and in the unclean act of generation, Christ call'd me into the

Covenant, and made me the childe of Christian parents? Could I call upon him, to do either of these for me? Or if I may seem to have made any step towards Baptism, because I was within the Covenant; or towards the Covenant, because I was of Christian parents: yet where was I, when God call'd me, when I was not, as though I had been, in the Eternal Decree of my Election? What said I for my self, or what said any other for me then, when neither I, nor they had any being? God *is found of them that sought him not: Non venit occurrere,* He came not to meet them who were, of themselves, set out before.

Isa. 65.1

But then, *non venit cogere,* He came not to force and compel them, who would not be brought into the way: Christ saves no man against his will. There is a word crept into the later School, that deludes many a man; they call it *Irresistibility;* and they would have it mean, that when God would have a man, he will lay hold upon him, by such a power of grace, as no perversness of that man, can possibly resist. There is some truth in the thing, soberly understood: for the grace of God is more powerful then any resistance of any man or devil. But leave the word, where it was hatcht, in the School, and bring it not home, not into practice: for he that stays his conversion upon that, God, at one time or other, will lay hold upon me by such a power of Grace, as I shall not be able to resist, may stay, till Christ come again, to *preach to the Spirits that are in prison.* Christ beats his Drum, but he does not Press men; Christ is serv'd with Voluntaries. There is a *Compelle intrare,* A forcing of men to come in, and fill the house, and furnish the supper: but that was an extraordinary commission, and in a case of Necessity: Our ordinary commission is, *Ite, prædicate; Go, and preach the Gospel,* and bring men in so: it is not, *Compelle intrare,* Force men to come in: it is not, Draw the Sword, kindle the Fire, winde up the Rack: for, when it was come to that, that men were forc'd to come in, (as that Parabolical story is reported in this Evangelist) *the house was fill'd,* and the supper was furnisht, (the Church was fill'd and the Communion-table frequented) but it was *with good and bad too:* for men that are forc'd to come hither, they are not much the better in themselves, nor we much the better assur'd of their Religion, for that: Force and violence, pecuniary and bloudy Laws, are not the right way to bring men to Religion, in cases where there is

Non Cogere

1 Pet. 3.19

Luk. 14.23

[Mark 16.15]

Mat. 22.10

nothing in consideration, but Religion meerly. 'Tis true, there is a *Compellite Manere,* that hath all justice in it; when men have been baptiz'd, and bred in a Church, and embrac'd the profession of a Religion, so as that their allegiance is complicated with their Religion, then it is proper by such Laws to compel them to remain and continue in that Religion; for in the Apostacy, and Defection of such men, the State hath a detriment, as well as the Church; and therefore the temporal sword may be drawn as well as the spiritual; which is the case between those of the Romish perswasion, and us: their Laws work directly upon our Religion; they draw blood meerly for that, ours work directly upon their allegiance, and punish only where pretence of Religion colours a Defection in allegiance. But Christs end being meerly spiritual, to constitute a Church, *Non venit Occurrere,* as he came not to meet man, man was not so forward; so he came not to compel man, to deal upon any that was so backward; for, *Venit vocare, He came to call.*

Veni vocare

Now, this *calling,* implies a voice, as well as a Word; it is by the Word; but not by the Word read at home, though that be a pious exercise; nor by the word submitted to private interpretation; but *by the Word preached,* according to his Ordinance, and under the Great Seal, of his blessing upon his Ordinance. So that *preaching* is this *calling;* and therefore, as if Christ do appear to any man, in the power of a miracle, or in a private inspiration, yet he appears but in weakness, as in an infancy, till he speak, till he bring a man to the hearing of his voice, in a setled Church, and in the Ordinance of preaching: so how long soever Christ have dwelt in any State, or any Church, if he grow speechless, he is departing; if there be a discontinuing, or slackning of preaching, there is a danger of loosing Christ. *Adam* was not made in Paradise, but brought thither, call'd thither: the sons of *Adam* are not born in the Church, but call'd thither

August.

by Baptism; *Non Nascimur sed re-nascimur Christiani;* No man is born a Christian, but call'd into that state by regeneration. And therefore, as the Consummation of our happiness is in that, that we shall be call'd at last, into the Kingdom of Glory, in the *Venite Benedicti, Come ye blessed, and enter into your Masters joy:* so is it a blessed Inchoation of that happiness, that we are called into the Kingdom of

Grace, and made partakers of his Word and Sacraments, and other Ordinances by the way. And so you have his Action, and Errand, *He came,* and, *came to call.*

The next, is the persons upon whom he works, whom he calls; where we have first the Negative, the Exclusive, *Non Justos, Not the righteous.* In which, *Gregory Nyssene* is so tender, so compassionate, so loath, that this Negative should fall upon any man, that any man should be excluded from possibility of salvation, as that he carries it wholly upon Angels: *Christ took not the nature of Angels,* Christ came not to call Angels: But this Exclusion falls upon men; What men? upon the righteous: Who are they? We have two Expositions, both of Jesuites, both good; I mean the Expositions, not the Jesuites: they differ somewhat; for, though the Jesuites agree well enough, too well, in State-business, in Courts, (how Kings shall be depos'd, and how massacred; how Kingdoms shall be deluded with Dispensations, and how invaded with Forces, they agree well enough) yet in Schools, and in Expositions, they differ, as well as others. The first, *Maldonat,* he says, That as in that parable, where Christ says, that *the good shepherd left the ninety nine sheep, that had kept their pastures, and went to seek that one, which was strayed,* he did not mean, that there is but one sheep of a hundred, that does go astray; but that if that were the case, he would go to seek that one: so when Christ says here, *he came not to call the righteous,* he does not mean that there were any righteous; but if the world were full of righteous men, so that he might make up the number of his Elect, and fill up the rooms of the fallen Angels, out of them; yet he would come to call sinners too. The other Jesuite *Barradas,* (not altogether *Barrabas*) he says, Christ said, *Non Justos, Not the righteous,* because if there had been any righteous, he needed not to have come: according to that of S. *Augustine, Si homo non periisset, filius hominis non venisset;* If Man had not fallen, and lain irrevocably under that fall, the Son of God had not come to suffer the shame, and the pain of the Cross: so that they differ but in this; If there had been any righteous, Christ needed not to have come; and though there had been righteous men, yet he would have come; but in this, they, and all agree, that there were *none* righteous. None? Why, *whom he predestinated, those he called;* and were not they whom he predestinated, and elected to salvation, righteous? Even the

Non Justos
G. Nyssen.

[Heb. 2.16]

Maldonat
Mat. 18.12

Barradas

August.

Rom. 8.30

Elect themselves have not a constant righteousness in this world: such a righteousness, as does always denominate them, so, as that they can always say to their own conscience, or so as the Church can always say of them, This is a righteous man: No, nor so, as that God, who looks upon a sinner with the eyes of the Church, and considers a sinner, with the heart and sense of the Church, and speaks of him with the tongue of the Church, can say of him, then, when he is under unrepented sin, This man is righteous: howsoever, if he look upon him, in that Decree which lies in his bosom, and by which he hath infallibly ordain'd him to salvation, he may say so. No man here, though Elect, hath an equal and constant righteousness; nay, no man hath any such righteousness of his own, as can save him; for howsoever it be made his, by that Application, or Imputation, yet the righteousness that saves him, is the very righteousness of Christ himself.

S. *Hilaries* Question then, hath a full Answer, *Erant quibus non erat necesse ut veniret?* Were there any that needed not Christs coming? No; there were none; who then are these righteous? we answer with S. *Chrysostome* and S. *Hierome* and S. *Ambrose,* and all the stream of the Fathers; They are *Justi sua Justitia,* those who thought themselves righteous; those who relyed upon their own righteousness; those who mistook their righteousness, as the *Laodiceans* did their riches; they said, *They were rich, and had need of nothing; and they were wretched, and miserable, and poor, and blind, and naked.* So, these men, *being ignorant of Gods righteousness, and going about to establish a righteousness of their own, have not submitted themselves to the righteousness of God;* that is, depend wholly upon the righteousness of Christ. He calls it *Suam, their righteousness,* because they thought they had a righteousness of their own; either in the faculties of Nature, or in the exaltation of those faculties by the help of the Law: And he calls it *Suam, their righteousness,* because they thought none had it but they. And upon this Pelagian righteousness, it thought Nature sufficient without Grace; or upon this righteousness of the *Cathari,* the Puritans in the Primitive Church, that thought the Grace which they had received sufficient, and that upon that stock they were safe, and become impeccable, and therefore left out of the Lords Prayer, that Petition, *Dimitte nobis, Forgive us our trespasses;* upon this Pelagian righteousness, and this Puritan

Hilarie

Apoc. 3.17

Rom. 10.3

righteousness, Christ does not work. He left out the righteous, not that there were any such, but such as thought themselves so; and he took in sinners, not all effectually, that were simply so, but such as the sense of their sins, and the miserable state that that occasioned, brought to an acknowledgement, that they were so; *Non Justos, sed peccatores.*

Peccatores

Here then enters our Affirmative, our Inclusive, Who are called; *peccatores:* for here no man asks the Question of the former Branch: there we asked, Whether there were any righteous? and we found none; here we ask not whether there were any sinners, for we can finde no others, no not one. He came to call sinners, and only sinners; that is, only in that capacity, in that contemplation, as they were sinners; for of that vain and frivolous opinion, that got in, and got hold in the later School, That Christ had come in the flesh, though *Adam* had stood in his innocence; That though Man had not needed Christ as a Redeemer, yet he would have come to have given to man the greatest Dignity that Nature might possibly receive, which was to be united to the Divine Nature: of this Opinion, one of those Jesuites whom we named before, *Maldonat,* who oftentimes making his use of whole sentences of *Calvins,* says in the end, This is a good Exposition, but that he is an Heretick that makes it. He says also of this Opinion, That Christ had come, though *Adam* had stood; this is an ill Opinion, but that they are Catholicks that have said it. He came for sinners; for sinners onely; else he had not come: and then he came for all kind of sinners: for, upon those words of our Saviours, to the High Priests and Pharisees, *Publicans and Harlots go into the Kingdom of Heaven before you,* good Expositors note, that in those two Notations, *Publicans* and *Harlots,* many sorts of sinners are implyed: in the name of *Publicans,* all such, as by their very profession and calling, are led into tentations, and occasions of sin, to which some Callings are naturally more exposed then other, such as can hardly be exercised without sin; and then in the Name of *Harlots,* and prostitute Women, such as cannot at all be exercised without sin; whose very profession is sin: and yet for these, for the worst of these, for all these, there is a voice gone out, Christ is come to call sinners, onely sinners, all sinners. Comes he then thus for sinners? What an advantage had S. *Paul* then, to be of this *Quorum,* and the first of them; *Quorum Ego Maxi-*

Mat. 21.31

mus, That when Christ came to save sinners, he should be the greatest sinner, the first in that Election? If we should live to see that acted, which Christ speaks of at the last day, *Two in the field, the one taken, the other left,* should we not wonder to see him that were left, lay hold upon him that were taken, and offer to go to Heaven before him, therefore, because he had killed more men in the field, or robbed more men upon the Highway, or supplanted more in the Court, or oppressed more in the City? to make the multiplicity of his sins, his title to Heaven? Or, *two women grinding at the Mill, one taken, the other left;* to see her that was left, offer to precede the other into Heaven, therefore, because she had prostituted herself to more men, then the other had done? Is this S. *Pauls Quorum,* his Dignity, his Prudency; I must be saved, because I am the greatest sinner? God forbid: God forbid we should presume upon salvation, because we are sinners; or sin therefore, that we may be surer of salvation. S. *Pauls* title to Heaven, was, not that he was *primus peccator,* but *primus Confessor,* that he first accused himself, and came to a sense of his miserable estate; for that implies that which is our last word, and the effect of Christs calling, That whomsoever he calls, or how, or whensoever, it is *ad Resipiscentiam,* to repentance. It is not *ad satisfactionem,* Christ does not come to call us, to make satisfaction to the justice of God: he call'd us to a heavy, to an impossible account, if he call'd us to that. If the death of Christ Jesus himself, be but a satisfaction for the punishment for my sins, (for nothing less then that could have made that satisfaction) what can a temporary Purgatory of days or hours do towards a satisfaction? And if the torments of Purgatory it self, sustain'd by my self, be nothing towards a satisfaction, what can an Evenings fast, or an *Ave Marie,* from my Executor, or my Assignee, after I am dead, do towards such a satisfaction? Canst thou satisfie the justice of God, for all that blood which thou hast drawn from his Son, in thy blasphemous Oaths and Execrations; or for all that blood of his, which thou hast spilt upon the ground, upon the Dunghil, in thy unworthy receiving the Sacrament? Canst thou satisfie his justice, for having made his Blessings the occasions, and the instruments of thy sins; or for the Dilapidations of his Temple, in having destroyed thine own body by thine incontinency, and making that, the same flesh with a Harlot? *If he will contend with thee, thou*

Mat. 24.41

[1 Tim. 1.15]

Non ad satisfactionem

Job 9.3

canst not answer him one of a thousand: Nay, a thousand men could
not answer one sin of one man.

It is not then *Ad satisfactionem;* but it is not *Ad gloriam* neither.
Christ does not call us to an immediate possession of glory, without
doing any thing between. Our Glorification was in his intention, as
soon as our Election: in God who sees all things at once, both entred
at once; but in the Execution of his Decrees here, God carries us by
steps; he calls us to Repentance. The Farmers of this imaginary satisfaction, they that sell it at their own price, in their Indulgencies, have
done well, to leave out this Repentance, both in this text in S. *Matthew,*
and where the same is related by S. *Mark.* In both places, they tell us,
that Christ came *to call sinners,* but they do not tell us to what; as
though it might be enough to call them to their market, to buy their
Indulgencies. The Holy Ghost tells us; it is *to repentance:* Are ye to
learn now what that is? He that cannot define Repentance, he that
cannot spell it, may have it; and he that hath written whole books,
great Volumes of it, may be without it. In one word, (one word will
not do it, but in two words) it is *Aversio,* and *Conversio;* it is a turning from our sins, and a returning to our God. It is both: for in our
Age, in our Sickness, in any impotencie towards a sin, in any satiety
of a sin, we turn from our sin, but we turn not to God; we turn to a
sinful delight in the memory of our sins, and a sinful desire that we
might continue in them. So also in a storm at sea, in any imminent
calamity, at land, we turn to God, to a *Lord, Lord;* but at the next
calm, and at the next deliverance, we turn to our sin again. He onely
is the true Israelite, the true penitent, that hath *Nathaniel's* mark,
In quo non est dolus, In whom there is no deceit: For, to sin, and
think God sees it not, because we confess it not; to confess it as sin,
and yet continue the practise of it; to discontinue the practise of it,
and continue the possession of that, which was got by that sin; all
this is deceit, and destroys, evacuates, annihilates all Repentance.

To recollect all, and to end all: Christ justifies feasting; he feasts
you with himself: And feasting in an Apostles house, in his own
house; he feasts you often here: And he admits Publicans to this feast,
men whose full and open life, in Court, must necessarily expose them,
to many hazards of sin: and the Pharisees, our adversaries, calumniate
us for this; they say we admit men too easily to the Sacrament; with-

*Non ad
Gloriam*

[Joh. 1.47]

out confession, without contrition, without satisfaction. God in heaven knows we do not; less, much less then they. For Confession, we require publike confession in the Congregation: And in time of Sickness, upon the death-bed, we enjoyn private and particular Confession, if the conscience be oppressed: And if any man do think, that that which is necessary for him, upon his death-bed, is necessary, every time he comes to the Communion, and so come to such a confession, if any thing lie upon him, as often as he comes to the Communion, we blame not, we disswade not, we dis-counsel not that tenderness of conscience, and that safe proceeding in that good soul. For Contrition, we require such a contrition as amounts to a full detestation of the sin, and a full resolution, not to relapse into that sin: and this they do not in the Romane Church, where they have soupled and mollified their Contrition into an Attrition. For Satisfaction, we require such a satisfaction as Man can make to Man, in goods or fame; and for the satisfaction due to God, we require that every man, with a sober and modest, but yet with a confident and infallible assurance believe, the satisfaction given to God, by Christ, for all mankinde, to have been given and accepted for him in particular. This Christ, with joy and thanksgiving we acknowledge to be come; to be come actually; we expect no other after him, we joyn no other to him: And come freely, without any necessity impos'd by any above him, and without any invitation from us here: Come, not to meet us, who were not able to rise, without him; but yet not to force us, to save us against our wills, but come to call us, by his Ordinances in his Church; us, not as we pretend any righteousness of our own, but as we confess our selves to be sinners, and sinners led by this call, to Repentance; which Repentance, is an everlasting Divorce from our beloved sin, and an everlasting Marriage and super-induction of our ever-living God.

Number 10.

Preached at the funerals of Sir William Cokayne Knight, Alderman of London, December 12. 1626.

JOH. 11.21. *LORD, IF THOU HADST BEEN HERE, MY BROTHER HAD NOT DIED.*

GOD MADE the first Marriage, and man made the first Divorce; God married the Body and Soule in the Creation, and man divorced the Body and Soule by death through sinne, in his fall. God doth not admit, not justifie, not authorize such Super-inductions upon such Divorces, as some have imagined; That the soule departing from one body, should become the soule of another body, in a perpetuall revolution and transmigration of soules through bodies, which hath been the giddinesse of some Philosophers to think; Or that the body of the dead should become the body of an evill spirit, that that spirit might at his will, and to his purposes informe, and inanimate that dead body; God allowes no such Super-inductions, no such second Marriages upon such divorces by death, no such disposition of soule or body, after their dissolution by death. But because God hath made the band of Marriage indissoluble but by death, farther then man can die, this divorce cannot fall upon man; As farre as man is immortall, man is a married man still, still in possession of a soule, and a body too; And man is for ever immortall in both; Immortall in his soule by Preservation, and immortall in his body by Reparation in the Resurrection. For, though they be separated *à Thoro & Mensa,* from Bed and Board, they are not divorced; Though the soule be at the *Table of the Lambe,* in Glory, and the body but at the table of *the Serpent, in dust;* Though the soule be

219

Cant. 1.16

in lecto florido, in that bed which is alwayes green, in an everlasting spring, in *Abrahams bosome;* And the body but in that green-bed, whose covering is but a yard and a halfe of Turfe, and a Rugge of grasse, and the sheet but a winding sheet, yet they are not divorced; they shall returne to one another againe, in an inseparable re-union in the Resurrection. To establish this assurance of a Resurrection in us, God does sometimes in this life, that which he hath promised for the next; that is, he gives a Resurrection to life, after a bodily death here. God hath made two Testaments, two Wills; And in both, he hath declared his Power, and his Will, to give this new life after death, in this world. To the Widows sonne of *Zarephtha,* he bequeaths new life; and to the Shunamites sonne, he gives the same legacy, in the Old Testament. In the New Testament, to the widow of *Naims* sonne, he bequeaths new life; And to *Iairus* daughter he gives the same legacy: And out of the surplusage of his inexhaustible estate, out of the overflowing of his Power, he enables his Executors to doe as he did; for *Peter* gives *Dorcas* this Resurrection too. Divers examples hath he given us, of the Resurrection of every particular man, in particular Resurrections; such as we have named; And one of the generall Resurrection, in the Resurrection of Christ himselfe; for, in him, we all rose; for, he was All in All; *Con-vivificavit,* sayes the Apostle; and *Considere nos fecit, God hath quickned us,* (all us; not onely S. *Paul,* and his Ephesians, but all) and *God hath raised us,* and *God hath made us to sit together in heavenly places, in Christ Iesus.* They that are not faln yet by any actuall sinne, (children newly baptized) are risen already in him; And they that are not dead yet, nay, not alive yet, not yet borne, have a Resurrection in him, who was not onely the Lambe *slaine* from the beginning, but from before all beginnings was *risen* too; and all that shall ever have part in the second Resurrection, are risen with him from that time. Now, next to that great Propheticall action, that type of the generall Resurrection, in the Resurrection of Christ, the most illustrious Evidence, of the Resurrection of particular men, is this Resuscitation of *Lazarus;* whose sister *Martha,* directed by faith, and yet transported by passion, seeks to entender and mollifie, and supple him to impressions of mercy and compassion, who was himselfe the Mold, in which all mercy was cast, nay, the substance, of which all mercy does consist,

1 King. 17.
[22]
2 King. 4.
[35]
Luk. 7.15
[Luke 8.55]

Act. 9.40

Ephes. 2.5

Christ Jesus, with this imperfect piece of Devotion, which hath a tincture of Faith, but is deeper dyed in Passion, *Lord, if thou hadst been here, my brother had not dyed.*

This Text which you Heare, *Martha's* single words, complicated with this Text which you See, The dead body of this our Brother, makes up between them this body of Instruction for the soule; first, That there is nothing in this world perfect; And then, That such as it is, there is nothing constant, nothing permanent. We consider the first, That there is nothing perfect, in the best things, in spirituall things; Even *Martha's* devotion and faith hath imperfections in it; And we consider the other, That nothing is permanent in temporall things; Riches prosperously multiplied, Children honorably bestowed, Additions of Honor and Titles, fairly acquired, Places of Command and Government, justly received, and duly executed; All testimonies, all evidences of worldly happinesse, have a Dissolution, a Determination in the death of this, and of every such Man: There is nothing, no spirituall thing, perfect in this world; Nothing, no temporall thing, permanent and durable; And these two Considerations shall be our two parts; And then, these the branches from these two roots; First, in the first, we shall see in generall, The weaknesse of Mans best actions; And secondly, more particularly, The weaknesses in *Martha's* Action; And yet, in a third place, the easinesse, the propensnesse, the largenesse of Gods goodnesse towards us, in the acceptation of our imperfect Sacrifices; for, Christ does not refuse, nor discourage *Martha,* though her action have these imperfections; And in this largenesse of his Mercy, which is the end of all, we shall end this part. And in our second, That as in spirituall things nothing is perfect, so in temporall things nothing is permanent, we shall, by the same three steps, as in the former, looke first upon the generall consideration, the fluidnesse, the transitorinesse of all such temporall things; And then, consider it more particularly, in Gods Master-piece, amongst mortall things, the body of man, That even that flowes into putrefaction; And then lastly, returne to that, in which we determined the former part, The largenesse of Gods goodnesse to us, in affording even to mans body, so dissolved into putrefaction, an incorruptible and a glorious state. So have you the frame set up, and the roomes divided; The two parts, and the

Divisio

three branches of each; And to the furnishing of them, with meditations fit for this Occasion, we passe now.

1 Part.
*In spiritu-
alibus,
nihil per-
fectum.
Scientia*

In entring upon the first branch of our first part, That in spirituall
things nothing is perfect, we may well afford a kinde of spirituall
nature to knowledge; And how imperfect is all our knowledge?
What one thing doe we know perfectly? Whether wee consider
Arts, or Sciences, the servant knows but according to the proportion
of his Masters knowledge in that Art, and the Scholar knows but
according to the proportion of his Masters knowledge in that Science; Young men mend not their sight by using old mens Spectacles;
and yet we looke upon Nature, but with *Aristotles* Spectacles, and
upon the body of man, but with *Galens,* and upon the frame of the
world, but with *Ptolomies* Spectacles. Almost all knowledge is rather
like a child that is embalmed to make Mummy, then that is nursed
to make a Man; rather conserved in the stature of the first age, then
growne to be greater; And if there be any addition to knowledge,
it is rather a new knowledge, then a greater knowledge; rather a
singularity in a desire of proposing something that was not knowne
at all before, then an emproving, an advancing, a multiplying of
former inceptions; and by that meanes, no knowledge comes to be
perfect. One Philosopher thinks he is dived to the bottome, when
he sayes, he knows nothing but this, That he knows nothing; and
yet another thinks, that he hath expressed more knowledge then he,
in saying, That he knows not so much as that, That he knows nothing. S. *Paul* found that to be all knowledge, To know Christ; And
Mahomet thinks himselfe wise therefore, because he knows not,
acknowledges not Christ, as S. *Paul* does. Though a man knew not,
that every sin casts another shovell of Brimstone upon him in Hell,
yet if he knew that every riotous feast cuts off a year, and every
wanton night seaven years of his seventy in this world, it were some
degree towards perfection in knowledge. He that purchases a Mannor, will thinke to have an exact Survey of the Land: But who thinks
of taking so exact a survey of his Conscience, how that money was
got, that purchased that Mannor? We call that a mans meanes, which
he hath; But that is truly his meanes, what way he came by it. And
yet how few are there, (when a state comes to any great proportion)
that know that; that know what they have, what they are worth?

We have seen great Wills, dilated into glorious uses, and into pious uses, and then too narrow an estate to reach to it; And we have seen Wills, where the Testator thinks he hath bequeathed all, and he hath not knowne halfe his own worth. When thou knowest a wife, a sonne, a servant, a friend no better, but that that wife betrayes thy bed, and that sonne thine estate, and that servant thy credit, and that friend thy secret, what canst thou say thou knowest? But we must not insist upon this Consideration of knowledge; for, though knowledge be of a spirituall nature, yet it is but as a terrestriall Spirit, conversant upon Earth; Spirituall things, of a more rarified nature then knowledge, even faith it selfe, and all that grows from that in us, falls within this Rule, which we have in hand, That even in spirituall things, nothing is perfect.

We consider this therefore *in Credendis,* In things that we are bound to Beleeve, there works our faith; And then, *in Petendis,* In things that we are bound to pray for, there works our hope; And lastly, *in Agendis,* In things that we are bound to doe, and there works our charity; And there is nothing in any of these three perfect. When you remember who they were, that made that prayer, *Domine adauge,* That the Apostles themselves prayed, that their faith might receive an encrease, *Lord increase our faith,* you must necessarily second that consideration with a confession, That no mans faith is perfect. When you heare Christ so often upbraid, sometimes whole Congregations, with that, *Modicæ fidei, O yee of little faith;* And sometimes his Disciples alone, with the same reproach, *Modicæ fidei, O yee of little faith;* when you may be perplexed with the variety of opinions amongst the ancient Interpreters, whether Christ spoke but to the incredulous Jewes, or to his own Disciples, when he said, *O faithlesse and perverse generation, how long shall I be with you? how long shall I suffer you?* (for many Interpreters goe one way, and many the other) And when you may be cleared without any colour of perplexity, that to whom soever Christ spoke in that place, he spoke plainly to his owne Disciples, when he said, *Because of your unbeliefe you cannot doe this;* In which Disciples of his, he denies also, that there is such a proportion of faith, as a graine of Mustard-seed, can ye place a perfectnesse of faith in any? When the Apostle takes knowledge of the good estate and condition of the

Fides

Luk. 17.5

Mat. 6.30
Mat. 8.26

Mat. 17.17

Vers. 20

1 Thes. 1.2
Thessalonians, and gave God thanks for their *Workes of faith,* for *their labours of love,* for their *patience of hope, in our Lord Iesus Christ:* does he conclude them to be perfect? No; for after this he
3.10
sayes, *Night and day we pray exceedingly, that we may perfect that which is lacking in your faith.* And after this, he sees the fruit of
2 Thes. 1.3
those prayers, *We are bound to thanke God alwayes, because your faith groweth exceedingly;* still, at the best, it is but a growing faith,
Iames 2.5
and it may be better. There are men that are said to be *Rich in faith;*
Galat. 4.9
men that are come from the *weake and beggarly elements of Nature, or of the Law,* to the knowledge of the precious and glorious *Gospell,* and so are *Rich in faith,* enriched, emproved by faith. There are men
2 Cor. 8.7
that *Abound in faith;* that is, in comparison of the emptinesse of other men, or of their owne emptinesse before they embraced the
Rom. 12.3
Gospell, they abound now; But still it is, *As God hath given the measure of faith to every man;* Not as of his Manna, a certaine measure, and an equall measure, and a full measure to every man; no man hath such a measure of faith, as that he needs no more, or that he may not lose at least some of that. When Christ speakes
Luke 18.8
so doubtfully, *When the Son of man commeth, shall he finde faith upon earth?* Any faith in any man? If the Holy Ghost be come into this presence, into this Congregation, does he find faith in any? A perfect faith he does not.

Deceive not your selves then, with that new charme and flattery of the soule, That if once you can say to your selves you have faith, you need no more, or that you shall alwaies keepe that alive; The
Rom. 3.27
Apostle sayes, *All boasting,* that is, all confidence, *is excluded; By what Law?* sayes he, *by the Law of faith,* Not by faith, but by the Law of faith; There is a Law of faith; a rule that ordinates, and regulates our faith; by which law and rule, the Apostle cals upon
2 Cor. 13.5
us, To examine our selves whether we be in the faith, or no; not onely by the internall motions, and private inspirations of his blessed Spirit, but by the Law and the Rule, which he hath delivered to us in the Gospell. The Kings pardon flowes from his meere grace, and from his brest; but we must have the writing and the Seale, that we may plead it: So does faith from God; But we must see it our selves, and shew it to others, or else we doe not observe the Law of
Rom. 4.11
faith. *Abraham received the Seale of the righteousnesse of faith,*

sayes the Apostle; Hee had an outward testimony to proceed by; And then, *Abraham* became an outward testimony and Rule to the faithfull, *Walke in the steps of the faith of Abraham,* sayes that Apostle in that place; Not a faith conceived onely, but a faith which you saw, The faith of *Abraham;* for, so the Apostle proposing to us the example of other men sayes, *Their faith follow you,* Not faith in generall, but their faith. So that it is not enough to say, I feele the inspiration of the Spirit of God, He infuses faith, and faith infused cannot be withdrawne; but, as there is a Law of faith, and a practise of faith, a Rule of faith, and an example of faith, apply thy selfe to both; Regulate thy faith by the Rule, that is, the Word, and by Example, that is, Beleeve those things which the Saints of God have constantly and unanimely beleeved to be necessary to salvation: The Word is the Law, and the Rule, The Church is the Practise, and the Precedent that regulates thy faith; And if thou make imaginary revelations, and inspirations thy Law, or the practise of Sectaries thy Precedent, thou doest but call Fancie and Imagination, by the name of Reason and Understanding, and Opinion by the name of Faith, and Singularity, and Schisme, by the name of Communion of Saints. The Law of thy faith is, That that that thou beleevest, be Universall, Catholique, beleeved by all; And then, that the Application be particular, To beleeve, that as Christ dyed sufficiently for all, so he dyed effectually for thee. And of this effectuall dying for thee, there arises an evidence from thy selfe, in thy conformity to him; Thy conformity consists in this, That thou art willing to live according to his Gospell, and ready to dye for him, that dyed for thee. For, till a man have resisted unto blood, he cannot know experimentally what degrees towards perfection his faith hath: And though he may conceive in himselfe a holy purpose to dye for Christ, yet till he have dyed for Christ, or dyed in Christ, that is, as long as we are in this valley of tentations, there is nothing, no not in spirituall things, not in faith it selfe, perfect.

It is not *In credendis,* in our embracing the object of faith; we doe not that perfectly; It is not *In petendis,* in our directing our prayers faithfully neither; we doe not that; our faith is not perfect, nor our hope is not perfect; for, so argues the Apostle, *Ye aske, and receive not, because ye aske amisse;* you cannot hope constantly, because you

Ver. 12

Heb. 13.7

Spes

Iames 4.3

doe not pray aright: And to make a Prayer a right Prayer, there go
so many essentiall circumstances, as that the best man may justly
suspect his best Prayer: for, since Prayer must bee of faith, Prayer
can be but so perfect, as the faith is perfect; and the imperfections
of the best faith we have seene. Christ hath given us but a short
Prayer; and yet we are weary of that. Some of the old Heretiques of
the Primitive Church abridged that Prayer, and some of our later
Schismatiques have annihilated, evacuated that Prayer: The Cathari
then, left out that one Petition, *Dimitte nobis, Forgive us our tres-*
passes, for they thought themselves so pure, as that they needed no
forgivenesse, and our new men leave out the whole Prayer, because
the same Spirit that spake in Christ, speakes in their extemporall
prayers, and they can pray, as well as Christ could teach them. And
(to leave those, whom we are bound to leave, those old Heretiques,
those new Schismatiques) which of us ever, ever sayes over that
short Prayer, with a deliberate understanding of every Petition as
we passe, or without deviations, and extravagancies of our thoughts,
in that halfe-minute of our Devotion? We have not leasure to speake
of the abuse of prayer in the Roman Church; where they wil antidate
and postdate their prayers; Say to morrows prayers to day, and to
dayes prayers to morrow, if they have other uses and employments
of the due time betweene; where they will trade, and make merchandise of prayers by way of exchange, My man shall fast for me, and
I will pray for my man; or my Atturney, and Proxy shall pray for
us both, at my charge; nay, where they will play for prayers, and
the loser must pray for both; To this there belongs but a holy scorne,
and I would faine passe it over quickly. But when we consider with
a religious seriousnesse the manifold weaknesses of the strongest devotions in time of Prayer, it is a sad consideration. I throw my selfe
downe in my Chamber, and I call in, and invite God, and his Angels
thither, and when they are there, I neglect God and his Angels, for
the noise of a Flie, for the ratling of a Coach, for the whining of a
doore; I talke on, in the same posture of praying; Eyes lifted up;
knees bowed downe; as though I prayed to God; and, if God, or his
Angels should aske me, when I thought last of God in that prayer,
I cannot tell: Sometimes I finde that I had forgot what I was about,
but when I began to forget it, I cannot tell. A memory of yesterdays

pleasures, a feare of to morrows dangers, a straw under my knee, a noise in mine eare, a light in mine eye, an any thing, a nothing, a fancy, a Chimera in my braine, troubles me in my prayer. So certainly is there nothing, nothing in spirituall things, perfect in this world.

Not *In credendis,* In things that belong to Faith; not *In petendis,* In things that belong to Hope; nor *In agendis,* In things that belong to Action, to Workes, to Charity, there is nothing perfect there neither. I would be loath to say, That every good is a sin; That were to say, That every deformed, or disordered man were a beast, or that every corrupt meat were poyson; It is not utterly so; not so altogether; But it is so much towards it, as that there is no worke of ours so good, as that wee can looke for thanks at Gods hand for that worke; no worke, that hath not so much ill mingled with it, as that wee need not cry God mercy for that worke. There was so much corruption in the getting, or so much vaine glory in the bestowing, as that no man builds an Hospitall, but his soule lies, though not dead, yet lame in that Hospitall; no man mends a high-way, but he is, though not drowned, yet mired in that way; no man relieves the poore, but he needs reliefe for that reliefe. In all those workes of Charity, the world that hath benefit by them, is bound to confesse and acknowledge a goodnesse, and to call them good workes; but the man that does them, and knows the weaknesses of them, knows they are not good works. It is possible to Art, to purge a peccant humour out of a sick bodie; but not possible to raise a dead bodie to life. God, out of my Confession of the impuritie of my best actions, shall vouchsafe to take off his eyes from that impurity, as though there were none; but no spirituall thing in us, not Faith, not Hope, not Charitie, have any puritie, any perfection in themselves; which is the generall Doctrine wee proposed at first; And our next Consideration is, how this weakenesse appeares in the Action, and in the Words of *Martha* in our Text, *Lord, if thou hadst beene here, my brother had not dyed.*

Now lest we should attribute this weakenesse, onely to weake persons, upon whom we had a prejudice, to *Martha* alone, we note to you first, that her sister *Mary,* to whom in the whole Story very much is ascribed, when she comes to Christ, comes also in the same voice of infirmity, *Lord, if thou hadst beene here, my brother had*

Charitas

Marthæ fides

Ver. 32

not died. No person so perfect, that hath not of these imperfections; Both these holy Sisters, howsoever there might be differences of degrees in their holinesse, have imperfections in all three, in the consideration of their Faith, and their Hope, and their Charity; though in all three they had also, and had both, good degrees towards perfection. Looke first upon their Faith; they both say, *Lord, if thou hadst beene here, our brother had not died.* We cannot say so to any Consultation, to any Colledge of Physitians; not to a *Chiron,* to an *Esculapius,* to a God of Physicke, could any man say, If you had beene here, my friend had not died? though surely there be much assistance to be received from them, whom God had endowed with knowledge to that purpose. And yet there was a weakenesse in these Sisters, in that they said but so, and no more to Christ. They thought Christ to be the best amongst good men; but yet they were not come

Verse 22

to the knowledge that he was God. *Martha* saies, *I know, that even now, whatsoever thou askest of God, God will give it thee;* but she does not know him to be God himselfe. I doe not here institute a confutation, but here, and every where I lament the growth, and insinuation of that pestilent Heresie of Socinianisme; That Christ was a holy, a thrice-holy man, an unreproachable, an irreprehensible, an admirable, an incomparable man; A man, to whom, he that should equall any other man, were worse then a Devill; A man worthy to bee called God, in a farre higher sense then any Magistrate, any King, any Prophet; But yet hee was no God, say they, no Son of God; A Redeemer, by way of good example; but no Redeemer, by way of equivalent satisfaction, say those Heretiques. S. *Paul* sayes,

Ephes. 2.12

He is an Atheist, that is without Christ; And he is as much an Atheist still, that pretends to receive Christ, and not as God; For if the receiving of Christ must redeeme him from being an Atheist, there can no other way be imagined, but by receiving him as God, for that onely, and no other good opinion of Christ, overcomes, and removes his Atheisme. After the last day, whatsoever is not Heaven, is Hell; Hee that then shall be where the Sunne is now, (if he be not then in heaven) shall be as farre from heaven, as if hee were where the Center of the earth is now; Hee that confesses not all Christ, confesses no Christ. *Horribile dictu, dicam tamen,* sayes S. *Augustine* in another case; There belongs a holy trembling to the saying of it, yet I must say it, *If Christ were not God, hee was a devill that durst say he was God.* This then was one weaknesse in these Sisters faith, that it carried them not up to the consideration of Christ as God; And then another rose out of that, That they insisted so much, relied so much, upon his corporall, and personall presence, and promised themselves more from that, then hee had ever given them ground for; which was that which Christ diverted *Mary* from, when after his Resurrection manifesting himselfe to her, and shee flying unto him with that impatient zeale, and that impetuous devotion, *Rabboni, Master, My Master,* Christ said to her, *Touch mee not, for I am not ascended to my Father;* that is, Dwell not upon this passionate consideration of my bodily, and personall presence, but send thy thoughts, and thy reverence, and thy devotion, and thy holy amorousnesse up, whither I am going, to the right hand of my Father, and consider me, contemplate mee there. S. *Peter* had another holy distemper of another kinde, upon the personall presence of Christ; He was so astonished at his presence in the power of a Miracle, that he fell downe at his feet, and said, *Depart from me, for I am a sinfull man, O Lord.* These Sisters longed for him, and S. *Peter* longed as much to be delivered of him; both out of weaknesse and error. So is it an error, and a weaknesse to attribute too much, or too little to Christs presence in his Sacraments, or other Ordinances. To imprison Christ *in Opere operato,* to conclude him so, as that where that action is done, Christ must necessarily bee, and necessarily work, this is to say weakly with these Sisters, *Lord, if thou hadst beene here, our brother had not died.* As long as we are present at thine Ordinance, thou art present with us. But to banish Christ from those holy actions, and to say, That he is no otherwise present, or works no otherwise in those actions, then in other times, and places, this is to say with *Peter,* in his astonishment, *Exi à me Domine, O Lord depart from me;* It is enough that thy Sacrament be a signe; I do not look that it should be a Seal, or a Conduit of Grace; This is the danger, this is the distemper, to ascribe too much, or too little to Gods visible Ordinances, and Institutions, either to say with those holy Sisters, *Lord, if thou hadst been here, our brother had not died,* If we have a Sacrament, if we have a Sermon all is well, we have enough; or else with *Peter, Exi à me,* Leave me to my selfe, to my

Ioh. 20.16

Luke 5.8

private motions, to my bosome inspirations, and I need no Church-
work, no Sermons, no Sacraments, no such assistances.

Marthæ
spes

So there was weaknesse in their Faith, there was so too in their
Hope, in their confidence in Christ, and in their manner of expressing it. For, they did not goe to him, when their brother was sick,

Joh. 3.1
Mat. 8.5
Mark 5.22
and 25

but sent. *Nicodemus* came in person for his sick soule; And the
Centurion in person, for his sick servant; And *Iairus* in person, for
his sick daughter; And the woman with the bloody Issue in person,
for her sick selfe. These sisters did but send, but piously, and rever-
endly; Their Messenger was to say to Christ, not *Lazarus,* not *Our*
Brother, but *He whom thou lovest, is sick;* And they left this inti-
mation to work upon Christ; But that was not enough, we must
bring Christ and our necessities neerer together then so. There is
good instruction in the severall expressings of Christs curings of

Mark 1.30

Peters mother in the Euangelists. S. *Marke* sayes, *They told him of*
her; And S. *Luke* sayes, *They brought him up to her;* And S. *Mat-*

[Mat. 8.14
and 15]

thew sayes, *He saw her, and tooke her by the hand.* I must not wrap
up all my necessities in generall termes in my prayers, but descend
to particulars; For this places my devotion upon particular considerations of God, to consider him in every Attribute, what God hath
done for me in Power, what in Wisedome, what in Mercy; which
is a great assistance, and establishing, and propagation of devotion.
As it is a degree of unthankfulnesse, to thank God too generally,
and not to delight to insist upon the waight, and measure, and proportion, and the goodnesse of every particular mercy: so is it an
irreverent, and inconsiderate thing, not to take my particular wants
into my thoughts, and into my prayers, that so I may take a holy
knowledge, that I have nothing, nothing but from God, and by
prayer. And as God is an accessible God, as he is his owne *Master*
of Requests, and is ever open to receive thy Petitions, in how small
a matter soever: so is he an inexhaustible God, he can give infinitely,
and an indefatigable God, he cannot be pressed too much. Therefore

Luke 11.5
18.5
Matt. 15.22

hath Christ given us a Parable of getting *Bread at midnight* by
Importunity, and not otherwise; And another of a *Iudge* that heard
the widows cause by *Importunity,* and not otherwise; And, not a
Parable, but a History, and a History of his own, of a woman of
Canaan, that overcame him in the behalfe of her daughter, by *Im-*

portunity; when, but by importunity, she could not get so much as an answer, as a deniall at his hands. Pray personally, rely not upon dead nor living Saints; Thy Mother the Church prayes for thee, but pray for thy selfe too; Shee can open her bosome, and put the breast to thy mouth, but thou must draw, and suck for thy selfe. Pray personally, and pray frequently; *David* had many stationary times of the day, and night too, to pray in. Pray frequently, and pray fervently; God took it not ill, at *Davids* hands, to be *awaked,* and to be called up, as though hee were asleepe at our prayers, and to be called upon, *to pull his hand out of his bosome,* as though he were slack in relieving our necessities. This was a weaknesse in those Sisters, that they solicited not Christ in person; still get as neare God as you can; And that they declared not their case particularly; It is not enough to pray, nor to confesse in generall termes; And, that they pursued not their prayer earnestly, thorowly; It is not enough to have prayed once; Christ does not onely excuse, but enjoine Importunity.

[Psa. 44.23]

[Psa. 74.11]

And then a weaknesse there was in their Charity too, even towards their dead brother. To lament a dead friend is naturall, and civill; and he is the deader of the two, the verier carcasse, that does not so. But inordinate lamentation implies a suspition of a worse state in him that is gone; And if I doe beleeve him to be in heaven, deliberately, advisedly to wish him here, that is in heaven, is an uncharitable desire. For, for me to say, He is preferred by being where he is, but I were better, if he were againe where I am, were such an indisposition, as if the Princes servant should be loath to see his Master King, because he should not hold the same place with him, being King, as he did when he was Prince. Not to hope well of him that is gone, is uncharitablenesse; and at the same time, when I beleeve him to be better, to wish him worse, is uncharitablenesse too. And such weaknesses were in those holy and devout Sisters of *Lazarus;* which establishes our Conclusion, There is nothing in this world, no not in spirituall things, not in knowledge, not in faith, not in hope, not in charity perfect. But yet, for all these imperfections, Christ doth not refuse, nor chide, but cherish their piety, which is also another circumstance in that Part.

Marthæ charitas

Non rejicit Christus

There is no forme of Building stronger then an Arch, and yet an

Arch hath declinations, which even a flat-roofe hath not; The flat-roofe lies equall in all parts; the Arch declines downwards in all parts, and yet the Arch is a firme supporter. Our Devotions doe not the lesse beare us upright, in the sight of God, because they have some declinations towards natural affections: God doth easilier pardon some neglectings of his grace, when it proceeds out of a tendernesse, or may be excused out of good nature, then any presuming upon his grace. If a man doe depart in some actions, from an exact obedience of Gods will, upon infirmity, or humane affections, and not a contempt, God passes it over oftentimes. For, when our Saviour Christ says, *Be pure as your Father in heaven is pure,* that is a rule for our purity, but not a measure of our purity; It is that we should be pure so, not that we should be so pure as our Father in heaven. When we consider that weaknesse, that went through the Apostles, even to Christs Ascension, that they looked for a temporall Kingdome, and for preferment in that; when we consider that weaknesse in the chiefe of them, S. *Peter,* at the *Transfiguration,* when, as the Text sayes, *He knew not what to say;* when we consider the weaknesse of his action, that for feare of death, he renounced the Lord of Life, and denied his Master; when in this very story, when Christ said that *Lazarus* was *asleepe,* and that *he would goe to awake him,* they could understand it so impertinently, as that Christ should goe such a journey, to come to the waking of a man, asleep at that time when he spoke; All these infirmities of theirs, multiply this consolation upon us, That though God look upon the Inscription, he looks upon the metall too, Though he look that his Image should be preserved in us, he looks in what earthen vessels this Image is put, and put by his own hand; and though he hate us in our rebellions, yet he pities us in our grievances; though he would have us better, he forsakes us not for every degree of illnesse. There are three great dangers in this consideration of perfectnesse, and purity; First to distrust of Gods mercy, if thou finde not this purity in thy selfe, and this perfectnesse; And then to presume upon God, nay upon thine own right, in an overvaluing of thine own purity, and perfectnesse; And againe, to condemne others, whom thou wilt needs thinke lesse pure, or perfect then thy selfe. Against this diffidence in God, to thinke our selves so desperately impure, as that God will not look upon us; And this presumption in

[Mat. 5.48, misquoting "pure" for "perfect"]

Mar. 9.6

God, to thinke our selves so pure, as that God is bound to look upon us; And this uncharitablenesse towards others, to think none pure at all, that are not pure our way; Christ armes us by his Example, He receives these sisters of *Lazarus,* and accomplishes as much as they desired, though there were weaknesses in their Faith, in their Hope, in their Charity, expressed in that unperfect speech, *Lord, if thou hadst been here, my brother had not dyed:* for, there is nothing, not in spirituall things perfect. This we have seen out of the Text we have Heard; And now out of the Text, which we See, we shall see the rest, That as in spirituall things, there is nothing Perfect, so in temporall, there is nothing Permanent.

I need not call in new Philosophy, that denies a settlednesse, an   2 Part
acquiescence in the very body of the Earth, but makes the Earth to move in that place, where we thought the Sunne had moved; I need not that helpe, that the Earth it selfe is in Motion, to prove this, That nothing upon Earth is permanent; The Assertion will stand of it selfe, till some man assigne me some instance, something that a man may relie upon, and find permanent. Consider the greatest Bodies upon Earth, The Monarchies; Objects, which one would thinke, Destiny might stand and stare at, but not shake; Consider the smallest bodies upon Earth, The haires of our head, Objects, which one would thinke, Destiny would not observe, or could not discerne; And yet Destiny, (to speak to a naturall man) And God, (to speake to a Christian) is no more troubled to make a Monarchy ruinous, then to make a haire gray. Nay, nothing needs be done to either, by God, or Destiny; A Monarchy will ruine, as a haire will grow gray, of it selfe. In the Elements themselves, of which all sub-elementary things are composed, there is no acquiescence, but a vicissitudinary transmutation into one another; Ayre condensed becomes water, a more solid body, And Ayre rarified becomes fire, a body more disputable, and in-apparant. It is so in the Conditions of men too; A Merchant condensed, kneaded and packed up in a great estate, becomes a Lord; And a Merchant rarified, blown up by a perfidious Factor, or by a riotous Sonne, evaporates into ayre, into nothing, and is not seen. And if there were any thing permanent and durable in this world, yet we got nothing by it, because howsoever that might last in it selfe, yet we could not last to enjoy it; If our goods were not amongst Moveables,

yet we our selves are; if they could stay with us, yet we cannot stay with them; which is another Consideration in this part.

Corpus hominis

The world is a great Volume, and man the Index of that Booke; Even in the body of man, you may turne to the whole world; This body is an Illustration of all Nature; Gods recapitulation of all that he had said before, in his *Fiat lux,* and *Fiat firmamentum,* and in all the rest, said or done, in all the six dayes. Propose this body to thy

[1 Cor. 6.19]

consideration in the highest exaltation thereof; as it is the *Temple of the Holy Ghost:* Nay, not in a Metaphor, or comparison of a Temple, or any other similitudinary thing, but as it was really and truly the very body of God, in the person of Christ, and yet this body must wither, must decay, must languish, must perish. When *Goliah* had armed and fortified this body, And *Iezabel* had painted and perfumed this body, And *Dives* had pampered and larded this body, As God

[Ezek. 37.3]

said to *Ezekiel,* when he brought him to the *dry bones, Fili hominis, Sonne of Man, doest thou thinke these bones can live?* They said in their hearts to all the world, Can these bodies die? And they are dead. *Iezabels* dust is not Ambar, nor *Goliahs* dust *Terra sigillata,* Medicinall; nor does the Serpent, whose meat they are both, finde any better relish in *Dives* dust, then in *Lazarus.* But as in our former part, where our foundation was, That in nothing, no spirituall thing, there was any perfectnesse, which we illustrated in the weaknesses of Knowledge, and Faith, and Hope, and Charity, yet we concluded, that for all those defects, God accepted those their religious services; So in this part, where our foundation is, That nothing in temporall things is permanent, as we have illustrated that, by the decay of that which is Gods noblest piece in Nature, The body of man; so we shall also conclude that, with this goodnesse of God, that for all this dissolution, and putrefaction, he affords this Body a Resurrection.

Resurrectio

The Gentils, and their Poets, describe the sad state of Death so, *Nox una obeunda,* That it is one everlasting Night; To them, a Night; But to a Christian, it is *Dies Mortis,* and *Dies Resurrectionis,* The day of Death, and The day of Resurrection; We die in the light, in the sight of Gods presence, and we rise in the light, in the sight of his very Essence. Nay, Gods corrections, and judgements

[Isa. 10.3]

upon us in this life, are still expressed so, *Dies visitationis,* still it is a Day, though a *Day of visitation;* and still we may discerne God to be

in the action. The *Lord of Life* was the first that named *Death; Morte* Gen. 2.[17]
morieris, sayes God, Thou shalt die the Death. I doe the lesse feare,
or abhorre Death, because I finde it in his mouth; Even a malediction
hath a sweetnesse in his mouth; for there is a blessing wrapped up in
it; a mercy in every correction, a Resurrection upon every Death.
When *Iezabels* beauty, exalted to that height which it had by art, or
higher then that, to that height which it had in her own opinion,
shall be infinitely multiplied upon every Body; And as God shall
know no man from his own Sonne, so as not to see the very righteousnesse of his own Sonne upon that man; So the Angels shall know no
man from Christ, so as not to desire to looke upon that mans face,
because the most deformed wretch that is there, shall have the very
beauty of Christ himselfe; So shall *Goliahs* armour, and *Dives* fulnesse, be doubled, and redoubled upon us. And every thing that we
can call good, shall first be infinitely exalted in the goodnesse, and
then infinitely multiplied in the proportion, and againe infinitely
extended in the duration. And since we are in an action of preparing
this dead Brother of ours to that state, (for the Funerall is the
Easter-eve, The Buriall is the depositing of that man for the Resurrection) As we have held you, with Doctrine of Mortification, by
extending the Text, from *Martha* to this occasion; so shall we dis-
misse you with Consolation, by a like occasionall inverting the Text,
from passion in *Martha's* mouth, *Lord, if thou hadst been here, my
Brother had not dyed,* to joy in ours, *Lord, because thou wast here,
our Brother is not dead.*

The Lord was with him in all these steps; with him in his life; *In vita*
with him in his death; He is with him in his funerals, and he shall
be with him in his Resurrection; and therefore, because the Lord
was with him, our Brother is not dead. He was with him in the
beginning of his life, in this manifestation, That though he were of
Parents of a good, of a great Estate, yet his possibility and his expectation from them, did not slacken his own industry; which is a
Canker that eats into, nay that hath eat up many a family in this
City, that relying wholly upon what the Father hath done, the Sonne
does nothing for himselfe. And truly, it falls out too often, that he
that labours not for more, does not keepe his own. God imprinted
in him an industrious disposition, though such hopes from such par-

Psa. 81.10
[11, *F,* as
in Vulg.]

ents might have excused some slacknesse, and God prospered his industry so, as that when his Fathers estate came to a distribution by death, he needed it not. God was with him, as with *David* in a Dilatation, and then in a Repletion; God enlarged him, and then he filled him; He gave him a large and a comprehensive understanding, and with it, A publique heart; And such as perchance in his way of education, and in our narrow and contracted times, in which every man determines himselfe in himselfe, and scarce looks farther, it would be hard to finde many Examples of such largenesse. You have, I thinke, a phrase of Driving a Trade; And you have, I know, a practise of Driving away Trade, by other use of money; And you have lost a man, that drove a great Trade, the right way in making the best use of our home-commodity. To fetch in Wine, and Spice, and Silke, is but a drawing of Trade; The right driving of trade, is, to vent our owne outward; And yet, for the drawing in of that, which might justly seeme most behoofefull, that is, of Arts, and Manufactures, to be imployed upon our owne Commodity within the Kingdome, he did his part, diligently, at least, if not vehemently, if not passionately. This City is a great Theater, and he Acted great and various parts in it; And all well; And when he went higher, (as he was often heard in Parliaments, at Councell tables, and in more private accesses to the late King of ever blessed memory) as, for that comprehension of those businesses, which he pretended to understand, no man doubts, for no man lacks arguments and evidences of his ability therein, So for his manner of expressing his intentions, and digesting and uttering his purposes, I have sometimes heard the greatest Master of Language and Judgement, which these times, or any other did, or doe, or shall give, (that good and great King of ours) say of him, That he never heard any man of his breeding, handle businesses more rationally, more pertinently, more elegantly, more perswasively; And when his purpose was, to do a grace to a Preacher, of very good abilities, and good note in his owne Chappell, I have heard him say, that his language, and accent, and manner of delivering himselfe, was like this man. This man hath God accompanied all his life; and by performance thereof seemes to have made that Covenant with him, which he made to

Gen. 17.2

Abraham, Multiplicabo te vehementer, I will multiply thee exceed-

ingly. He multiplied his estate so, as was fit to endow many and
great Children; and he multiplied his Children so, both in their
number, and in their quality, as they were fit to receive a great Estate.
God was with him all the way, In *a Pillar of Fire,* in the brightnesse   [Exod.
of prosperity, and in the *Pillar of Clouds* too, in many darke, and   13.21]
sad, and heavy crosses: So great a Ship, required a great Ballast, So
many blessings, many crosses; And he had them, and sailed on his
course the steadier for them; The *Cloud* as well as the *Fire,* was a
Pillar to him; His crosses, as well as his blessings established his
assurance in God; And so, in all the course of his life, *The Lord was
here,* and therefore *our Brother is not dead;* not dead in the evidences
and testimonies of life; for he, whom the world hath just cause to
celebrate, for things done, when he was alive, is alive still in their
celebration.

The Lord was here, that is, with him at his death too. He was   *In morte*
served with the Processe here in the City, but his cause was heard
in the Country; Here he sickned, There he languished, and dyed
there. In his sicknesse there, those that assisted him, are witnesses, of
his many expressings, of a religious and a constant heart towards
God, and of his pious joyning with them, even in the holy declaration of kneeling, then, when they, in favour of his weakenesse, would
disswade him from kneeling. I must not defraud him of this testimony from my selfe, that into this place where we are now met, I
have observed him to enter with much reverence, and compose himselfe in this place with much declaration of devotion. And truly it
is that reverence, which those persons who are of the same ranke
that he was in the City, that reverence that they use in this place,
when they come hither, is that that makes us, who have now the
administration of this Quire, glad, that our Predecessors, but a very
few yeares before our time, (and not before all our times neither)
admitted these Honourable and worshipfull Persons of this City, to
sit in this Quire, so, as they do upon Sundayes: The Church receives
an honour in it; But the honour is more in their reverence, then in
their presence; though in that too: And they receive an honour, and
an ease in it; and therefore they do piously towards God, and pru-
dently for themselves, and gratefully towards us, in giving us, by
their reverent comportment here, so just occasion of continuing that

honour, and that ease to them here, which to lesse reverend, and unrespective persons, we should be lesse willing to doe. To returne to him in his sicknesse; He had but one dayes labour, and all the rest were Sabbaths, one day in his sicknesse he converted to businesse; Thus; He called his family, and friends together; Thankfully he acknowledged Gods manifold blessings, and his owne sins as penitently: And then, to those who were to have the disposing of his estate, joyntly with his Children, he recommended his servants, and the poore, and the Hospitals, and the Prisons, which, according to his purpose, have beene all taken into consideration; And after this (which was his Valediction to the world) he seemed alwaies loath to returne to any worldly businesse, His last Commandement to Wife and Children was Christs last commandement to his Spouse the Church, in the Apostles, *To love one another.* He blest .them, and the Estate devolved upon them, unto them: And by Gods grace shall prove as true a Prophet to them in that blessing, as he was to himselfe, when in entring his last bed, two dayes before his Death, he said, *Help me off with my earthly habit, and let me go to my last bed.* Where, in the second night after, he said, *Little know ye what paine I feele this night, yet I know, I shall have joy in the morning;* And in that morning he dyed. The forme in which he implored his Saviour, was evermore, towards his end, this, *Christ Iesus, which dyed on the Crosse, forgive me my sins; He have mercy upon me:* And his last and dying words were the repetition of the name of Jesus; And when he had not strength to utter that name distinctly and perfectly, they might heare it from within him, as from a man a far off; even then, when his hollow and remote naming of Jesus, was rather a certifying of them, that he was with his Jesus, then a prayer that he might come to him. And so *The Lord was here,* here with him in his Death; and because *the Lord was here, our Brother is not dead;* not dead in the eyes and eares of God; for as the blood of *Abel* speaks yet, so doth the zeale of Gods Saints; and their last prayers (though we heare them not) God continues still; and they pray in Heaven, as the Martyrs under the Altar, even till the Resurrection.

He is with him now too; Here in his Funerals. Buriall, and Christian Buriall, and Solemne Buriall are all evidences, and testimonies

[Joh. 13.34]

[Heb. 12.24]

In funere

of Gods presence. God forbid we should conclude, or argue an absence of God, from the want of Solemne Buriall, or Christian Buriall, or any Buriall; But neither must we deny it, to be an evidence of his favour and presence, where he is pleased to afford these. So God makes that the seale of all his blessings to *Abraham, That he should be buried in a good age;* God established *Iacob* with that promise, *That his Son Ioseph should have care of his Funerals:* And *Ioseph* does cause his servants, *The Physitians, to embalme him, when he was dead.* Of Christ it was Prophecied, *That he should have a glorious Buriall;* And therefore Christ interprets well that profuse, and prodigall piety of the Woman that poured out the Oyntment upon him, *That she did it to Bury him;* And so shall *Ioseph* of Arimathea be ever celebrated, for his care in celebrating Christs Funerals. If we were to send a Son, or a friend, to take possession of any place in Court, or forraine parts, we would send him out in the best equipage: Let us not grudge to set downe our friends, in the Anti-chamber of Heaven, the Grave, in as good manner, as without vaine-gloriousnesse, and wastfulnesse we may; And, in inclining them, to whom that care belongs, to expresse that care as they doe this day, *The Lord is with him,* even in this Funerall; And because *The Lord is here, our brother is not dead;* Not dead in the memories and estimation of men.

And lastly, that we may have God present in all his Manifestations, *Hee that was, and is, and is to come,* was with him, in his life and death, and is with him in this holy Solemnity, and shall bee with him againe in the Resurrection. God sayes to *Iacob, I will goe downe with thee into Egypt, and I will also surely bring thee up againe.* God goes downe with a good man into the Grave, and will surely bring him up againe. When? The Angel promised to returne to *Abraham* and *Sarah,* for the assurance of the birth of *Isaac, according to the time of life;* that is, in such time, as by nature a woman may have a childe. God will returne to us in the Grave, *according to the time of life;* that is, in such time, as he, by his gracious Decree, hath fixed for the Resurrection. And in the meane time, no more then the God-head departed from the dead body of our Saviour, in the grave, doth his power, and his presence depart from our dead bodies in that darknesse; But that which *Moses* said to the whole Congregation, I

Gen. 15.[15]
Gen. 46.[4]

Gen. 50.[26]
Esay. 11.10

Matt. 26.
[12]

*In resur-
rectione*
[Apoc. 1.4]

Gen. 46.4

Gen. 18.10

say to you all, both to you that heare me, and to him that does not, *All ye that did cleave unto the Lord your God, are alive, every one of you, this day;* Even hee, whom we call dead, is alive this day. In the presence of God, we lay him downe; In the power of God, he shall rise; In the person of Christ, he is risen already. And so into the same hands that have received his soule, we commend his body; beseeching his blessed Spirit, that as our charity enclines us to hope confidently of his good estate, our faith may assure us of the same happinesse, in our owne behalfe; And that for all our sakes, but especially for his own glory, he will be pleased to hasten the consummation of all, in that kingdome which that Son of God hath purchased for us, with the inestimable price of his incorruptible blood. *Amen.*

Prayers and Meditations

O LORD, I most humbly acknowledg and confesse, that I have understood sin, by understanding thy laws and judgments; but have done against thy known and revealed will. Thou hast set up many candlesticks, and kindled many lamps in mee; but I have either blown them out, or carried them to guide me in by and forbidden ways. Thou hast given mee a desire of knowledg, and some meanes to it, and some possession of it; and I have arm'd my self with thy weapons against thee: Yet, O God, have mercy upon me, for thine own sake have mercy upon me. Let not sin and me be able to exceed thee, nor to defraud thee, nor to frustrate thy purposes: But let me, in despite of Me, be of so much use to thy glory, that by thy mercy to my sin, other sinners may see how much sin thou canst pardon....

(Essays in Divinity, ed. Simpson, p. 97)

O GLORIOUS beauty, infinitely reverend, infinitely fresh and young, we come late to thy love, if we consider the past daies of our lives, but early if thou beest pleased to reckon with us from this houre of the shining of thy grace upon us; and therefore O God, as thou hast brought us safely to the beginning of this day, as thou hast not given us over to a finall perishing in the works of night and darkness, as thou hast brought us to the beginning of this day of grace, so defend us in the same with thy mighty power, and grant that this day, this day of thy visitation, we fall into no sin, neither run into any kind of danger, no such sinne, no such danger as may separate us from thee...

(Sermons, I, 250–251)

ON THE DEATH OF THE RIGHTEOUS

THEY SHALL awake as *Jacob* did, and say as *Jacob* said, *Surely the Lord is in this place,* and *this is no other but the house of God, and the gate of heaven,* And into that gate they shall enter, and in that house they shall dwell, where there shall be no Cloud nor Sun, no darkenesse nor dazling, but one equall light, no noyse nor silence, but one equall musick, no fears nor hopes, but one equal possession, no foes nor friends, but one equall communion and Identity, no ends nor beginnings, but one equall eternity. Keepe us Lord so awake in the duties of our Callings, that we may thus sleepe in thy Peace, and wake in thy glory . . .

(*Sermons,* VIII, ´191)

FORGIVE ME *O Lord, O Lord* forgive me my sinnes, the sinnes of my youth, and my present sinnes, the sinne that my Parents cast upon me, Originall sinne, and the sinnes that I cast upon my children, in an ill example; Actuall sinnes, sinnes which are manifest to all the world, and sinnes which I have so laboured to hide from the world, as that now they are hid from mine own conscience, and mine own memory; Forgive me my crying sins, and my whispering sins, sins of uncharitable hate, and sinnes of unchaste love, sinnes against *Thee* and *Thee,* against thy Power O Almighty Father, against thy Wisdome, O glorious Sonne, against thy Goodnesse, O blessed Spirit of God; and sinnes against *Him* and *Him,* against Superiours and Equals, and Inferiours; and sinnes against *Me* and *Me,* against mine own soul, and against my body, which I have loved better then my soul; Forgive me *O Lord, O Lord* in the merits of thy *Christ* and my *Jesus,* thine Anointed, and my Saviour; Forgive me my sinnes, all my sinnes, and I will put Christ to no more cost, nor thee to more trouble, for any reprobation or malediction that lay upon me, otherwise then as a sinner. I ask but an application, not an extention of that Benediction, *Blessed are they whose sinnes are forgiven;* Let me be but so blessed, and I shall envy no mans Blessednesse: say thou to my sad soul, *Sonne be of good comfort, thy sinnes are forgiven thee,* and I shall never trouble thee with Petitions, to take any other Bill off of the fyle, or to reverse any other Decree, by which I should be accurst, before I was created, or condemned by thee, before thou saw'st me as a sinner ...

(*Sermons,* VII, 361–362)

Now, this Bell tolling softly for another, saies to me, Thou must die.

PERCHANCE hee for whom this *Bell* tolls, may bee so ill, as that he knowes not it *tolls* for him; And perchance I may thinke my selfe so much better than I am, as that they who are about mee, and see my state, may have caused it to toll for mee, and I know not that.... As therefore the *Bell* that rings to a *Sermon,* calls not upon the *Preacher* onely, but upon the *Congregation* to come; so this *Bell* calls us all: but how much more *mee,* who am brought so neere the *doore* by this *sicknesse....* No man is an *Iland,* intire of it selfe; every man is a peece of the *Continent,* a part of the *maine;* if a *Clod* bee washed away by the *Sea, Europe* is the lesse, as well as if a *Promontorie* were, as well as if a *Mannor* of thy *friends,* or of *thine owne* were; Any Mans *death* diminishes *me,* because I am involved in *Mankinde;* And therefore never send to know for whom the *bell* tolls; It tolls for *thee.*

(*Devotions upon Emergent Occasions,* 1624,
Meditation 17)

Textual Notes to the Sermons

Sermon 6, p. 152. Knife is evidently the wrong word here. It was suggested in *Sermons* III, 433, that *knife* might be a mistake for *knitch*, "a word now obsolete except in dialect, but used from the fourteenth to the seventeenth century to denote a bundle of wood, flax, or hay tied together, or a faggot (see N. E. D.)."

Sermon 6, p. 155. "...in lesse then seaven *years apprentissage,* which your occupations cost you, you shall learn, not the Mysteries of your *twelve Companies,* but the Mysteries of the *twelve Tribes,* of the *twelve Apostles...*"

In this peroration Donne addressed himself particularly to that section of his audience which comprised the representatives of the twelve great livery companies of London who accompanied the Lord Mayor and the Sheriffs to St. Paul's for Divine Service on Christmas Day and six other days in the year (see Stow, *Survey of London,* ed. Kingsford, II, 190). These companies were the Mercers, the Grocers, the Drapers, the Fishmongers, the Goldsmiths, the Skinners, the Merchant Tailors, the Haberdashers, the Salters, the Ironmongers, the Vintners, and the Clothworkers. Their members served an apprenticeship of seven years. Donne had a strong personal link with the companies in the fact that his father had been a member of the Ironmongers Company, and had become its Warden in 1574.

Sermon 8, Text, p. 178. The Folio mentions only *Isa.* 7.14, but *Mat.* 1.23, which quotes *Isa.* 7.14, is included in the heading for two reasons. First, when a text occurs twice, it is Donne's practice to give only the first reference. Whenever he refers to a passage in *Matthew* which is found also in *Mark,* or perhaps in both *Mark* and *Luke,* he gives only the reference to *Matthew.* Secondly, the whole sermon is a Christmas one, devoted to the Virgin Birth of Christ, and it is the union of the two texts which is the foundation of Donne's discourse.

Sermon 8, pp. 190–191. The references here to Gellius, Pliny, and Genebrard, with the quotations from Cyprian and Tertullian, are taken from the commentary of Cornelius à Lapide on the four major prophets.